STUDIES IN CHRISTIAN HISTORY AND THOUGHT

Peace, Toleration and Decay

The Ecclesiology of Later Stuart Dissent

STUDIES IN CHRISTIAN HISTORY AND THOUGHT

A complete listing of all titles in this series will be found at the close of this book.

STUDIES IN CHRISTIAN HISTORY AND THOUGHT

Peace, Toleration and Decay

The Ecclesiology of Later Stuart Dissent

Martin Sutherland

Wipf and Stock Publishers
199 W 8th Ave, Suite 3
Eugene, OR 97401

Peace, Toleration and Decay
The Ecclesiology of Later Stuart Dissent
By Sutherland, Martin

ISBN: 1-59752-791-2
Publication date 6/23/2006
Previously published by Paternoster, 2003

This Edition Published by Wipf and Stock Publishers
by arrangement with Paternoster

Paternoster
9 Holdom Avenue
Bletchley
Milton Keyes, MK1 1QR
Great Britain

Studies in Christian History and Thought

Series Preface

This series complements the specialist series of *Studies in Evangelical History and Thought* and *Studies in Baptist History and Thought* for which Paternoster is becoming increasingly well known by offering works that cover the wider field of Christian history and thought. It encompasses accounts of Christian witness at various periods, studies of individual Christians and movements, and works which concern the relations of church and society through history, and the history of Christian thought.

The series includes monographs, revised dissertations and theses, and collections of papers by individuals and groups. As well as 'free standing' volumes, works on particular running themes are being commissioned; authors will be engaged for these from around the world and from a variety of Christian traditions.

A high academic standard combined with lively writing will commend the volumes in this series both to scholars and to a wider readership.

Series Editors

For my Mum and Dad,
Pauline and Keith Sutherland
and my brother, David

Contents

Dates, Quotations and References

Unless there is confusion over the date, each reference has followed the modern practice of commencing the year on 1 January. I have not, however, 'corrected' the contemporary English dating to the later-adopted continental system.

In all quotations from printed works, the spelling, punctuation and type of the edition cited are reproduced where possible. This has meant that Howe's works often appear in modern spelling (or, at least, that favoured by his nineteenth-century editors). Following standard practice, omissions are indicated by dots and square brackets enclose words and capitals not found in the cited edition.

Howe's published works are cited by their original titles in the first instance, with a further reference to the collected edition employed. Thereafter, the citation will be by an abbreviated title. In all cases the page numbers will relate to the collected edition.

Current practice is to use capitals to begin words only, as in the case of a person's name, when one is essential. I have therefore avoided capitals for loose groupings or movements (so, 'puritan', 'nonconformist', 'dissent') but used them for more defined entities (Presbyterians, Independents, Quakers). 'Church' is a special case. I have used lower case for all uses other than references to the established Church of England.

ABBREVIATIONS

The following abbreviations are used in the notes:

BL	British Library
Calamy	E. Calamy, *Memoirs of the Life of the Late Rev*[d] *Mr John Howe* (London, 1724).
CH	*Church History*
CR	A.G. Matthews, *Calamy Revised: Being a Revision of Edmund Calamy's Account of the Ministers and Others Ejected and Silenced, 1660-2*, Oxford, 1934 (1988).
C.S.P.D.	*Calendar of State Papers Domestic*
DNB	*The Dictionary of National Biography*, ed. L. Stephens and S. Lee, 63 vols. (1885-1900)
EHR	*English Historical Review*
EMH	*Early Modern History*
HJ	*Historical Journal*
JEH	*Journal of Ecclesiastical History*
JBS	*Journal of British Studies*
JRH	*Journal of Religious History*
LACT	*Library of Anglo-Catholic Theology*
P&P	*Past and Present*
RB	Richard Baxter, *Reliquiae Baxterianae*, ed. Sylvester (1696)
TRHS	*Transactions of the Royal Historical Society*
Whole Works	J. Hunt (ed.) *The Whole Works of the Rev. John Howe, M.A.* 8 vols. (London: 1827).
Works	E. Calamy (ed.) *The Works of the Rev. John Howe, M.A. as Published during his Life* (London, 1724), 3 vols., (1848), reprint: Ligonier PA: Soli Deo Gloria, 1990).

PREFACE

English religion in the Stuart period was a complex phenomenon. Anyone who approaches it must come to terms with a confusing array of positions, alliances, arguments and failures. The challenge is magnified by the fact, initially strange to inhabitants of the twenty-first century, that religion was intimately bound to political structures and concepts which themselves underwent massive change in the period. It is thus a fundamental position of this book that Stuart religion cannot be understood apart from its political context and that, in turn a more sophisticated grasp of the theology of the time will inform our knowledge of other ideas and developments.

What follows is not, of course, a global study of Stuart life. Rather it is an attempt to explain the tests, trials and traumas of one group of religious people, over just the later part of the Stuart age, and largely through the theology of one key leader. The very complexity of the issues demands a focused approach. Even so, the political turmoil of the times provides a key interpretative structure and there are implications for wider questions.

The success or otherwise of this enterprise is for the reader to judge. Any gaps in the argument must be claimed fully as my own, as I have had only the best of assistance and advice. This study has grown out of doctoral research on the theology of John Howe. Numerous mentors, friends and family made that study possible.

I was singularly fortunate to benefit from the supervision of Glenn Burgess, then of the University of Canterbury, New Zealand, whose own research is in the political theory of the seventeenth century. I thus gained access to aspects of Stuart thought, the significance of which for my study I might have missed. Glenn was in all respects an exemplary supervisor and made an incalculable contribution to the development of whatever historical skills I have acquired. The presence of other historians at Canterbury with interests in my area added further advantage. Mandy Capern lent her knowledge of theological debates in the early Stuart period and was a willing advisor and reliable critic. For a time I was a research assistant for Marie Peters. Marie's example taught me much about record keeping and attention to detail and her knowledge of Restoration and Hanoverian history was of immense value. Such mentors made the PhD experience almost pleasant.

The move from thesis to monograph is not always smooth. Carey Baptist College and Epsom Baptist Church provided research leave to enable new enquiry and rewriting. David Bebbington and N.H. Keeble made comments and suggested further lines of enquiry with a degree of interest and thoroughness which I had no right to expect, but for which I am extremely thankful. The analysis of the controversies of 1680 in chapter four draws in part on material first published in the *Journal of Religious History* in 1997. I am grateful to the editors for permission to use elements of that article. David Field graciously allowed me to refer to his unpublished thesis on John Howe, completed at a time similar to my own.

All this professional advice and guidance was augmented by the interest of friends. Brian Smith, my theological college principal, underwrote my post-graduate study with spiritual and practical support. To have someone backing the idea before it even seemed possible was a true blessing. John Hitchcock, Paul Windsor, Tim Cooper, Keith Clark and Kevin Ward all gave encouragement at crucial moments. Esther McInnis, Sylvia Baldwin and Marion Bradfield committed themselves to practical provision, as did the Jenkins trust and our friends at Avonhead Baptist Church. Our pastors, Chris Finlay and Ilene Allan, stood with us at the most difficult times. More recently Lesley and Ray Utting and Tim and Barbara Bulkeley have provided environments for writing and reflection.

For our families, doctoral research was something unprecedented and the problems of Stuart religion very foreign. Nevertheless we experienced unflagging encouragement from this quarter. My wife's grandmother and various of our uncles and aunts backed us through the process. Yvonne's parents, Roger and Shirley, and her brother and sisters with their families, provided an environment of care and love which we cannot quantify.

I owe a deep personal debt, of course, to Yvonne and our children. Louisa, Andrew and Sarah. For three years their lives were determined by 'Dad's thesis'. Inevitably this meant the limitation of opportunities and living arrangements which were not always ideal. That we got through those years owes much to their patience and generosity of spirit.

From my parents and brother I want to acknowledge not a few years but a lifetime of unwavering confidence in me and my aspirations. I dedicate this book to them.

Introduction

> But when we consider, that every one must give an account of himself to God…this will bring the matter with weight upon our own spirits, lest we should be found transgressors in Bethel, and to have offered strange fire, instead of a sacrifice, on the one hand; or needlessly, on the other, set on fire the temple itself. (John Howe, 1702)[1]

Later Stuart dissent decayed from within.

This study examines a story of decline, alienation and lost opportunity. Within a generation of the Restoration, dissent was marginalised and fragmented, a disparate assemblage of competing nonconformities. Just as nonconformists achieved relative peace and toleration, their unity unraveled. This experience bore the marks of tragedy. Dissent was cut down by its own inherent weaknesses.

Through the later Stuart period leading thinkers generated a vigorous discourse of church and conscience. As it came to terms with toleration, dissent was called to an irenic ecclesiology, radically focused on the invisible church. A drive for harmony based on loving forbearance would for a season energise dissent. Ironically, this theology would betray the very unity it sought. It was 'strange fire' – an offering which would led to destruction.

The development of that distinctive view of the church is the central concern of this study. At its core was a bold confidence in immediate encounter with a transcendent God. Its supreme expression was found in the theology of John Howe (1630-1705). In the first decade of the eighteenth century it would be powerfully promulgated as the 'moderate nonconformity' of Edmund Calamy Jnr (1671-1732). Calamy, however, merely continued Howe's earlier vision. Howe's ideas are thus central to the analysis which follows.

1 John Howe, *Some Consideration of a Preface to an Inquiry Concerning the Occasional Conformity of Dissenters etc* (London: 1702), *Works* III, 536-552, 538. Howe alludes to an incident in Leviticus 10.

They will be shown to have had a profound, though ultimately detrimental, impact on the fate of dissent.

Key Premises

Four convictions inform and underpin the interpretation advanced in this book.

1. *Dissent was a religious phenomenon.* This essential characteristic must be fully acknowledged if dissent is not to be reduced to a political, economic or sociological curiosity. Accepting the insights of other approaches, the historian cannot elude the fact that it was a particular religious consciousness which drove nonconformists. Whatever else they imagined themselves to be, above all they defined themselves by their perceived relationship to God the Father through Jesus Christ and the Holy Spirit.

2. *Theology played a critical role in Stuart history.* Historians of the Stuart age have been wary of theology. Nicholas Tyacke laments that this indifference can amount even to hostility.[2] Theology can be seen as esoteric, too subject to the vagaries of sectarian commitment, not sufficiently open to investigation and evidence. Almost any other explanation of events has been preferred. There was no such discomfort in the seventeenth century. Theology provided the language of intellectual debate. It was the stuff of the public square. No interpretation of the tortured history of later Stuart dissent, however insightful, can be complete if the preferred discourse of dissenters themselves is misunderstood or ignored.

3. *The deep structures of theological discourse must be recognised.* The importance of theology is increasingly acknowledged. In fact, the historiography has shifted profoundly in recent years. Tyacke has been a major catalyst in this recovery. Yet the results have been inconclusive at best and sometimes confusing. In part this is because the parameters are set too narrowly. Tyacke and others have concentrated on the tension between 'Calvinism' and 'Arminianism'. Allowing for problems of definition, this was clearly a major contemporary debate, but that does not mean it was the only, or even the most significant, fault line in Stuart theology. This study approaches later Stuart dissent through its ecclesiology, but the analysis goes beyond arguments over structure and authority. Underpinning conflicting ecclesiological stances was a range of understandings of how God works in the world. This substratum of

2 N. Tyacke, 'Arminianism and the Restoration Church' in *idem*, *Aspects of English Protestantism c 1530-1700* (Manchester: Manchester University Press, 2001), 320-339, 320.

theology was determinative. Indeed, differing degrees of commitment to the transcendent or immanent action of God lay at the core of a number of Stuart theological debates.

4. Theology is a creature of historical context. Religious ideas do not develop solely by their own momentum. In the Stuart age they were fully integrated with political and philosophical discourse. New theologies were also galvanized by historical experience. To disregard these contexts would be merely to reverse the error of historians who have ignored theology. Some helpful models are emerging, most notably the interpretation proffered by Jonathan Scott.

Destruction, Reconstruction, Innovation and Dissent

The analysis in Scott's recent work, *England's Troubles,* 'begins from the proposition that we need to take contemporary beliefs seriously.'[3] In this overview of seventeenth-century English political history, Scott identifies three key processes at work: 'destruction', 'reconstruction' and 'innovation'. The combination of these was what caused the instability of the era. As examples of the first, Scott points to 'the causes of the English civil war, the exclusion crisis and the glorious revolution. Periods of 'reconstruction', characterised by efforts to restore what was perceived to be lost, took place in response to each of these - in 1660-65, following the Restoration, in 1681-85, after moves to exclude the Duke of York from the succession failed, and in 1689-94. The third process, 'innovation,' was primarily a phenomenon of ideas. As such it both underlaid and overlapped movements of destruction and reconstruction. The interaction of the three processes was complex. Periods of destruction were both the outcome of, and the stimulus for, new ideas. In turn, reconstructions did not merely replicate the past but incorporated new theories. In Scott's analysis, of the three reconstructions, only the third, which followed the 'glorious revolution' of 1688-9, was successful in securing stability. There was, thus, no consequent period of destruction.

Scott's framework informs a large part of this study. The story of religious dissent was not the same as that of political instability. There were inescapable connections, but these were tempered by a fundamental dislocation. This vital difference arises from the fact that dissent experienced at crucial times the *obverse* of the processes identified by Scott in the political sphere. Thus, one of the first moments of 'destruction' (viewed from the perspective of the political

---

3 J. Scott, *England's Troubles: Seventeenth-Century English Political Instability in European Context* (Cambridge; CUP, 2000), 4.

nation) - the 1640s and the Interregnum which followed – was, for radical puritans, a 'reconstruction', a true reformation. By contrast, the return of Charles II was a defeat for nonconformity. As N.H. Keeble has recently noted, the maypoles and opulent celebrations of 1660 'declared that this was no longer a Puritan age.'[4] Likewise, the exclusion crisis represented a significant opportunity for the comprehension of dissent within the Church of England. For nonconformists, this period (the second main 'destructive' episode in Scott's analysis) represented a potential 'reconstruction' of what they had sought earlier in the century – a broader, more inclusive, Church. Sadly for dissent, the potential was unfulfilled and the second political 'restoration' which followed from 1681-1685 was, like the first, a set-back for dissent, a 'destructive' process. Conversely, the revolution of 1688-9 provided a further opportunity to advance nonconformist interests. Thus it can be argued that the experience of dissent shadowed that of the political nation as a whole. The effect was like the impress of a stamp on soft clay, where the high points on one match depressions on the other. What was 'destruction' for the political state was opportunity for nonconformists. Similarly, political 'restoration' meant set-back for the dissenting interest.

We reach with this a crucial point. Dissent continued to negatively mirror the experience of the political state after 1689. The final phase of 'reconstruction' which Scott identifies was the settlement reached in the years 1689-1694. This time, in contrast to earlier attempts, lasting political institutions were put in place. The key point for this study – indeed, a principal argument of the book – is that such stability did *not* emerge for dissent.

The reasons for this turn on the third of Scott's processes: 'innovation'. Whereas, for the political state, the extent of innovation in political theory narrowed sufficiently to allow a workable consensus to emerge in the 1690s, this was not true of the ecclesiology of dissent. Innovation occurred, but with a markedly different outcome. Early in the Restoration period, dissent sought an ecclesiastical settlement which would return to them some of the gains won in previous decades. This phase, well covered in the historiography, was dominated by the approaches of such as Richard Baxter (1615-91) and John Owen (1616-83). Baxter desired a broadly-based Church of England, which could include or 'comprehend' most dissenters; Owen sought toleration for autonomous congregations. Crucially, both men were motivated by ideas which had been forged in the 1640s and 1650s. Innovation was required, and it emerged as

4 N.H. Keeble, *The Restoration: England in the 1660s* (Oxford: Blackwell, 2002) 43.

the waning of the exclusion crisis signaled an end to hopes for comprehension. From 1680 toleration supplanted comprehension as the principal ambition. Importantly, this quest was not driven by the aggressive independency of Owen. A younger group of theologians was taking a quite different ecclesiological line. By the 1690s this irenic new ecclesiology, radically centred on the invisible church, and the transcendent action of God, was predominant. However, unlike the political state, dissent did not achieve stability. The new ecclesiology, which by its very nature relegated the importance of institutions, was not capable of sustaining a unified movement, able to take full advantage of toleration.

Dissent was now facing decay. As Scott points out, Stuart England was a place in which 'institutions were fragile and ideas powerful.'[5] Dissenters' institutions were *extremely* fragile, in large part because the powerful idea of an invisiblist ecclesiology kept them so. Whilst the state was on a trajectory towards stability by 1694, dissent was on a path to self-destruction. Strength would not return until, by the infusion of further ideas and with new opportunities, dissent gave way to evangelicalism as bearer of the puritan impulse.

The Structure of this Book

In Chapter One, we 'approach' later Stuart dissent by first outlining the some key features of its history and assessing a range of explanations proffered by historians. The need for close attention to theology is identified and explored. In the second part of this chapter the specific challenges of seventeenth-century ecclesiology are outlined and the deep structure of the debates is explained. In Chapter Two, attention turns to the central individual in this study, John Howe. Howe has an historiographical 'history' of his own. Reasons why he has not been recognised as a major figure in earlier treatments, and why he is unsatisfactorily treated in more recent studies, are considered. His intellectual background and career until ejection in 1662 are then examined.

For Howe personally, as for dissent in general, the early Restoration was a troubled time. He was not yet a significant figure in seeking peace for dissent, though he was anxious for peace himself. This was found, physically and intellectually, during an interlude in Ireland in the early 1670s. In Chapter Three this period and the first of Howe's major works are discussed. It will be shown that the 1676 publication, *The Living Temple,* laid an essential foundation for Howe's developed ecclesiology.

5 Scott, *England's Troubles,* 24.

Howe's writings during the exclusion crisis are the focus of Chapter Four. As attitudes towards dissent within the established church began to harden once more, signs of a new approach began to emerge among some nonconformists. A divergence of views between older and younger leaders is identified in a major controversy of 1680. Official pressure on dissent increased as moves for exclusion faltered. Among the results was a burst of innovation among younger dissenters. In the early 1680s Howe developed a sophisticated case for tolerance and for a unity which transcended institutions. He was not the only one working on new ideas. Chapter Five compares Howe's approaches with those of John Locke (1632-1704).

With the glorious revolution, a bright future seemed to beckon. But the 1690s did not fulfill their promise. Dissent did not grow strong with toleration. Howe was at the centre of nonconformist affairs in this decade. Chapter Six examines his efforts towards unity and his response to their failure. Faced with the collapse of his schemes, he resorted to eschatological, rather than structural solutions. These provide a platform for another comparison. Chapter Seven makes an assessment of the points of difference between Howe and Richard Baxter.

The comparative studies of Chapters Five and Seven are crucial. Locke and Baxter have been advanced as the key influences on later dissent. There is no doubting their significance. However, their hegemony has been overstated. Each was compromised, in opposite ways. Locke was a radical innovator, though of questionable orthodoxy; Baxter was doctrinally sound, but no innovator. Howe was both an ecclesiological innovator and orthodox in piety and doctrine. His approach represents an essential third element in the theology of dissent. In Chapter Eight, the impact of this 'moderate nonconformity' is traced through the final period in 'the decay of the dissenting interest'. John Howe died in 1705 but his ecclesiology was picked up by Edmund Calamy and can be seen to have been influential in the thinking of Phillip Doddridge and Isaac Watts.

In the concluding chapter an attempt is made to describe the dynamics of later Stuart ecclesiology in general, employing the categories identified in the main part of the book. Specific attention is then given to the fate of dissent. What emerges is, in many respects, a sobering picture. The ecclesiology of later Stuart nonconformity was gravely flawed. Whatever the irenic visions of Howe and Calamy, dissent would need something more.

CHAPTER 1

Approaching Later Stuart Dissent

In the four decades following the collapse of the Republic in 1659, dissent experienced determining crises, both in its relationships with the Church of England and within itself. The period was a crucible in which theological differences became irreconcilable and the fragmentation of dissent gathered a fatal momentum.

This chapter is in three sections. The first provides an overview of the troubled relationship between dissent and Church until 1689 and the subsequent turbulence within dissent itself. Particular note will be taken of the several proposals for comprehension and/or toleration which alternated with periods of intensified persecution through the Restoration period. The second part examines the historiography of these events. After reviewing significant recent scholarship I will contend that an understanding of nonconformist theology is a vital adjunct to other approaches. I then turn to the concepts which provide the framework for this study. Key terms are introduced and the range of Stuart views of the church are outlined.

1.1 Dissent's Troubles, 1660-1730

The course of events which resulted in the re-establishment of the Church of England and culminated in the Act of Uniformity and the great ejection of 1662 has been well described in modern scholarship.[1] From the outset, ecclesiology was a centre of debate. A

1 See particularly R.S. Bosher, *The Making of the Restoration Settlement* (Westminster: Dacre Press, 1951); A. Whiteman, 'The Restoration of the Church of England' and R. Thomas, 'Comprehension and Indulgence', both in G. Nuttall and O. Chadwick (eds), *From Uniformity to Unity 1662-1962* (London: SPCK, 1962), 19-88 and 191-253; A.H. Wood, *Church Unity without Uniformity: A Study of Seventeenth-century English Church Movements and of Richard Baxter's Proposals for a Comprehensive Church* (London: Epworth, 1963) 118-240; I.M. Green, *The Re-establishment of the Church of England, 1660-1663* (Oxford: OUP 1978); R. Hutton, *The Restoration: a Political and Religious History of*

satisfactory settlement of the religious question was crucial to the success of the revived monarchy. The re-establishment of the Church of England was expected, even welcomed by 'Churchmen' and 'Presbyterians' alike,[2] but key questions remained. 'What form would the new edifice take?' and (closely related) 'Who would place themselves under its cover?'.

Essential to these questions were the concepts of 'comprehension' and 'toleration'. On the comprehension debate hinged the 'who's in' issue. Would the new Church take a form which was acceptable to a variety of interested parties, or would the settlement reflect the concerns of those who sought a narrow base, similar to the Church under Laud? Comprehension was thus an essentially ecclesiological problem. It entailed arguments over structure and ecclesiastical authority and depended upon fundamental views of what the church represented.

The toleration debate presented slightly different concerns. More directly political than comprehension, it sought to determine the official attitude to those who ended up outside the established Church. Should they be allowed to gather, to preach, to proselytise; or should the external practise of their religious views be constrained, even forbidden? The focus was more on civil than on ecclesiastical authority. However, the basic matters at stake in toleration were not as far apart from those of comprehension as might be imagined. As will be seen, in the seventeenth century, attitudes to toleration related very closely to fundamental images of the church.

The church question was confused from the start of the Restoration. From Breda on 4 April 1660 Charles II had declared 'a liberty to tender consciences, and that no man shall be disquieted or called into question for differences of opinion in matter of religion, which do not disturb the peace of the Kingdom.' To those nervous about the return to prominence of such hardliners as Gilbert Sheldon (1598-1677), this sounded promising. But the declaration was vague on details. It was unclear whether Charles intended a broad comprehension within one structure, or a generous toleration, or a combination of the two. It was also unclear what power Charles

---

England and Wales 1658-1667 (Oxford: Clarendon Press, 1985); P. Seaward, *The Cavalier Parliament and the Reconstruction of the Old Regime, 1661-1667* (Cambridge: CUP, 1989); J. Spurr, *The Restoration Church of England 1646-1689* (New Haven: Yale University Press, 1991), 29-42 and most recently in Keeble, *Restoration*, 109-20.

2 Whiteman, Restoration' 84; Thomas, 'Comprehension', 191; Spurr, *Restoration Church*, 44.

would have to implement his policies. The general religious settlement was, ultimately, to be a matter for Parliament.

The first meaningful negotiations took place at Worcester House in London during October 1660. Significantly, although spokesmen for the Court, the Churchmen and the Presbyterians were present, the Independents stayed away.[3] The main discussion was directed towards comprehension. The Declaration which followed offered a settlement generally acceptable to the Presbyterians whilst proposing few fundamental departures from the pre-interregnum Church structure.[4] Significant positions in the new structure were offered to leading Presbyterians.[5]

Final legislative approval of the Declaration fell to the Convention. This interim body was ill-equipped to provide clear direction. It was not the unequivocally 'Presbyterian' body sometimes assumed. The majority appears to have been at least moderately royalist, and most were willing to accept a form of episcopacy. Members recognised as Independent stood against the measure, thereby assuring its defeat.[6]

---

3 See N.H. Keeble, *The Literary Culture of Nonconformity in Later Seventeenth-Century England* (Leicester: Leicester University Press, 1987) 26-7 on divisions between Presbyterians and Independents over the Worcester House meetings and their results.

4 *RB* I. ii, para 276. Whiteman 'Comprehension', 66-8. Wood (*Church Unity*, 151) records Baxter's 'surprised delight' at the contents of the Declaration. See also Thomas, 'Comprehension', 192-4; Spurr, *Restoration Church*, 34-6.

5 Baxter, Reynolds and Calamy were offered bishoprics, Manton and Bates Deaneries. Baxter declined within two days. Reynolds accepted before the Declaration was rejected. As Lamont points out, Reynolds' acceptance of the see of Norwich was thus on the basis of an expected settlement incorporating a reduced episcopacy, along the lines earlier proposed by Archbishop Ussher. See W. M. Lamont, *Richard Baxter and the Millennium: Protestant Imperialism and the English Revolution* (London: Croom Helm, 1979), 235-6. Baxter was offered Hereford which was near to his old charge of Kidderminster. This may not have been a great catch. It had been described as 'the worst endowed bishopric in England.' - *Dictionary of English Church History* (London: 1912), 267. There is no record of any similar offer of a post to Howe, who was only thirty in 1660.

6 The traditional view was that Presbyterians had considerable sway in the Convention - see C.G. Bolam and J. Goring, 'Presbyterians in Separation: The Cataclysm' in C.G. Bolam, J. Goring, H.L. Short and R. Thomas (eds) *The English Presbyterians: From Elizabethan Puritanism to Modern Unitarianism* (London: Allen & Unwin, 1968), 73-112, 73-8 and Wood, *Church Unity*, 122. This confidence was misplaced. Bosher (*Restoration Settlement*, 146-7) accepts the view that 'Presbyterians' (as distinguished from 'Churchmen' and 'Independents') were a minority and that the balance of power was 'always

The fate of the Worcester House Declaration highlights important divisions among the dissenting groups. Its demise also marked the turning point of the Restoration Church settlement. Despite some rear-guard action by the Court[7], the election of the 'Cavalier' Parliament in 1661 removed any possibility of a broadly-based outcome.

The 1662 Act of Uniformity endorsed a Church that was essentially the same as the pre-Interregnum 'Laudian' institution. John Spurr has shown how varied were the motivations of those who did not conform. Though, for most, nonconformity was attended more by sadness than anger, for many there was no option.[8] Baxter left his post before St Bartholomew's Day deadline arrived.

The high degree of nonconformity demonstrated the failure of the Act of Uniformity to force comprehension. Almost immediately there was an abortive attempt to ameliorate the impact of this default. On 26 December, 1662 Charles II declared an 'Indulgence' in the spirit of Breda. The Court sought Parliamentary sanction of a Royal prerogative to set aside the penalties of the Act of Uniformity. Among dissenters, the reaction was mixed. The move was vigorously opposed by Sheldon and the eventual Bill had no chance of success in the Commons.[9]

Other, quite different legislation was successful in this period. The Conventicles Act of 1664 and the Five Mile Act of 1665 made sectarian activity very difficult. It was not until 1667 that either comprehension or toleration would again be formally proposed.

An apparent softening towards dissent among some Churchmen was emerging as early as November 1666.[10] An interesting formal

---

precarious'. Hutton notes the failure of the Presbyterians to gain control of the Convention (*Restoration* 105, 113, 117-8, 144-5). See also G. R. Cragg, *Puritanism in the Period of the Great Persecution 1660-1688* (Cambridge: CUP, 1957), 238-9; M.R. Watts, *The Dissenters: from the Reformation to the French Revolution* (Oxford: OUP, 1978), 213-5; Spurr, *Restoration Church*, 31-33.

7 Bosher, *Restoration Settlement*, 250-64; Hutton, *Restoration*, 175-6.

8 Spurr, *Restoration Church*, 43-5. See also Bolam and Goring, 'Presbyterians in Separation', 79-84; Watts, *Dissenters*, 227-238.

9 Bosher, *Restoration Settlement*, 270; N. Sykes, *From Sheldon to Secker: Aspects of English Church History 1660-1768* (Cambridge: CUP, 1959), 70-1; Wood, *Church Unity*, 233-4; Thomas, 'Comprehension', 195; R.A. Beddard, 'The Restoration Church' in J.R. Jones (ed.), *The Restored Monarchy 1660-1688* (London: Macmillan, 1979), 155-175, 167-168; Watts, *Dissenters*, 225; Hutton , *Restoration*, 193-197 (see also 175-6); Spurr, *Restoration Church*, 50-1.

10 Not too much can be built on this as the principal evidence is the sermon preached to the House of Lords by Reynolds, Bishop of Norwich, who had earlier identified with moderate Presbyterians. See W.G. Simon, 'Comprehension in the Age of Charles II', *CH*, Vol. 31, 1962, 440-448, 440. Barlow of

move began in January 1668. The chief architect was Dr John Wilkins (1614-72), Oliver Cromwell's brother-in-law and later Bishop of Chester. Wilkins proposed both comprehension and a parallel indulgence of those still unable to come into the established Church.[11]

The level of official support for this move is unclear.[12] In any case, the most important questions relate to the nonconformist response. Wilkins' negotiations were with Presbyterians. Accord was relatively quickly reached and a Bill drafted. But the Presbyterians had confined themselves to the comprehension side of the equation.[13] Conversely, the Independents, led by John Owen, were interested only in indulgence. Owen rejected Wilkins' proposals for toleration and independently advanced his own scheme. The Wilkins plan did not necessarily exclude Papists; Owen made strict Protestant orthodoxy a test.[14]

In the event, neither measure received a hearing in the Cavalier Parliament. As had happened after the 1663 attempt at indulgence, the 1668 Bills were followed by a call for even sterner measures

---

Lincoln appears to have drafted a 'Comprehensive Bill' in October 1667 - see Thomas, 'Comprehension', 197.

11 Thomas, 'Comprehension', 199.

12 The King appears to have endorsed it. Simon suggests no less than eight Bishops were involved. He lists them as Piers (Bath and Wells), Ironsides (Bristol), Nicholson (Gloucester), King (Chichester), Fuller (Lincoln), Croft (Hereford), Reynolds (Norwich) and Blandford (Worcester). He erroneously includes Wilkins, as at Chester, but this elevation did not take place until later in the year. Spurr has cast doubt on the manuscript evidence for this list. See Simon, 'Comprehension', 442; Beddard, 'Restoration Church', 168; J. Spurr, 'The Church of England, Comprehension and the Toleration Act of 1689', *EHR*, 104, 1989, 927-946, 941 n 4; G.J. Schochet, 'From Persecution to 'Toleration' in J.R. Jones (ed) *Liberty Secured? Britain Before and After 1688* (Stanford: Stanford University Press, 1992), 122-157, 143.

13 Thomas Manton, William Bates and, later, Baxter were involved. See Simon, 'Comprehension', 442-3; Wood, *Church Unity*, 247-9; Thomas, 'Comprehension', 198-202. The chronology outlined by Simon and Thomas does not support Spurr's suggestion of 'long negotiations' - 'Comprehension', 934.

14 Thomas, 'Comprehension', 200. Both Sykes (*Sheldon to Secker*, 74-5) and D.R. Lacey, in *Dissent and Parliamentary Politics in England, 1661-1689: A Study in the Perpetuation and Tempering of Parliamentarianism* (New Brunswick: Rutgers University Press, 1969) 287, n. 41) appear to confuse the two proposals, suggesting that Owen's Bill left the way open for Papacy. All refer to Barlow's account (Bodleian Library B. 14, 15, Linc; H. Thorndike *Works* (London: 1854) vol. 5., 304-5). Given the concerns of Owen, Thomas is probably correct to ascribe the less doctrinally rigid proposal to Wilkins.

against dissenters. A new Conventicles Act was passed, though it struggled to receive the King's assent.[15]

The magnitude of the opportunity lost in 1668 is hard to gauge.[16] Nevertheless, the various moves signal important differences within dissent. This division was not limited to a neat line, drawn between Presbyterian and Independent. Different approaches had been developing within Presbyterianism since the Five Mile Act had forced a choice of compliance or defiance. This became more marked and obvious after the collapse of the 1668 effort. By 1671 Sir Joseph Williamson could identify two parties which he christened 'Dons' and 'Ducklings'. Baxter, Manton and Bates, principal negotiators in 1668, were 'Dons' - conservative leaders who actively sought comprehension and disliked Independency. The 'Ducklings' were a group of generally younger men, closer to the Independents, who preferred some form of indulgence as a solution to their difficulties.[17] It will be seen that these different concerns reflected more than obvious disagreements over church polity. Deeper ecclesiological forces were at play.

Charles' Declaration of Indulgence of 15 March 1672 was of immense consequence. It suspended enforcement of laws against those Protestant nonconformists who gained licences and allowed private worship to Roman Catholics. Again, the significance of the Indulgence lies less in its specific provisions than in the varying responses of nonconformists to the toleration offered. Growing fundamental differences were laid bare.

On a simple reading of the figures, the Indulgence appears to have been welcomed eagerly.[18] Declining to recognise the Crown's jurisdiction over matters of conscience, many Baptists and all Quakers refused to apply.[19] Presbyterians varied widely in their enthusiasm. 'Don' types accepted the measure reluctantly. Baxter waited until October to take a licence and would do so only if described as merely 'nonconformist'. John Howe was by this time in

---

15 Thomas, 'Comprehension', 203.

16 Some historians of the period (e.g. Wood and H.G. Plum, *Restoration Puritanism: A Study of the Growth of English Liberty* (Chapel Hill, NC: University of North Carolina Press, 1943)) barely mention the Bills of 1668. Among those who do, assessments of their importance vary according to the account followed. Those preferring Baxter (e.g. Spurr) give the attempt little prominence. Those giving greater weight to Barlow's record (Simon and Lacey) accord it more significance.

17 Thomas, 'Comprehension' 207-9; Lacey, *Dissent*, 64 (following Thomas); Spurr, *Restoration Church*, 61-2.

18 For such an interpretation see e.g. Lacey, *Dissent*, 64.

19 Wood, *Church Unity*, 252-3; *CR* xv; Watts, *Dissenters*, 247-8.

Ireland. Calamy asserts that, on his return to London in 1676, he 'made a quiet and peaceable use of King Charles's Indulgence'.[20] The Indulgence had been abrogated by this time but this may suggest some continuing degree of *de facto* toleration, at least in London.[21]

The most eager licensees were the Independents. Moreover, a drift toward the Independent position was now readily discernible among the many younger Presbyterians who also applied. Ordinations, suspended since 1660, recommenced, though necessarily in a 'independent' style. Watts notes at least one case in which 'a regular church' was set up. In 1680 Edward Stillingfleet would assert that the Indulgence marked the beginning of Presbyterian separation. After the fillip provided by the Indulgence, enthusiasm for comprehension among nonconformists waned considerably.[22] This was a sign of a significant shift. N.H. Keeble has identified the gradual supplanting of 'nonconformist' by 'dissent' as the preferred self description, the latter term carrying with it a greater sense of 'willing choice, with no desire for reunion'.[23] I will suggest that this growing self-confidence can be identified in the fresh thinking which emerged in leaders such as Howe from the late 1670s onwards.

A similar decline in interest can be detected in the Church. Although a Bill 'for the Ease of Protestant dissenters', passed the lower house after the King had been forced to withdraw the Indulgence in 1673, this was very much a Commons (rather than Church) initiative and was effectively defeated in the Lords after determined efforts against it by Sheldon and his supporters. In any case, its main thrust was for toleration.[24]

Comprehension did not disappear as a theoretical option. It was discussed almost continuously from 1675-1681. Yet those with a positive interest in the idea were few: Tillotson and Stillingfleet from

---

20 *CR* 67.

21 On the rigour or otherwise of enforcement of the Conventicle Acts in the country see A. Fletcher, 'The Enforcement of the Conventicle Acts 1664-1679' in W.J. Sheils (ed) *Persecution and Toleration*, Studies in Church History 21 (Oxford: B. Blackwell, 1984), 235-246. For London see G.S. De Krey, 'The First Restoration Crisis: Conscience and Coercion in London, 1667-73', *Albion* 25, (Winter 1993) 565-580.

22 Watts, *Dissenters*, 248-9; Wood, *Church Unity*, 255; Spurr, 'Comprehension', 944-5; *Restoration Church*, 61-62; Thomas, 'Comprehension', 209-210.

23 Keeble, *Literary Culture*, 40-44.

24 Nonconformists (notably the ubiquitous Baxter) were consulted on the shape of the Bill but it was always a lay initiative and was closely related to the Constitutional issues presented by the Indulgence. See Sykes, *Sheldon to Secker*, 76-78; Thomas 'Comprehension', 210-214; Lacey, *Dissent*, 67-69; Spurr, 'Comprehension', 935 and *Restoration Church*, 64.

the Church; Baxter, Manton, Bates and Howe from dissent.[25] The Church displayed interest only to the degree that it felt threatened. The experience of 1672 had shown how quickly parishioners might change allegiance if toleration were put in place.[26] Even more frightening was the prospect of 'popery'. It was no coincidence that the 1675 discussions commenced in response to the Duke of York's proposals for indulgence and that the strongest moves for both comprehension and indulgence in this period (1680) fell within the exclusion crisis.[27]

Moves towards both comprehension and indulgence came to an end in 1680. From 1681 until 1686 dissent suffered the greatest persecution of the Restoration period.

Constant harassment was the reason given by Howe for abruptly leaving his congregation for Holland in August 1685.[28] However, yet another shift in alliances began under James II, who came to the throne in 1685. When James offered his own Declaration of Indulgence on 4 April 1687, the reaction among nonconformist clerics was as mixed as it had been in 1672. Many (including Baxter, Bates and Howe) refused to thank the King publicly, as he desired. Yet, a sizable number of Presbyterians and Independents did subscribe to Addresses of at least qualified acceptance of the measure.[29] Moreover, in a marked change from 1672, Quakers and many Baptists were prominent in welcoming the Indulgence.[30]

The Catholic James, by now clearly estranged from the Church of England, continued to build alliances among 'whig collaborators'. Mark Goldie has demonstrated the alacrity with which many lay

25 Little encouragement could be taken from the fact that the discussions in 1675 were prompted by two Bishops. Morley and Ward were unlikely peacemakers. See Thomas, 'Comprehension', 219-221.

26 Beddard, 'Restoration Church', 169; Spurr, *Restoration Church*, 63.

27 Sykes, *Sheldon to Secker*, 75-76, 82-3; Thomas, 'Comprehension', 222-228; H. Horwitz, 'Protestant Reconciliation in the Exclusion Crisis', *JEH*, vol. 15, 1964, 201-217; Watts, *Dissenters*, 249-51; Spurr, 'Comprehension', 936-7.

28 See Howe's 'Letter to His Congregation and Friends on Setting Out to Travel with Lord Wharton', (1685), *Works III*, 556-60. This letter and its implications are discussed in chapter five.

29 J. Stoughton, *History of Religion in England, from the Opening of the Long Parliament to the End of the Eighteenth Century* (London: Hodder & Stoughton, 1881), Vol. IV, 119-121; Cragg, *Puritanism*, 29; Thomas, 'Comprehension', 236; Lacey, *Dissent*, 180-2; R. A. Beddard, 'Vincent Alsop and the Emancipation of Restoration Dissent', *JEH*, vol. XXIV, No. 2, April 1973, 161-184, 179.

30 Thomas, 'Comprehension', 174-5; Lacey, *Dissent*, 182-4; Watts, *Dissenters*, 257-8; Beddard, 'Vincent Alsop', 174-5.

nonconformists cooperated with the new King's measures.[31] Clerical dissent was wooed from all sides. James renewed his Declaration in 1688 and actively sought nonconformist support. He already had significant allies among the Quakers and Baptists but had made little headway among the more cautious Presbyterians and Independents. Twice, during the final months of his reign, James made direct approaches to Howe and others but failed to convince them to back his cause.[32]

These holdouts had other commitments. Negotiations with the Church on terms for comprehension were apparently enjoying a renaissance. The Petition of the Seven Bishops (presented in May against the King's direction to read the second Indulgence in the Churches) raised the prospect of some willingness to seek an acceptable settlement. Detailed discussions were held during July 1688, but nothing resulted.[33]

James and the Church were not the only suitors. In 1687 there were secret discussions with an envoy of William of Orange.[34] The complexity of the situation led many to be wary of all overtures. When William eventually landed, nonconformist leaders were slow to endorse him before his victory seemed certain.[35]

With the glorious revolution, and a new Convention Parliament, came early legislative moves for both comprehension and indulgence. The Bills were a Church package, designed to complement

---

31 See M. Goldie, 'John Locke's Circle and James II', *HJ*, 35, 3 (1992), 557-586 and 'James II and the Dissenters' Revenge: the Commission of Enquiry of 1688', *HR*, vol. 66, No. 159, Feb 1993, 53-88.

32 William Penn the Quaker and Stephen Lobb, a Congregationalist were James's agents on the first of these occasions (May 23) see Lacey, *Dissent*, 211-2, 220; Thomas, 'Comprehension', 238.

33 The undertaking by the Churchmen was vague and noncommittal. It included a reference to Convocation and was given little credence by dissenters. Lacey, *Dissent*, 187, 210-211 (see note 5); Spurr, *Restoration Church*, 94. See also Sykes, *Sheldon to Secker*, 83-85; Wood, *Church Unity*, 265; Watts, *Dissenters*, 259; Spurr, 'Comprehension', 937; N. Tyacke, 'The `Rise of Puritanism' and the Legalizing of Dissent, 1571-1719', in O.P. Grell, J.I. Israel and N. Tyacke (eds), *From Persecution to Toleration: The Glorious Revolution and Religion in England* (Oxford: Clarendon, 1991), 17-49, 39.

34 Both Howe and Bates were involved. Morrice records some caution on the part of nonconformists about their prospects if both William and Mary were to come to the throne. - see Lacey, *Dissent*, 186-187, 343 n 41.

35 Lacey (*Dissent*, 221-2) cites Morrice's frustration that dissenters 'did not more openly and publicly rise for, and serve the Prince of Orange'. Baptists and Quakers, many of whom had collaborated with James II, 'were most notably absent' from William's supporters.

each other.[36] Their respective fates are instructive. The Comprehension Bill was narrow, in many respects not acceptable even to moderate nonconformists who put together an alternative proposal. In an apparent deal between 'tory' and 'whig' groups, only the indulgence measure was seen through the parliamentary process, becoming the vaunted 'Act of Toleration'. The comprehension issue was referred to a Church Convocation, from which it did not emerge.[37]

It is clear that the Act settled few matters of importance in what B.R. White calls 'the twilight of puritanism'.[38] The Presbyterians and Independents experimented with a 'Happy Union' in the early 1690s, but this attempt at institutional co-operation quickly unravelled. There were minor attempts at reconciliation with the Church of England. These too were fruitless. By John Howe's death in 1705, all prospect of a broad, nationally-unified Church in England was gone.

In the decades which followed, dissent gradually broke up into competing nonconformities. It became 'fragmented, highly argumentative and individualistic'.[39] The watershed event was a division at Salters' Hall in 1719 when the loose grouping of dissenters in London fragmented amid argument and recrimination. Deep concern at these developments was felt among dissenters themselves, encapsulated in Strickland Gough's indictment in *An Enquiry into the Causes of the Decay of the Dissenting Interest* (1730). Isaac Watts (1674-1748) and Phillip Doddridge (1702-51) would attempt to recover the situation, but by the 1740s it is estimated that the numerical strength of dissenters was half what it had been in 1690.[40]

36 Spurr, *Restoration Church*, 103; Lacey, *Dissent*, 234-7.

37 Thomas, 'Comprehension', 251-3.

38 B.R. White, 'The Twilight of Puritanism in the Years Before and After 1688' in Grell *et al From Persecution to Toleration*, 307-330.

39 R. Brown, *Church and State in Modern Britain 1700-1850* (London: Routledge, 1991), 110-111.

40 J.C.D. Clark, *English Society 1688-1832: Ideology, social structure and political practice during the ancien regime* (Cambridge: CUP, 1985), 137. Holmes argues that the true relative weakness of dissent was not appreciated by defenders of the establishment - G. Holmes, *Religion and Party in Late Stuart England,* London: Historical Assn, 1975), *passim* and *The Making of a Great Power: Late Stuart and Early Georgian Britain 1660-1722* (London: Longman, 1993), 350-365. See also J. Goring, 'The Break-Up of Old Dissent' in Bolam *et al The English Presbyterians*, 175-218.

1.2 Explaining the Troubles

Key events in this history remain without satisfactory explanation. The reasons for the failure of the Worcester House Declaration, the severity of the Act of Uniformity and its supporting legislation and the failure of Charles' attempts at Indulgence are neither simple nor obvious. The rise and fall of various attempts to construct a more comprehensive religious settlement are as complex. Why was the Church apparently open to the possibility from 1675-80, only to abandon promising discussions as the exclusion crisis faded? Why was toleration the only major fruit of the glorious revolution, whilst comprehension, despite renewed negotiations during 1688, withered on the vine? Why did Quakers, Baptists and more radical Independents exploit the policies of the Catholic James II? In the aftermath of the glorious revolution, why were nonconformists unable to forge lasting formal bonds? How are we to interpret the division at Salters' Hall in 1719? In this study, developments in theology will be employed to provide a fresh view of these and other aspects of later Stuart dissent. However, it is necessary first to assess other recent approaches. As this is a particularly fertile field there are almost endless variations on the causes of these events. So, acknowledging that there are numerous subtleties, the available interpretations have been grouped according to what they identify as the key forces at work

A desire for 'peace' has long been recognised as an important element in Restoration religious issues. The view clearly has some merit. After the turmoil and uncertainty of the preceding two decades, there was unquestionably a strong yearning for 'the quiet life' in 1660.[41] Moreover, this interpretation suggests a logical link between perceived threats to national stability (such as the Yorkshire uprising (1663), the Rye House Plot (1683) and Monmouth's rebellion (1685)) and moves against dissent.[42] The call for peace was matched by moves to restore structures of power. Nowhere was this

---

41 Spurr, *Restoration Church*, 29 records the relief of Henry Newcome and Robert South. Cragg, *Puritanism*, 3 and Keeble, *Literary Culture*, 24-5 note similar feelings among puritans.

42 D.J. Milne, 'The Results of the Rye House Plot and their Influence Upon the Revolution of 1688', *T.R.H.S.*, Fifth Series, Vol. 1, 1951, 91-108; Cragg, *Puritanism*, 25-27; Watts, *Dissenters*, 221-229; Seaward, *Cavalier Parliament*, 189-90; J. Barry, 'The Politics of Religion in Restoration Bristol' in T. Harris, P. Seaward and M. Goldie (eds), *The Politics of Religion in Restoration England* (Oxford: B. Blackwell, 1990), 163-189, 176-7; J. Spurr, 'Virtue, Religion and Government: the Anglican Uses of Providence', in Harris et al, *The Politics of Religion in Restoration England*, 29-47, 34-35 and *Restoration Church*, 51, 81, 88.

more apparent than among the gentry who made up the bulk of the Cavalier Parliament. Green asserts that this group 'attacked those forces which challenged the ecclesiastical hierarchy and the existing order of society.'[43] Hutton describes this drive for the restoration of order as the 'tremendous unifying force' of early Restoration developments. The gentry 'fought to have Crown, Church, towns, Catholics, dissenters and vagrants all equally within their control, so that no force could remain within society capable of destroying its stability again.'[44] An 'unwillingness to allow the extension of political rights' may have been a telling reason for the ultimate failure of the 1689 Bill for Comprehension.[45] Yet, interpretations based on such motivations are hardly sufficient. They do not account for moves towards toleration within the Commons after 1680. Almost by definition they have nothing to say of the motivations of the dissenters and shed no light on the apparent waxing and waning of interest in comprehension among conformists. Recognising this, historians have brought other factors into the picture.

The 'puritans' and their successors have often been linked to the merchant classes. None would now cast the disputes between gentry Churchmen and 'middling' nonconformists as simple class conflict.[46] However a 'prosperity' interpretation has encouraged the idea that moves to toleration in particular were related to commercial concerns. By this view, the economic importance of the nonconformists (particularly in London) made persecution ultimately untenable. Economic arguments were certainly employed. The London MP and merchant, Sir William Thompson, supported toleration in 1668 'be-

---

43 Green, *Re-establishment*, 180. Green holds that 'the zeal of the gentry for the episcopal Church of England' was 'the most important single influence' on the church settlement (200). Seaward, *Cavalier Parliament*, 194-5, suggests that a profound identification of stability with uniformity was found in only 'a powerful minority' in the Cavalier Parliament but was nevertheless a factor 'among the country gentry as a whole'. See Hutton, *Restoration*, 183; Beddard, 'Restoration Church', 156.

44 Hutton, *Restoration*, 289.

45 Spurr, *Restoration Church*, 103. This concession to the political realities of parliament is interesting, given Spurr's preference for a theological explanation of the Church's attitude to the Bill - see Spurr, 'Church of England', 944.

46 Although Christopher Hill comes close. He asserts of a group which includes Richard Baxter that, during the Restoration, 'one common factor in the lives of these conservative Puritan ministers is the crucial importance to them of tithes' - *The Experience of Defeat: Milton and Some Contemporaries* (London: Faber, 1984), 217. Much of the framework for Hill's study depends upon economic stratification. As already noted, Green almost identifies parliamentary 'Anglicanism' with the country gentry.

cause...restraint would prove destructive to trade'.[47] Despite such sentiments, the 'prosperity' view is the weakest of the available explanations. It is now recognised that both Churchmen and nonconformists were to be found throughout all strata of society.[48] Paul Seaward has shown that the merchant elites of London gave substantial support to Sheldon's push for uniformity.[49] The fluctuations of nonconformist fortunes during the period demand a more subtle understanding.

Subtlety is certainly not lacking in the many-faceted 'political' interpretations of Restoration events. Several related themes emerge. The first is constitutional: the ongoing conflict between Crown and Parliament. Here the Indulgences of both Charles and James are understood as claims to prerogative power. The subsequent defeat or withdrawal of each represents victory for anti-absolutists within Parliament. The reluctance of many nonconformists to accept the Indulgences reflects constitutional qualms. For this last there is considerable support in the statements of the moderate dissenters.

In many ways a Court version of the 'peace and power' views, a second political theme lies in both monarchs' need to secure their position. Thus, Charles' 1662 efforts to soften the provisions of the Act of Uniformity related to his fear of nonconformist reaction. There was some basis for this. In 1671, arguing that dissenting ministers had more sway over the populace than did the parish clergy, John Hickes (Howe's brother-in-law) revised James I's maxim 'No Bishop, no King' to read 'No Non-conformist, no King'.[50] Charles II's chronic need for finance is used to explain his eventual capitulation to Parliament over the 1672 Indulgence. Support for comprehension from Charles and the dramatic overtures to dissent by James can be taken to reflect their desire to broaden the Crown's constituency, or

---

47 Lacey, *Dissent*, 448. For further examples (including one from John Owen) see C.E. Whiting, *Studies in English Puritanism from the Restoration to the Revolution, 1660-1688* (London: SPCK, 1962), 477, 495-6; R. Greaves, *Enemies Under His Feet: Radicals and Nonconformists in Britain, 1662-1677* (Stanford: Stanford University Press, 1990), 153; Tyacke, 'The Rise of Puritanism', 34-6.

48 T. Harris, 'Introduction: Revising the Restoration' in Harris *et al*, *The Politics of Religion in Restoration England*, 1-28, 20-22.

49 P. Seaward, 'Gilbert Sheldon, the London Vestries, and the Defence of the Church', in Harris *et al*, *The Politics of Religion in Restoration England*, 49-73, esp. 50-1.

50 J. Hickes, *A True and Faithful Narrative of the Unjust and Illegal Sufferings of many Christians...in Devon* (1671). See also C. *Wolsely, Liberty of Conscience the Magistrate's Interest* (1668).

at least to divide the opposition.[51] When the personal ambitions and machinations of other leading Restoration figures are incorporated it is clear that political explanations can be found for many of the twists and turns in the tortuous course of the religious disputes.

The most confident proponents of this interpretation relegate religious concerns to a minor role. J.R. Jones proclaims 'the demotion of religion from its previously dominant position'.[52] That view has recently been challenged by a raft of historiography which seeks 'to restore a lively sense of the tensions and the conflicts, the high stakes and the stern pieties, involved in the religious politics of Charles II's reign.'[53] There are, in any case, significant holes in the 'political' interpretation. As with the 'status-quo' explanations, little can be positively said by this approach about the attitudes of the nonconformists. The choice of so many not to conform in 1662 makes no clear sense by this view. Constitutional grounds could be adopted for more than one purpose.[54] Most importantly, the divisions within dissent over 'comprehension' versus 'toleration' and (on the Church side) the stands taken by such figures as Sheldon and Sancroft, defy mere political explanation. The laborious debates which attended the ecclesiological disputes and the weight of polemical writing from divines with no apparent political ambition require historians to attend directly to the more obviously religious forces at work.

Interpretations which highlight concerns over real or perceived threats from 'popery' might appear to address religious issues more directly. This is not necessarily so. John Miller identifies politics as the primary factor behind the 1678-1681 'popish plot' disturbances, suggesting that the immediate dangers of 'popery' were more imagined than real.[55] M.G. Finlayson argues that anti-Catholicism was a cypher for a complex web of constitutional, nationalistic and economic fears as well as theological concerns.[56] Along with the

---

51 J. Miller, 'The Later Stuart Monarchy' in Jones (ed.), *The Restored Monarchy, 1660-1688*, 30-47, 35; Beddard, 'Restoration Church' 161, 172.

52 J.R. Jones, 'Introduction' in Jones (ed), *The Restored Monarchy, 1660-1688*, 1-29. In the same volume Beddard suggests religion merely seconded 'secular grievance' - 'Restoration Church', 156.

53 'Preface' to Harris et al, *The Politics of Religion in Restoration England.*

54 See Lacey, *Dissent*, 65 on Philip Nye's argument in favour of the 1672 Indulgence.

55 John Miller, *Popery and Politics in England, 1660-88* (Cambridge: CUP 1973), 181-2.

56 M.G. Finlayson, *Historians, Puritanism and the English Revolution: The Religious Factor in English Politics before and after the Interregnum* (Toronto: University of Toronto Press, 1983), 123-141.

'politics' school in general, this relegation of strictly religious aspects has recently been challenged. By taking the arguments of protestant polemicists seriously, Jonathan Scott has built an impressive case for genuine religious factors in anti-Catholicism, at least in the 1678-83 'Restoration crisis'. He argues that, when put in a European (rather than merely English) context, the concern of Protestants sprang from anxiety over the advance of the Counter-Reformation.[57]

In this form, the 'popery' view explains well the discussions about comprehension between Church and dissent in the 1670s and again in 1687-88. The advances of Catholicism on the Continent raised fears about a Catholic succession. James II's actions once King seemed to confirm the threat.[58] A general opposition to Catholicism may have sealed the Parliamentary fate of the Indulgences.[59] However, some features of the narrative remain inexplicable by this approach. The Church abruptly broke off negotiations in 1680, just as James' succession was secured and before the end of the popular disruptions over Catholicism. Further, nonconformist groups like the Baptists and Quakers (whose theology clearly eschewed 'popery') supported the Indulgence efforts of James. With its religious aspects properly understood, anti-Catholicism accounts for a number of the concerns of Protestants. Yet, as a heuristic device for explaining the course of relations between Church and dissent in the Restoration period, it too is incomplete.

Whatever their individual limitations, might not these perspectives, if taken together, provide a rounded and sophisticated portrait of church disputes in the Restoration period? Each has its strengths and can supplement the light shed by the others. In particular, the actions of Court and Parliament receive considerable illumination. However, even so combined, these approaches do not provide the full picture. They leave significant shadows, the darkest of which, ironically, fall on those of whose opinions we have an unparalleled written record: the divines.

The theologians and leaders of both Church and dissent have not been taken seriously enough. Individuals like Howe, Baxter, Owen,

---

57 J. Scott, 'England's Troubles: Exhuming the Popish Plot' in Harris et al, *The Politics of Religion in Restoration England*, 107-131; most fully in *England's Troubles*.

58 Calamy 70-1; Cragg, *Puritanism*, 22-3; Horwitz, 'Protestant Reconciliation', 201-2; Watts, *Dissenters*, 249-50; Spurr, *Restoration Church*, 65-7. Sykes (*Sheldon to Secker*, 84) quotes Wake (in 1710) to the effect that, in 1688, most Church leaders were 'at the height of our labours, defending the Church of England against the assaults of Popery and thought of nothing else'.

59 Thomas, 'Comprehension', 209-211.

Bates, Alsop and their Church counterparts were religious, in most cases devout, men to whom theological questions were of the highest importance. Writing with Baxter in mind, Lamont has recently conceded that 'we can understand why historians have become heartily sick of the godly, but there is a price...to be paid for not listening to their voice.'[60] In Restoration historiography the price has been an inadequate understanding of the alienation of dissent.

The picture is only marginally different for the period following 1688. Several interpretations have been placed on the apparent decline of dissent. In 1975 J.W. Wilkes could explain its fate almost entirely in terms of 'secularisation'.[61] In different ways Geoffrey Holmes and J.C.D. Clark have pointed to the social and institutional alienation of nonconformists from political power.[62] Clark adds the impact of 'assertive Anglicanism'.[63] Michael Watts notes the effect of toleration itself in reducing the need for sacrificial zeal and thus weakening nonconformity at its heart. There are elements, he suggests, of the history of dissent which fit Neibuhr's model of an inexorable sociological shift from ascetic 'sect' to complacent and organised 'denomination'.[64] Most, though, acknowledge the debilitating effects of doctrinal disputes. The division at Salters' Hall in 1719 has been explained in terms of a split between rationalism and confessionalism.[65]

These latter interpretations appear to concede the importance of theology. Indeed they throw up significant insights. Nevertheless they deal primarily with surface manifestations rather than fundamental issues. The theological dynamics of nonconformity are not fully described merely by mapping public disputes. A full appreciation of the relationships between the various groups within dissent must go beyond their differences to acknowledge the corrosive effects of their underlying similarities. In this study an attempt will be made to identify the roots of 'dissent's troubles' in developments in ecclesiology. The roots of these innovations run a long way back into

60 W. Lamont, 'Arminianism: the controversy that never was' in N. Phillipson and Q. Skinner (eds), *Political Discourse in Early Modern Britain* (Cambridge: CUP, 1993), 45-66, 66.

61 J.W. Wilkes, 'The Transformation of Dissent: a Review of the Change from the Seventeenth to the Eighteenth Centuries' in C.R. Cole and M.E. Moody (eds), *The Dissenting Tradition: Essays for Leland H. Carlson* (Athens, Ohio: Ohio University Press, 1975), 108-122.

62 Holmes, *Making of a Great Power*, 355-6; Clark, *English Society*, 315-324, 376-7.

63 Clark, *English Society*, 137.

64 Watts, *Dissenters*, 388-91.

65 E.g. R. Thomas 'Presbyterians in Transition', in Bolam *et al* (eds) *The English Presbyterians*, 113-174, 169.

the history of Christian theology. However, tensions reached a critical mass in England in the first half of the seventeenth century.

1.3 The Early Stuart Church

For at least two centuries what has recently been termed 'England's long reformation'[66] threw up tensions which, when combined with political, dynastic and international pressures, placed unrelenting stress on public culture. The effect on the English Church was enormous and irreversible. In the seventeenth century a tide of division reached its flood in the series of disputes which began in the 1620s and culminated with the ejection of 1662. These were in part reflections of wider aspects of the instability which affected England for almost the entire century. There were also internal stresses. A complex web of ecclesiastical conflicts helped precipitate the mid-century crises. In the aftermath, these conflicts were recast and intensified.

The later Stuart period saw a divergence of ideas on fundamental questions of ecclesiology. The conformist position had gained theological strength during the Interregnum. By contrast, as they were propelled into separatism in 1662, nonconformists were in need of a new understanding of themselves, one which would sustain and justify their separation. The story of later Stuart dissent is in part the story of that search.

The conflicts of the early Stuart Church continue to be the subject of vigorous debate. Dualistic 'Anglican/puritan' interpretations are almost universally rejected but the acknowledged complexity of the issues has hindered the emergence of satisfactory alternatives. In Nicholas Tyacke's influential 'Anti-Calvinist' analysis the key provocation was Archbishop Laud's supposed 'Arminianism'.[67] However the implication that attitudes to predestination and free will provide a key has proved inadequate. Tyacke himself has conceded that Arminianism was 'essentially secondary to the sacramental reorientation of English religious life'.[68] Peter Lake has

66 See the debate in N. Tyacke (ed), *England's Long Reformation 1500-1800* (London: U.C.L. Press, 1998), especially Tyacke's 'Introduction: Rethinking the 'English Reformation,' 1-32.

67 See N. Tyacke, 'Puritanism, Arminianism and Counter-Revolution' in C. Russell (ed.) *The Origins of the English Civil War* (London: Macmillan, 1973), 119-43 and more fully in *Anti-Calvinists: the Rise of English Arminianism c1590-1640* (Oxford: Clarendon Press, 1987).

68 N. Tyacke, 'Archbishop Laud' in K. Fincham (ed), *The Early Stuart Church 1603-1640* (Basingstoke: Macmillan, 1993), 51-70, 69.

gone further, suggesting that a 'bizarre obsession with predestination is threatening to obscure...the real issues at stake' and that 'a wider context' is urgently required.[69]

The parameters of that vision were emerging even as Lake made his plea. He himself gave a hint, in identifying the 'Laudian style' as 'a coherent, distinctive and polemically aggressive vision of the Church, the divine presence in the world, and the appropriate ritual response to that presence.'[70] However, it has been Anthony Milton who has gone the furthest in reconstructing the necessary 'wider context'. In a groundbreaking 1995 monograph he examines attitudes to the Roman church and Reformed churches of the continent in the polemical discourse of the English Church.[71] By this analysis he is able to identify not two conflicting parties, but a confused spectrum of positions, influenced by a range of factors but able to be identified by means of the treatment in their discourse of such concepts as the 'true' church, the 'invisible church' and the 'visible church'. The 'wider context' which Milton describes lies not with doctrines of grace, as in Tyacke's original suggestion, but with doctrines of the church.

Here we encounter a puzzling blind spot in seventeenth century historiography. Although theology in general has begun to return to favour, it's treatment is often unhelpfully confined to 'the fortunes of Calvinism'.[72] Ecclesiology is often dismissed as a source of confusion. There is even a tendency to divorce ecclesiology from theology altogether. Tyacke, for instance, attempting to extend his 'Arminianism' analysis into the later Stuart period, finds the resultant picture perplexing and suggests it is therefore necessary to 'distinguish sharply between theology and ecclesiology'.[73] Yet such a distinction is both unnecessary and misleading. Ecclesiology is every bit as theologically driven as the doctrines of grace. Indeed, it is perhaps the field most revealing of the fundamental structures of theological discourse.

69 P. Lake, 'The Laudian Style: Order, Uniformity and the Pursuit of the Beauty of Holiness in the 1630s' in Fincham (ed), *The Early Stuart Church*, 161-185, 162.

70 Lake, 'Laudian Style', 162.

71 A. Milton, *Catholic and Reformed: The Roman and Protestant Churches in English Protestant Thought, 1600-1640* (Cambridge: CUP, 1995).

72 See e.g. J. Spurr, *English Puritanism 1603-1689* (Basingstoke: Macmillan, 1998), 153-170.

73 Tyacke, 'Arminianism and the Restoration Church', 334. Though with different interests, Mark Goldie similarly distinguishes ecclesiologial from theological arguments in his study of 'Religious Intolerance in Restoration England' in Grell *et al* (eds.), *From Persecution to Toleration*, 331-368.

1.4 The Deep Structures of Ecclesiology

Milton's extensive work has clearly advanced our understanding of the issues at stake in the early Stuart conflicts. Nevertheless, further theological questions remain. A clearer picture still may emerge if we push deeper, beneath the categories Milton identifies. Constructions such as the 'visible' and 'invisible' churches depend on even more fundamental concepts. Once again the historiography throws up hints of ideas at work at this lower stratum. Tyacke acknowledges a 'sacramental reorientation'; Lake cites the importance of 'the divine presence in the world'; John Fielding asserts that 'the concept of a holy visible church' finds its logic in 'a perceived divine immanence'.[74] Fincham notes that Laud himself held the altar to be 'the greatest place of God's residence upon earth'.[75] These insights point us to issues which lie beneath the landscape Milton has so thoroughly mapped.

Ecclesiologies depend on more than ideas about structure and authority, on more even than descriptions of the church. These surface issues are supported by a theological sub-stratum which deals with the nature of divine interaction with creation. Here, the crucial concepts are the 'immanence' and the 'transcendence' of God. The competing ecclesiologies of the Stuart period had their roots in this basic level.

In the deep structure of Christian theology there lies a tension between ideas which emphasise the 'otherness' of God - his 'transcendence' - and those which stress God's presence within the world - his 'immanence'. Transcendent views tend to expect God's work to be a 'breaking in' to a fallen, corrupt system, to effect spiritual rescue. Conversely, ideas based on immanence emphasise the view that the Spirit of God pervades all of creation and that the grace of God operates through apparently natural means. The first approach can regard nature as an impediment to God's work, the second sees nature as the principal channel. Transcendence imagines God's activity as a lightning bolt; immanence represents it as a mist rising from the bowels of the earth.

The implications of these two emphases are easily observed in Christology. In theory, Christians believe that salvation is rooted in the entire Christ event. Often, however, the stress is put on one or other of two aspects. Those who emphasise God's transcendence look primarily to the drama of the cross, holding that some eternal

---

74 J. Fielding, 'Arminianism in the Localities: Peterborough Diocese, 1603-1642' in Fincham (ed) *The Early Stuart Church*, 93-113, 103-4.

75 Cited by K. Fincham, 'Episcopal Government, 1603-1640', in K. Fincham (ed), *The Early Stuart Church*, 71-91, 81.

transaction took place which rescued the universe from sin. On the other hand, those who emphasise the immanence of God hold the crucial aspect of Christ to be the incarnation, the divine becoming human, the ultimate example of God working through creation.

These fundamental categories have proved useful in the history of ideas. John Sommerville links early modern 'secularisation' to a shift in emphasis from divine immanence to transcendence.[76] Carolyn Merchant applies the concepts to the history of science in the seventeenth century.[77] Particularly illuminating is Francis Oakley's extensive examination of a medieval defence against determinism.[78] Oakley identifies a distinction, drawn between the 'absolute' and 'ordinary' powers of God. The crucial issue was whether God can effect what is 'naturally' impossible. The scholastic Pierre d'Ailly, was

> prone to speak of God as acting 'naturally' when he acts in accordance with his ordained power, and as acting 'supernaturally or miraculously' when he acts by his absolute power, breaching thereby the 'common law' or 'common course of nature'.[79]

This distinction coheres almost exactly with the immanence/transcendence framework. In the normal course, God works immanently, through 'common laws', 'laws of nature' which he has decreed and maintains. Nevertheless, God can 'break in' and override his 'ordinary' power through the transcendent operation of his 'absolute' power.

The related concepts of immanence and transcendence or, rather, a spectrum of relative emphases on these divine qualities, lends added clarity to our understanding of the Stuart religion. It is important to recognise that there was no sharp dichotomy between 'transcendentalists' and 'immanentalists'. N.H. Keeble has identified a strong note of immanence in nonconformist literature of the period, which rejoiced that 'God's glory was as evident in the '*ordinary*' and in the 'extraordinary'. As will be seen, Howe reserved some of his richest prose to celebrate this truth. Spurr has shown that 'puritans' had a developed 'a sense of the holy'.[80] The determining factor,

---

76 C.J. Sommerville, *The Secularization of Early Modern England: From Religious Culture to Religious Faith* (New York: OUP, 1992), esp. 3-11, 165-187.

77 C. Merchant, *The Death of Nature: Women, Ecology and the Scientific Revolution* (San Francisco: Harper & Row, 1980), 202.

78 F. Oakley, *Omnipotence, Covenant and Order: An Excursion in the History of Ideas from Abelard to Leibniz* (Ithaca, NY: Cornell University Press, 1984), esp. ch. 2, 41-65.

79 Oakley, *Omnipotence*, 56.

80 Spurr, *English Puritanism*, 178-186.

though, was order and priority. 'The puritan life, the holy life, was all about giving precedence to the regenerate conscience.' God's presence in the world did not sneak up on one unawares; it was recognised by the redeemed. Thus communion was a privilege of the already converted, rather than a 'converting ordinance.' Crucially, 'it was not the liturgy or the Sabbath, images or providences, in themselves which mattered to puritans, it was the fact that God's word had invested them with significance, had made them holy or unholy.'[81]

There are profound implications for the debates of the Stuart church, especially those concerning ecclesiology. Those who gave priority to immanence also tended to lay great store on the church as the vehicle of God's grace. This 'visible' church was empirical, observable and typically (though not necessarily) identified with the institutions and hierarchies of ecclesiastical organisation. Its sacraments and forms mediated encounter with God. Conversely, the ecclesiology of those who emphasised transcendence was centred on the invisible church - a spiritual reality, not to be identified with any organisation or structure. Rather than a vehicle, the invisible church was the product of God's grace. It consisted of the elect, the truly saved. Here the quest was for immediacy; sacraments were relegated and preaching (with its promise of a direct word from God) elevated.

1.5 Conformist Ecclesiology

Anthony Milton has shown that the English Church was irretrievably fractured by 1640.

> Religion...was no longer in a position to unite the forces of the realm - now it could only further divide them. This was a truth that would haunt not just the following decade, but the rest of the century.[82]

This assessment is surely sound. The trauma of the middle decades of the seventeenth century would further polarise English ecclesiology. In the 1640s Church of England loyalists had personal crises which would be matched by those of the nonconformists in the 1660s. The shock waves would not subside quickly. Dissent developed an ever-stronger desire for unmediated encounter with God and an increasing orientation to the invisible church. The part played in this evolution by John Howe is the focus of this study. But dissent was not alone in its drift to a more extreme position. Within the Church of England, too, there were conflicting understandings of

---

81 Spurr, *English Puritanism*, 185-6.

82 Milton, *Catholic and Reformed*, 546.

authority and divine action. In their extreme forms, these differed from each other as decidedly as they both rejected nonconformity.

Milton has shown how 'avant-garde conformists' and 'Laudians' developed a pronounced aversion to discourse about the invisible church. In a 1993 essay he concluded that, under the 'Laudians' 'there was no longer to be any confusion in the use of the word 'church' - it would now only refer to visible institutions.'[83] This shift would be hugely influential over Restoration conformist ecclesiology. However, not one but two streams flowed out of this catchment. Both emphasised divine immanence, but they differed as to its locus and operation. Only to the first may be properly ascribed the familiar label of 'high church'. For reasons which will become clear I will term the second the 'Constantinian' view. It was with an amalgam of these ideas that the leaders of Restoration dissent had to contend. The basic concerns of each feature again and again in the arguments employed by Churchmen in Restoration debates over comprehension and toleration. Before proceeding we will note the characteristics of these two approaches.

A broad historiographical consensus identifies a marked evolution of 'high church' ecclesiology during the Interregnum.[84] The most important elements in this development were the further reinforcement of episcopacy and the refinement by Henry Hammond of

---

83 A. Milton, 'The Church of England, Rome and the True Church: The Demise of the Jacobean Consensus' in K. Fincham (ed), *The Early Stuart Church*, 187-210, 196-7. See also Milton, *Catholic and Reformed*, 296-300. The reluctance to employ invisiblist language arose in part from its association with allegations that the 'true' Church had at times become 'invisible'. This was an argument used primarily against Rome but it was also a powerful tool to be used against any visible ecclesiastical authority regarded as heretical. Because of this danger Laud, notes Milton (*Catholic and Reformed*, 298), 'had effectively deprived [the purer sense of the invisible Church of the elect] of any practical importance outside the particular visible Church.'

84 The interpretation has a long pedigree. Baxter noted the rise of 'New Prelatists' , identified with Hammond - see Whiteman, 'Restoration', 43-44 and 37-49 generally. John Keble discerned 'a marked distinction' between Hooker's view of the episcopate and 'the bolder and completer view' of such as Laud and Hammond - 'Editor's Preface', R. Hooker, *Works*, Vol. 1, Oxford, 1841, (Seventh ed. - 1888), ix-cxvi, lxxxv. See also N. Sykes, *Old Priest, and New Presbyter: The Anglican attitude to episcopacy, presbyterianism and papacy since the Reformation* (Cambridge: CUP, 1956), 58-117 and *Sheldon to Secker*, 105-139; G. Every covers some of the issues in *The High Church Party 1688-1718* (London: SPCK, 1956), 1-18; P. Avis, *Anglicanism and the Christian Church* (Edinburgh: T&T Clark, 1989), 139-153 is useful, although more descriptive than analytical. The best available analysis is found in Spurr's work, esp. *Restoration Church* 1-28, 105-165.

the idea of the 'national church'. The latter concept supplied a much needed external defence against the Roman charge of schism.[85] Its internal impact was to intensify, rather than diminish, the 'high church' commitment to the visible church.

This may be most readily observed in the writings of Herbert Thorndike. Thorndike (1598-1672) was one of the few truly systematic thinkers in the Interregnum and Restoration Church. He was the quintessential 'high church divine.'[86] Writing in 1659, he displayed a typical preoccupation with visible unity.

> [U]nity in the Church is of so great advantage to the service of God, and that Christianity from whence it proceedeth, that it ought to overshadow and cover very great imperfections in the laws of the Church....Especially, seeing I maintain that the Church, by divine institution, is in point of right one visible body, consisting in the communion of all Christians, in the offices of God's service; and ought, by human administration, in point of fact to be the same.[87]

So crucial were visible communion and uniformity that their absence called into question the veracity of the faith.

> [W]ere not the Church...one society, one visible body, communion or corporation from the beginning - the communion whereof always confin[ing] the profession and conversation of Christians to some certain visible rule - I should think it impossible to make evidence of any common truth received of all Christians.[88]

It was thus incumbent on the church, through its leaders, to determine the proper interpretations of scripture and institute appropriate forms and rituals.[89] The alternative was the anarchy of the Interregnum.

> But if all the world should do as men do now in England, make every fancy taken up out of the Bible a law to their faith - not questioning whether ever professed, owned or enjoined by the Church, or not - it would soon become questionable whether there be indeed any such thing as Christianity or not, those that profess it agreeing in noth-

---

85 Bosher, *RestorationSettlement*, 83-4; Sykes, *Old Priest*, 66-84; Whiteman, 'Restoration', 43-48; Avis, *Anglicanism*, 139-154. Spurr, (*Restoration Church* 163-4) suggests that the National Church concept was crucial as it 'simultaneously repudiated Rome's accusations [of schism] and condemned the Nonconformists whilst remaining compatible with the Royal supremacy' as well as providing a focus for unity. See Milton, *Catholic and Reformed*, 322-340 on the antecedents of Hammond's view among the Laudians.

86 On Thorndike see *D.N.B.*; Stoughton, *Religion in England* IV, 254-265; Avis, *Anglicanism*, 147-150.

87 H. Thorndike, *Of the Principles of Christian Truth*, (1659), *Works*, 2, pt I, 6.

88 Thorndike, *Principles*, pt I, 102.

89 Thorndike, *Principles*, pt I, 114-6.

ing....All churches should be linked together by a law of visible communion in the service of God, and so to make one Church.[90]

With one eye on Rome, Thorndike asserted that the church was not infallible. However, dissension was warranted only when its rulings were 'destructive to the common faith'. In all other cases, especially those relating to forms and structures, submission was required.[91] There was thus no ground for nonconformity. If dissenters received harsh punishment, they had only themselves to blame.

[W]here...unity is once broken to pieces and destroyed, and palliating cures are out of date, the offence which is taken at shewing the true cure, is imputable to them that cause the fraction, not to him that would see it restored.[92]

Thorndike was a useful, if extreme, case of what Spurr describes as 'a shift in the Church of England's ecclesiological centre of gravity toward a more Catholic understanding of the nature of the church.'[93] His attitude to what would become dissent is indicative of the approach taken by many during the later Stuart period.

Samuel Parker (1640-1688) attacked dissent from a different direction. His was an heroically 'Constantinian' vision. Like Thorndike, Parker stressed the immanent work of God. Direct, immediate, divine action was discounted; the age of miracles was dead. In only one period in history had God acted intrusively: in the crucial first centuries of the Christian church. At that time, he says,

[Christians] were not capable of any coercive Power; tis wonderfully remarkable how God himself was pleased to supply their want of civil jurisdiction by his own immediate Providence, and in a Miraculous way to inflict the Judgments they denounced.[94]

However, this age of frequent transcendent activity ended once 'coercive Power' through 'civil jurisdiction' became available - that is: with Constantine. As soon as Emperors became sympathetic to the Christian cause 'then began the Divine Providence to withdraw the miraculous Power of the Church...as being now well supplied by the natural and ordinary Power of the Prince.'[95]

The prince, the successor to Constantine, was central to Parker's thought. Whereas Thorndike located immanence in the church, Parker identified it with the magistrate. Princes were paramount because they were part of the God-ordained natural order. No

90 Thorndike, *Principles*, pt II, 400.
91 Thorndike, *Principles*, pt II, 511.
92 Thorndike, *Principles*, pt I, 6.
93 Spurr, *Restoration Church*, 113.
94 S. Parker, *A Discourse of Ecclesiastical Politie*, London, 1669, 44.
95 Parker, *Ecclesiastical Politie*, 49.

scripture was needed to establish their authority as 'from the first ages of the World, Monarchy was its only Government, necessarily arising out of the constitution of Humane Nature.'[96]

There were obvious implications for the question of religious authority. Conscience could be dismissed as fickle and unreliable; its elevation led inexorably to arrogance, rebellion and anarchy. This was what Parker held to be the fundamental crime of dissenters. Their message was not merely wrong, it was dangerous, and not to be tolerated.

Although he was accused of 'Hobbism', Parker's vision was radically different from what he called the 'Malmsbury Philosophy'. Hobbes saw Leviathan arising as the only practicable way of dealing with a bad situation. To Parker, the goodness of God precluded the possibility of there ever being a bad situation in Nature. Humans were created with a drive to set up princes, that they did so was merely proof of God's providence. It is inaccurate to suggest either that Parker had no theological foundation to his ideas or that he was caught in a 'dilemma' when seeking to reconcile natural law and strong political authority.[97] His position was the natural product of his location of immanent divine action in the prince. Although clothed in the discourse of theology, Hobbes' commitment to the sovereign was fundamentally pragmatic; Parker's lay at the heart of his religion. Moreover, a major concern in Hobbes' thought was to remove unnecessary 'fear' by placing God at a considerable remove from humans.[98] For Parker the movement was in the opposite direction - the *nearness* of God was secured in the magistrate. For Hobbes, immanence played no active part; for Parker, it was everything.

---

96 Parker, *Ecclesiastical Politie*, 29.

97 For such suggestions see G. Schochet, 'Between Lambeth and Leviathan: Samuel Parker on the Church of England and political order' in Phillipson and Skinner (eds) *Political Discourse in Early Modern Britain*, 189-208 and 'Samuel Parker, religious diversity, and the ideology of persecution' in R.D. Lund (ed) *The Margins of Orthodoxy: Heterodox Writing and Cultural Response* (Cambridge: CUP, 1995), 119-148, 135-6; J. Parkin, 'Hobbism in the Later 1660s: Daniel Scargill and Samuel Parker', *HJ* 42, I, (1999), 85-108, 107. For other comparisons of Parker and Hobbes see R. Ashcraft, *Revolutionary Politics & Locke's 'Two treatises of Government'* (Princeton: Princeton University Press, 1986), 48-52 and J.G.A. Pocock, 'Thomas Hobbes: Atheist or Enthusiast? His Place in a Restoration Debate', *History of Political Thought*, Vol. XI, No. 4, Winter 1990, 737-749.

98 Richard Tuck has shown how Hobbes ultimately achieved this in *Leviathan*. See R. Tuck, 'The civil religion of Thomas Hobbes' in Phillipson and Skinner (eds), *Political Discourse in Early Modern Britain*, 120-138.

Thorndike and Parker are extreme cases, useful for appraisal and example but not necessarily representative of the majority. Not all or even most Anglicans were as eccentric in their commitments as these two. Most held versions of both the 'high church' and 'Constantinian' views in tension. These ideas may be observed to varying degrees among many Churchmen of the Restoration. High churchmanship akin to Thorndike's drove the Seven Bishops in 1689.[99] It was found in moderate form in Edward Stillingfleet (1635-99). Parker's Constantinian view probably reflected that of his patron, Archbishop Gilbert Sheldon[100] and was paralleled in Parker's contemporary and fellow-defender of James II, Thomas Cartwright (1634-1689).[101] It would find an attenuated echo in John Tillotson (1630-94). Traces of each approach thus appeared across the range of Anglican polity, from Archbishops to 'latitudinarians'.[102]

1.6 Nonconformist Ecclesiology by 1660

Developments in dissent to some extent mirrored those in the established Church. Laud and his followers did not create a new 'puritanism' in the 1620s and 1630s. Rather, a discernible 'Laudian' tilt towards the visible reactivated concerns among 'the Godly'

---

99 On this see M. Goldie, 'The Political Thought of the Anglican Revolution' in R.A. Beddard (ed), *The Revolution of 1688* (Oxford: Clarendon Press, 1991), 102-136, esp. 124-132. See also J.A.I. Champion, *The Pillars of Priestcraft Shaken: The Church of England and its enemies 1660-1730* (Cambridge: CUP, 1992).

100 Whiting, *Studies in English Puritanism,* 502, asserts that Parker's *Discourse* was published at Sheldon's request. See also Ashcraft, *Revolutionary Politics,* 44. Parker was Sheldon's Chaplain. He appears to have had some responsibility for assessing books for imprimatur see L. Kirk, *Richard Cumberland and Natural Law: Secularisation of Thought in Seventeenth-Century England* (Cambridge: James Clarke, 1987), 15 & esp. 78-9.

101 Cartwright was appointed to Chester at about the same time as Parker was to Oxford. Both appointments were resisted by Sancroft. Burnet notes that Cartwright 'had set himself long to raise the king's authority above law...their authority was from God, absolute and superior to law'. In Burnet's assessment, Parker and Cartwright were 'the two worst men that could be found out'. See G. Burnet, *History of My Own Time* (London, 1838), 442-3 and Goldie, 'Political Thought', 135-6. For a sympathetic view of Cartwright see R.A. Beddard, 'Bishop Cartwright's Death-Bed', *Bodleian Library Record,* Vol. 11, 1984, 220-230.

102 I have outlined some of the implications of the presence of these two strands in conformist ecclesiology in Martin Sutherland, 'Protestant Divergence in the Exclusion Crisis', *JRH,* vol. 21, No. 3, October 1997, 285-301. See also the discussion of the controversies of 1680 in chapter four.

which had never completely disappeared.[103] Snapshots of self-consciously different nonconformist ecclesiologies can be derived from the Presbyterian Westminster Confession (1647) and the Independent Savoy Declaration (1658). In direct contrast to the views of such as Thorndike and Parker, both of these statements emphasised the invisible church. Importantly, however, they differed in the degree of that bias.

The Presbyterian system preserved a significant role for the visible church. The definition in the Westminster Confession is instructive.

> The visible Church...consists of all those, throughout the world, that profess the true religion, and of their children; and is the kingdom of the Lord Jesus Christ, the house and family of God, out of which there is no ordinary possibility of salvation. (XXV.2)

Yet it was the *invisible* church which was 'the spouse, the body, the fullness' of Christ (XXV.1). The prime function of the visible church was the 'gathering and perfecting of the Saints' (XXV.3) The Confession maintained a traditional Reformed concern for the visible measure of 'discipline' but nevertheless signalled that the visible was to be determined by invisible categories (i.e. the 'saints', the elect). Further, the 'visibility' of the church fluctuated according to its purity (XXV.4). The importance of the visible church thus flowed from its relation to the invisible. There was little sense of it having its own *raison d'être*.[104]

A subtly different picture emerges among the Independents. Immediately prior to his death, Cromwell had reluctantly sanctioned what would be the Savoy Conference (29 September to 12 October 1658). Howe attended this gathering, though as an observer rather than a participant.[105] Neal records that the Protector and some in his court were unhappy with this conference of Independents 'as tending to establish a separation between them and the Presbyterians'.[106] At the time, Cromwell retained hopes for a union of the two parties.[107]

---

103 P. Christianson, 'Reformers and the Church of England under Elizabeth I and the Early Stuarts', *JEH*, vol. 31, no. 4, Oct. 1980, 463-482, 480-481.

104 E.G. Jay, *The Church: Its Changing Image Through Twenty Centuries* (London, SPCK, 1977), vol. 1, 210-211.

105 R.F. Horton, himself a Congregationalist, endeavours to make Howe an Independent on the basis of his attendance at Savoy. See R.F. Horton, *John Howe* (London, Methuen, 1895) 55-6.

106 D. Neal, *The History of The Puritans, or Protestant Nonconformists* (4 vols., London: 1732-9) abridged in 2 vols. by E. Parsons (London, 1811), II, 434.

107 A.G. Matthews, *The Savoy Declaration of Faith and Order 1658* (London: Independent Press, 1959), 16. This is borne out by the comments of Howe in a letter to Richard Baxter on April 13 1658 (*Baxter Correspondence* III, 198).

The Savoy Declaration displayed an even greater relegation of the visible church than is evident among the Presbyterians. As the Declaration was based upon the Westminster document, its differences are important. Chapter XXV.2 of the Confession (quoted above) was replaced with the following statement.

> The whole body of men throughout the world, professing the faith of the Gospel and obedience unto God by Christ according to it, not destroying their own profession by any Errors everting the foundation, or unholiness of conversation, are, and may be called the visible Catholique Church of Christ, although as such it is not intrusted with the administration of any ordinances or have any officers to rule or govern in, or over the whole Body. (XXVI. 2)

The Savoy clause placed a greater stress on godliness. There was no mention of children[108] and, significantly, the Westminster phrase 'out of which there is no ordinary possibility of salvation' was omitted. In keeping with this shift to the invisible, the Congregationalists proscribed any institutional authority of the wider church.

There were streams of dissent beyond Presbyterians and Independents. Of these, Baptists differed on only a few matters from the Independents. More extreme, 'spiritualist' types of ecclesiology, fellow travellers with the radical edge of continental Protestantism, had never played a major role in English Christianity. Though they enjoyed a brief, albeit spectacular, flowering in early years of the Interregnum, the only significant group to enter the Restoration period was the Quakers. Even here caution is necessary. At least partly because of the spiritualists' suspicion of organisation, attempts to trace their taxonomy are fraught with difficulty. Simple, diachronic connections may certainly be disregarded.[109] However, M.B. Endy has made a convincing case for regarding groups that were 'spiritualist' in a broad sense (such as the Quakers) as theologically distinct from those, such as the Presbyterians and Independents, labelled 'puritan'.[110]

Early Quaker thought displayed an extreme emphasis on the invisible church. However Quakerism underwent a fundamental transformation during the Restoration. Not only organisation but a

---

108 Although a clause similar to that in the Westminster Confession appears in the 1680 version. See Matthews, *Savoy Declaration*, 111 n 5.

109 For examples see G.H. Williams, *The Radical Reformation* (Philadelphia: Westminster Press, 1962), 465, 788-789; Jay 179.

110 M.B. Endy Jnr, *William Penn and Early Quakerism* (Princeton: Princeton University Press, 1973) *passim* and 'Puritanism, Spiritualism and Quakerism: An Historiographical Essay' in R.S. and M.M. Dunn (eds), *The World of William Penn* (Philadelphia: U. Pennsylvania Press, 1986), 381-301.

form of discipline developed. The second-generation Quakerism of such as William Penn took on the characteristics of a type of Protestant ecclesiology quite distinct from that of the thoroughgoing spiritualists. By the 1690s, as mainstream Protestantism had found necessary a hundred and fifty years before, Quaker thought was integrating the visible church into its ecclesiology.[111]

Of English religion at the start of the Restoration period a picture emerges which portends conflict and difficulty. The essential problem was one of disparate theological cultures. The re-established Church was dominated by those who stressed divine immanence in one form or another. The dissenters came from those groups which sought a more immediate relationship with God and thus emphasised the invisible church. Even so, nonconformists were far from homogeneous - fault lines extended into Restoration dissent. Along these, as theological leadership fell to a new generation of divines, ecclesiological tremors would be felt.

At the fore in that new generation would be John Howe.

111 See Endy, *William Penn*, 330-336; Watts, *Dissenters*, 325-335; B. Reay, *The Quakers and the English Revolution* (London: Temple Smith, 1985), 103-122; E.B. Bronner, 'Quaker Discipline and Order, 1680-1720: Philadelphia Yearly Meeting and London Yearly Meeting', in R.S. and M.M. Dunn (eds), *The World of William Penn*, 323-335; White, 'The Twilight of Puritanism,' 316-318.

CHAPTER 2

John Howe's Early Career

Through the night of 20 December, 1675, John Howe brooded on the dangers of travel. He examined his heart, wrestling with fears and expectations, weighing danger against opportunity. His questions reflected the uncertainties of the occasion.

Have I not an undue Design or Self-respect in [this journey]?

Am I not afraid of miscarrying in this undertaken voyage, by shipwreck, &c.?[1]

The hazardous winter journey on which he was embarked was from Antrim, Ireland to London. It would prove a critical turning point in Howe's life. From relative obscurity he would move to the centre of nonconformist affairs. His hitherto indifferent career was about to enter a phase of success and recognition.

The winter expedition of 1675 serves as a poignant opening to a study of John Howe's theology and significance. It was a moment of crisis, but the dangerous journey has symbolic meaning as well. Howe was 45 years old. His personal journey to this point had itself been hazardous. Early promise had met with disappointment and failure; juvenile confidence had been overwhelmed for a time by diffidence and uncertainty. There was little to suggest that the John Howe who had been ejected along with hundreds of others in 1662 would amount to much. Yet by 1675 he was a focus for the hopes of significant leaders in dissent. This chapter will examine Howe's early career and intellectual development. First, however, it is necessary to consider why it has been that Howe has been a peripheral figure in most interpretations of the later Stuart period.

2.1 The Howe Myth

In 1707 James Webster, minister of the Tolbooth church, Edinburgh, was concerned about the impact of the Treaty of Union on religion north of the border. The example of English nonconformity cheered

1 Calamy 59, 63.

him little. 'Were not their Great toping men their leaders, Richard Baxter, Mr How and Dr Bates for the lawfulness of Episcopacy?...from all which is evident, we have not many firm friends in England, we can rely on.'[2]

Webster's suspicion of Howe and the others' faithfulness to the Presbyterian vision signals the fluidity of English ecclesiology - a theme which appears frequently in this study. Of the three 'toping men' only Baxter has been prominent (indeed, I will argue, too prominent) in the historiography. Bates seems to have fallen into a black hole of neglect. John Howe suffered a different fate. In direct contrast to his older contemporary and friend Baxter, Howe left a dearth of manuscript sources. This was deliberate. His oldest son, George Howe, recorded that his father, on his deathbed, ordered the immediate destruction of 'the large memorials he had collected of the material passages of his own life, and of the times wherein he lived, which he most industriously conceal'd...stitch'd up in a multitude of small Volumes...which accordingly I did.'[3]

George Howe's regrettable compliance with his father's instruction caused a significant loss to Stuart historiography. The student of John Howe thus faces a scarcity of primary biographical sources. The situation is partially redeemed by the survival of a few manuscript letters and the ready availability of Howe's theological compositions. The latter fall into two categories. Most important is the quite extensive corpus of his published works, spanning forty-five years.[4] In addition, there are several series of lectures and sermons 'taken first in shorthand by the hand of a very ready and judicious writer' and published after his death.[5] Fortunately for the

2 J. Webster, *Lawful prejudices against an incorporating union with England; or, some modest considerations on the sinfulness of this union, and the danger flowing from it to the Church of Scotland* (Edinburgh: 1707), 8.

3 Dr George Howe to George Hughes. Cited by Calamy 227-8. Rogers (*Life*, 3) claims this letter to be addressed to Obadiah Hughes, George Hughes' father, George Howe's uncle, John Howe's brother-in-law. As Obadiah Hughes predeceased John Howe, Calamy's record is clearly to be preferred.

4 Howe's works have been collected in several combinations. The only version currently available is a reprint of Calamy's 1724 collection, *The Works of the Rev. John Howe, M.A.* (3 Vols. - Ligonier, PA: Soli Deo Gloria, 1990). References to the published works will be to this version.

5 Howe, *Whole Works*, V, 211. The posthumous sermons were first published in the 1720s. They may be found in J. Hunt (ed) *The Whole Works of the Rev. John Howe, M.A.* (Eight Volumes - London, 1827). All references to these sermons and lectures will be to this collection. For indications of Howe's major concerns, the published material must take precedence. The recorded sermons are, however, of considerable value. They are generally easier to read than Howe's own writ-

historical theologian, Howe covers a wide range of issues in his works and, with due care, the shape of his thought may be construed with some confidence.

If access to Howe is limited as to primary material it is confused by generations of hagiography. Christopher Hill's maxim that 'the principal headache…is not too few documents but too many predecessors' rings true for Howe.[6] His biographers have magnified Howe's personal and spiritual qualities to heroic proportions. Thus, although his publications are readily available, the construction of a life setting for these writings is not always straightforward. Perhaps because of this problem of context, very little modern analysis of Howe's theological work has been attempted.

The construction of what may be termed the 'Howe myth' is worth tracing. Little biographical detail is to be found in John Spademan's 1705 funeral sermon for Howe, neither is there much of the exaggerated respect for the deceased, common in such orations. Spademan notes that Howe 'hated the sounding a trumpet before him, living and dying'.[7] However, in his dedication to the published version, regretting that he had 'spoken so few things...concerning him', Spademan makes recompense by recalling that 'he was not only a shining light and ornament of his age, but an inviting example of universal goodness.'[8] Such an assessment was not exceptional following the death of a popular figure. What is at once intriguing and frustrating to the modern historian is that Howe's subsequent biographers continued in this vein with apparently increasing enthusiasm.

Of the several accounts of Howe, four are more or less full-scale biographies. By far the most important is the first: Edmund Calamy's *Memoirs of the Life of the Late Rev. Mr. John Howe*, published in 1724. Calamy, a crucial figure in the development of later Stuart dissent, was the pre-eminent historian of the movement and an ac-

---

ten style. Further, as dates and locations are often noted, they are of value in plotting Howe's movements.

6 C. Hill, 'History and Denominational History', reprinted in *idem*, *The Collected Essays of Christopher Hill - Volume Two: Religion and Politics in 17th Century England* (Brighton: Harvester Press, 1986), 3-10, 3.

7 J. Spademan, *A Sermon on the Occasion of the Justly Lamented Death of the Truly Reverend Mr John Howe, April 8, 1705*, in Howe's *Works* III, 609-624, 611. As was typical of such sermons, Spademan employs the example of the deceased to edify the living. See N.H. Keeble, *Richard Baxter: Puritan Man of Letters* (Oxford: Clarendon Press, 1982), 123-4.

8 Spademan, *Sermon*, 609.

tive polemicist.[9] He reissued Howe's published works, edited a version of Baxter's *Reliquiae* and produced the famous *Account* of nonconformists ejected following the Restoration. The importance of his connections with Howe will be discussed in detail in chapter eight of this book. The *Memoirs* supply the bulk of the information we have on Howe's life and laid the foundation for the subsequent veneration of Howe's memory. In particular, his portrayal of Howe as a man of reason and toleration provided the framework for all later assessments.

Neal's *History of the Puritans* (1732-9) contains very little reference to Howe. However, a Protestant form of beatification had taken place by 1809, when Bogue and Bennett published their *History of the dissenters*.

> Unfeigned and exalted piety filled the soul of John Howe. It would be difficult to say, if ever there was a better man in England....It would not be easy to find a man equal to him in love to all the disciples of Christ, in universal benevolence, and in that purity and humility which adorn the character of a man of God.[10]

This reverential tone is maintained consistently by Howe's subsequent biographers. Henry Rogers (1806-1877), a Congregational minister and man of letters who also produced an edition of Howe's published works (1862-3), is typical in declaring 'the light in which I regard him, is that of a signal trophy of the transforming power of the gospel....Thus viewed, his character well deserves the attentive contemplation of every Christian'.[11] From biographers of this persuasion, little serious criticism of Howe is to be expected. None is to be found. By the end of the nineteenth century Howe had become an icon of nonconformist piety.

In contrast to the considerable Victorian interest in his memory, Howe rarely gets more than a fleeting mention in modern historiog-

---

9 For Calamy's life see his own *An Historical Account of My Own Life, with some Reflections on the Times I have Lived In (1671-1731)* 2 vols. (London, 1829) and his entry in DNB.

10 D. Bogue and J. Bennett, *History of the Dissenters from the Revolution in 1688, to the Year 1808* 4 vols (London: 1808-1812), Vol. II, 220.

11 Rogers, *Life,* 12-13. Subsequent biographers: J.P. Hewlett ('A Brief Memoir etc' in Howe's *Works* I ix-xxix, 1848), R. F. Horton (1895) and W. Scott (1911) were just as admiring. See also the many references to Howe in John Stoughton's multivolume *History of Religion in England* (1881). Howe's example could have a profound personal effect. Rogers' admiration stemmed from reading Howe's *The Redeemer's Tears wept over lost Souls* (1684) at the age of seventeen. The DNB entry on Rogers records that this encounter 'diverted his attention from surgery [his intended trade] to theology' - DNB, Vol XVII, 121-3. See also Horton's testimony in R.F. Horton, *An Autobiography* (London: 1917) 157-8.

raphy. Two unpublished theses in the 1950s were followed by a 1975 essay which merely repeats the uncritical respect of the past.[12] Not until the 1990s was focused attention given to John Howe.[13] David Field's 1993 doctoral thesis is interesting, given the discussion of the wider historiography in the previous chapter. Field places Howe with Baxter, as one of the 'moderate Presbyterians' who modified the harsher features of Calvinism in the face of anti-Calvinist criticism. Howe's key contribution is thus cast in terms of the disputes over the doctrines of grace which form the framework for the interpretations of such as Tyacke. For the same reasons which, I suggest, make Tyacke's analysis inadequate, I contend that this is not the way to understand Howe. Rather, his thought is better approached through his ecclesiology. As this analysis will show (again, departing from Field), Howe developed a very different position from that of Baxter.

Two centuries of homage constructed around Howe an unblemished reputation on which more cynical generations have been strangely silent. The almost complete absence of detailed published analysis represents a void in the historiography of seventeenth-century England. It seems that the limited primary biographical material and the dense cloud of mythology have discouraged scholarly interest. There is another reason: Howe's works can be painfully difficult to read. Even such an admirer as Rogers admits that 'his excellencies seem happy accidents; his faults and negligences are systematic and habitual.'[14]

Ironically, given his stylistic failings, the outstanding recent treatment of Howe comes from the field of literary history. N.H Keeble includes Howe as a major figure in his study of late seven-

---

12 C. Farah, 'The Theological Thought of John Howe, 1630-1705' (Edinburgh: unpublished PhD thesis, 1958); W.W. Bass 'Platonic Influences on Seventeenth-Century English Puritan Theology as expressed in the thinking of John Owen, Richard Baxter and John Howe' (Univ. of Sthn California: unpublished PhD thesis, 1958); J.T. Carson, 'John Howe: Chaplain to Lord Massarene at Antrim Castle, 1671-1677', *Bulletin of the Presbyterian Historical Society of Ireland*, vii (1977), 11-16, 16.

13 Two doctoral theses were completed in isolation from each other. David Field's, '"Rigide Calvinism in a Softer Dresse" The Moderate Presbyteriansim of John Howe (1630-1705)' (Cambridge: unpublished PhD thesis, 1993) preceded my own by 18 months – Martin Sutherland, '*Strange Fire*: John Howe (1630-1705) and the Alienation and Fragmentation of Later Stuart Dissent' (Canterbury, NZ: 1995).

14 Rogers, *Life*, 333. Keeble, in *Literary Culture*, 22-3, includes Howe among the 'misplaced persons' of Restoration literature.

teenth-century nonconformist writing.[15] In more conventional historical works, if mentioned at all, Howe is typically quoted for his involvement in a significant event or in relation to some other personage but rarely as a figure of interest in his own right.[16]

This cursory treatment is regrettable. Howe was not an obscure player in the history of Stuart dissent. James Webster was not mistaken when he listed him as a 'toping man'. He was frequently involved in negotiations with the established Church,[17] was a confidant of William of Orange[18] and a leading figure within 1690s nonconformity. His published works were widely read by contemporaries.[19] Moreover, although primary sources are limited, they are

---

15 *Literary Culture*, passim. Keeble too concedes Howe's literary faults, contrasting his 'inelegancy' with the more attractive prose of such as Bates, Penn and Baxter - see *Literary Culture*, 246.

16 Thus Lamont, *Richard Baxter*, 162, 198, 222 quotes Howe to build a picture of Baxter's mind but omits him from his list of 'Baxter's friends and Enemies' (325-9). D.D. Wallace summarises Howe's thought in five lines (*Puritans and Predestination: Grace in English Protestant Theology 1525-1695*, Chapel Hill, NC: University of North Carolina Press, 1982), 160) and only mentions him again at any length because he features in a controversy over grace (179-80). Christopher Hill, in his essay 'Occasional Conformity and the Grindalian Tradition' (reprinted in *idem, Religion and Politics in 17th Century England*, 301-320), quotes the merest portion of one of Howe's later works (315-6). J.F.H. New in *Anglicans and Puritans: The Basis of Their Opposition, 1558-1640* (London, 1964), although extending his study to include much discussion of Baxter, ignores Howe altogether. Cragg, in *Puritanism* cites Howe on thirteen occasions, but never in depth and usually to effect a caricature of Howe's style and concerns. B.R. White, in his essay 'The Twilight of Puritanism', a study of the 1690s in which Howe might be expected to figure prominently, mentions him only in passing and with no analysis of his importance (313). I. Rivers, in *Reason, Grace, and Sentiment: A Study of the Language of Religion and Ethics in England, 1660-1780* (Cambridge: CUP, 1991), makes some useful comments but Howe is introduced primarily to illustrate analysis of such as Baxter, Doddridge, Watts and Wesley - see e.g. 100, 183, 191, 198, 216.

17 Calamy 72, records at least one occasion on which Howe was preferred to Baxter as negotiator by the Church party. See also Rogers, *Life*, 191-3; Thomas, 'Comprehension', 225-7; Wood, *Church Unity*, 260-1.

18 See Rogers, *Life*, 238-40.

19 Howe's *The Blessedness of the Righteous* (1668) ran to at least four editions. It was one of the books recommended by Richard Baxter (see Keeble, *Richard Baxter*, 37) and was especially favoured by the young Cotton Mather (*Diary of Cotton Mather*, New York, (1911), vol. 1, 56). At least three of Howe's works were owned by John Locke - see J.R. Harrison and Laslett, *The Library of John Locke* (Oxford: OUP, 1965), 159.

not totally absent. Enough evidence exists to inspire a fresh examination of this man's life and thought.

2.2 Education in Nonconformity

John Howe had clerical nonconformity in his blood. His grandfather, William Howe, had been incumbent at Tattershall, Lincolnshire.[20] One of William's sons, Obadiah Howe D.D. (1616?-1683), held charges in the same county under both Interregnum and Restoration regimes and was a minor polemicist.[21] Active dissent enters the family in the person of John Howe's father - another son of William, also named John. When the subject of this study was born on 17 May 1630, John Howe sen. held a curacy in Loughborough, Leicestershire.[22] He was ejected from this post in 1634, for his prayer during a service 'that the young prince might not be brought up in popery'. For this offence, the elder Howe was fined the then enormous sum of five hundred guineas, later reduced to twenty. The case achieved some notoriety, eventually being cited in the charges laid against Archbishop Laud. [23] The family spent some time in Ireland following this reversal. They returned to England in 1641-2, apparently to escape the Irish rebellion, and settled in Winwick, Lancashire, where John Howe jun. received his early education.

It is impossible accurately to assess the factors which may have influenced Howe in these early years. Exposure to the tumult of the 1630s and 1640s must have had some effect but, in his surviving works, Howe gives no direct clues. This uncertainty is in marked contrast to what may be affirmed of the next period of his life. The impact of his years at university can be confidently identified.

---

20 See DNB entry for Obadiah Howe. Calamy (6) mentions 'one Mr. *William Howe* of *Gedney* in [Lincolnshire] that was (I suppose) of the Family, tho I can't be positive how related to [John Howe].'

21 See DNB. Obadiah Howe's major controversy (1651-5) was with John Goodwin over Goodwin's Arminian tract, *The Pagan's Debt and Dowry* (1651).

22 J. and J.A. Venn (eds) *Alumni Cantabrigienses*, Pt I, vol. II (Cambridge: 1922), 417. W.G.D. Fletcher, *The Rectors of Loughborough* (Oxford: 1882), 19-21 notes that the Rector at this time was one of two named 'John Browne' who held the post in the early decades of the seventeenth century. John Howe jun.'s baptism was recorded on May 23 1630 - see W.G.D. Fletcher, 'The Parish Registers of Loughborough in the County of Leicester', *The Reliquary Quarterly Archaeological Journal and Review*, 1873, 194-202, 197.

23 See the *CSPD: Charles I*, 1634-1635, 318, 550; Calamy 6; W. Laud, *The Works of the Most Reverend Father in God, William Laud D.D.* (Oxford: LACT, 1854), vol. IV, 323-4.

The formal details of Howe's university career are quickly outlined. On 19 May, 1647 he entered Christ's College, Cambridge. In late 1648, apparently having gained a BA, he moved to Oxford. He was admitted to Brasenose College, took an Oxford BA in January 1650, to be made MA in 1652. Howe was appointed Chaplain at Magdalen in 1650 and was a Fellow there from 1652 until 1655.[24]

For the seventeenth century there is little that is remarkable about this progress. The full import of Howe's university years lies not in his academic record but in the teachers and fellow students he encountered. Attendance at both Cambridge and Oxford brought Howe into contact with two important groups, each of which had a profound impact on his thought.

At Cambridge, Howe encountered the Platonists. Benjamin Whichcote (1609-1683) was at King's and John Smith (1618-1652) at Queen's during Howe's Cambridge period. Ralph Cudworth (1617-1688) was Master of Clare Hall and Regius Professor of Hebrew. Most important of all was Henry More (1614-1687). More had been a Fellow at Howe's college, Christ's, since 1639. With More, Howe developed a friendship which lasted until More's death.[25] It is to these Cambridge connections that Calamy and others quite rightly trace Howe's '*Platonick* Tinkture'.[26]

Howe relished intellectual stimulation. He clearly spoke from his own experience when he described the joys of 'ratiocination' in his first major work, *The Blessedness of the Righteous* (1668).

> To the altogether unlearned it will hardly be conceivable, and to the learned it need not be told, how high a gratification... employment of his reason naturally yields to the mind of a man.... What a pleasure is it, when a man shall apprehend himself regularly led on...through the labyrinths of nature; when still new discoveries are successfully made, every further enquiry ending in a further prospect, and every new scene of things entertaining the mind with a fresh delight![27]

At Cambridge, fertile seeds of philosophical understanding were sown. However, in contrast to another who would be Cromwell's chaplain, Peter Sterry (d. 1672), Howe is rightly never cited as even a

---

24 See Venn (eds), *Alumni Cantabrigienses*, Pt I, Vol II, 417; A.A. Wood, *Athenae Oxonienses*, Vol 2, (New York: 1967) 589-91.

25 Calamy 8

26 Calamy (7-8) attributes significant influence to More and Cudworth; Rogers (*Life*, 19) wants to link Howe to Smith (perhaps because Smith's pious and gentle reputation accords best with Rogers' view of Howe). G.R. Cragg (ed) *The Cambridge Platonists* (New York: OUP, 1968), though he includes such as Theophilus Gale, does not mention Howe, even as a minor Platonist.

27 J. Howe, *The Blessedness of the Righteous*, [London, 1668], *Works* II, 1-260, 63-4.

peripheral figure in the Cambridge Platonist circle. That there were Platonic features to his thought is clear, but the philosophical school was not the dominant influence in Howe's maturity. The Platonism of such as Cudworth and More was combined with a powerful religious piety. So was Howe's, but of a particular type. His version of puritan piety came to be the determinative factor in his theology, dominating the 'tinkture' of Platonism he undoubtedly retained. In this process it was not the two years at Cambridge which were decisive, but the six years at Oxford.

At his second university Howe again met men who were to be friends for life. One, John Spilsbury (1630-1699), a Congregationalist, was also a Fellow at Magdalen. Spilsbury would be ejected in 1662 but licensed in 1672.[28] Howe was writing intimate letters to him until just months before Spilsbury's death.[29] The President of the College was Thomas Goodwin (1600-1680), another Congregationalist and a friend of John Owen (1616-1683). Calamy records an encounter between Howe and Goodwin which is important for the light it throws on the early breadth of Howe's sympathies. Goodwin, surprised at Howe's absence from his 'gather'd Church among the Scholars', questioned Howe as to the reasons.

> Mr. *Howe* with great frankness told him, that the true and only reason why he had been so silent about the matter, was because he understood they laid a considerable stress among them upon some distinguishing Peculiarities, of which he had no fondness, tho he could give others their Liberty to take their own way...; but that if they would admit him into their society upon *Catholick Terms*, he would readily become one of them.[30]

Howe was never a narrow sectarian. The apparent ease and range of his associations were an important feature of his university years. A theme had been established which would be constant through his career. His first clerical appointment set the pattern. In 1654 Howe took up a perpetual curacy at Great Torrington, in Devon. Though Howe had been ordained in 1652 by the Presbyterian Charles Herle of Winwick, he succeeded 'the famous Independent', Lewis Stucley

---

28 On Spilsbury see *CR*. Spilsbury, a member of the Worcestershire Association, may have been an important connection between Howe and Richard Baxter - see C.F. Nuttall, 'The Worcester Association: Its Membership', *JEH*, vol. 1, (1950), 197-206.

29 See letters J. Howe to J. Spilsbury April 20, 1695; Jan 25, [1698] 1699, *Works* III, 591-3. See also Calamy 9; Rogers, *Life*, 279-281, 291-2.

30 Calamy 10-11.

(1632?-1687) at Torrington.[31] The perpetual curacy itself was in the gift of Christ Church, Oxford, of which the Congregationalist John Owen was then Dean.

Howe left Oxford with a wide range of connections. He was also at this time apparently confident in his theology. According to Calamy, whilst at the universities he developed his own 'body of divinity'.[32] In subsequent years this confidence would be sorely tested.

2.3 The Torrington Ministry

The challenges began at Torrington. The Howe myth portrays this ministry as one of unblemished joy. There was certainly personal happiness - on 1 March 1655 Howe married Katherine, a daughter of the respected Devon Presbyterian, George Hughes (1603-1667). Calamy suggests the bliss extended beyond mere domestic circumstances when he asserts that 'the more he spent himself in his Master's service, the more was he belov'd by the Inhabitants of his Parish.'[33]

Howe was undoubtedly earnest in his endeavours. He described to Calamy his habit on fast days to preach for nearly three hours in total and lead his congregation in prayer for upwards of three more. Even Calamy conceded this would have produced 'inexpressible weariness' in most preachers and congregations.[34] Nevertheless, evidence of some mutual affection is not lacking. Howe maintained pastoral links with Torrington after he had left. As late as 1674 he dedicated his treatise *Delighting in God* to 'much valued friends' in his first charge. With a sentimentality common to the day he even confessed the need to restrain the passion of their relationship.

> I do very well understand your affection to me; and could easily be copious in the expression of mine to you, if I would open that sluice: but I do herein resolvedly...restrain myself; apprehending that...a gradual mortification ought to be endeavoured of such affection as is often between those so related as you and I have been.[35]

Yet, despite such protestations, there is evidence that the impression of pastoral contentment is misleading. In particular we must question Calamy's view that Howe 'had thought of no other, than of

---

31 Calamy 13. On Stucley or 'Stukely' see *CR*. Stucley later carried on considerable correspondence with Lord Wharton, with whom Howe was also closely acquainted.

32 Rogers, *Life*, 29-30.

33 Calamy 15.

34 Calamy 14-15.

35 J. Howe, *Delighting in God*, [London, 1674], *Works*, I, 474-664, 475.

living and dying [at Torrington].'[36] In a letter to Richard Baxter in 1658, Howe himself averred that 'when I settled there, I expressly reserved to myself a liberty of removing' if so led.[37] Indeed, a move came in 1656, only two and a half years into the Torrington ministry, when Howe became a Household Chaplain to Oliver Cromwell, in London. Moreover, the most plausible account of how he came to Cromwell's notice has Howe a candidate for a living in the larger Devon town of Dartmouth. Rogers discounts this version, largely because it does not fit the Howe myth, preferring the less likely account given by Calamy in the *Memoirs*. In this version Calamy suggests that the initiative lay with the Protector, after Cromwell noticed Howe in the congregation of a Whitehall service and 'discern'd something more than ordinary in his Countenance'. However, in his later (1727) *Continuation* Calamy gives the Dartmouth story.[38] This may actually have been the second time Howe was sought for another congregation. In 1655 Lord Paget, with whom, at least later in his career, Howe was connected, was active in seeking the appointment of a 'Mr How' for Merlow.[39]

There are indications that Howe's ministry at Torrington was not easy. In the preface to *Delighting in God*, in which (as noted above) Howe otherwise avowed great affection for his former parishioners, he referred to

> some who have...expressed more *contempt* of God...than *delight* in him. I know not how the case may be altered with such since I left you; or what blessing may have followed the endeavours of any other hand. Death I am sure will be making alterations, as I have heard it hath.[40]

A rift had developed under his predecessor.[41] Although Howe seems to have been able temporarily to calm this situation, soon after his departure he admitted to Richard Baxter that 'the people I left are breaking into parties; cannot meet in any one person as they profess

---

36 Calamy 14.

37 John Howe to Richard Baxter, May 25, [1658] *Baxter Corr.*, xi, 232. Also Rogers, *Life*, 69-71; N.H. Keeble and G.R. Nuttall (eds) *Calendar of the Correspondence of Richard Baxter*, 2 Vols. (Oxford: Clarendon, 1991), no. 453.

38 See Rogers, *Life*, 40 note; Calamy 16-17 and the *CR* entry for Allen Geare. A useful assessment of the merits of the two accounts is found in Hewlett's 'Brief Memoir', xiii-xv. Nevertheless, even Hewlett suggests that 'no-one who properly appreciates this great man will suspect him of seeking Dartmouth' (p. xv).

39 R. Spalding (ed), *The Diary of Bulstrode Whitelock* (Oxford: OUP, 1990), 403 (April 8, 9, 1655).

40 Howe, *Delighting in God*, 476.

41 Howe to Baxter, 1 June, [16]58, *Baxter Corr.*, iv, 79 (Rogers, *Life*, 71-3; Keeble, *Calendar*, no. 455).

they could in me; and are now wholly destitute; and, having heard of some inclinations on my part towards them, invite my return.'[42]

Howe's continued pastoral concern for the flock at Torrington was not simple affection. It arose, at least partially, from persistent difficulties in finding a suitable successor. (Torrington, it seems, was no 'plum'.) Moreover, his 'inclinations...towards them' were at least intensified by his real discomfort at Whitehall. In the same letter, he disclosed to Baxter his intention to cite the troubles at Torrington as a screen for his other concerns. 'I...resolve, to others, to insist upon the necessitous condition of the place I left as the reason of my removal (if I do remove [from Whitehall];) to yourself I state my case more fully.'[43]

Despite his obvious love for learning and scholarly pursuits, Howe's biographers have discounted any possibility of intellectual frustration at Torrington, away from the centres of academic and theological debate. Horton is confident that he 'was conscious of no limitation.'[44] Yet this sanguine picture too can be questioned. In one of his Torrington sermons Howe employed a telling metaphor.

> Let us now use ourselves much with God. Our knowledge of him must aim at conformity to him; and how powerful a thing is converse in order hereto! How insensibly is it wont to transform men, and mould anew their spirits, language, garb, deportment! To be removed from the solitude or rudeness of the country to a city or university, what an alteration it doth make! How is such a person divested by degrees of his rusticity, of his more uncomely and aggressed manners! Objects we converse with beget their image upon us.[45]

Care must be taken in applying rhetorical flourishes to the life of the speaker. Nevertheless, it would be surprising if Howe, trained among some of the best minds of the day, did not welcome a transfer to London.

Without doubt, Howe felt his ministry at Torrington to have been valuable. Yet it is significant that he identified this value in his peacemaking roles, both among parishioners and (in what sounds

---

42 Howe to Baxter, May 25, [1658].

43 Rogers' comment (71n) on this disingenuous approach is an instructive example of the need to preserve the Howe myth. 'The concluding paragraph of this letter would justly expose Howe to the charge of insincerity, had not the 'lamentable condition' of the people at Torrington, been a real and very powerful reason for his leaving Whitehall. Provided we state the real reason for our conduct, it is agreed by all casuists, that we are not bound to state *every* reason.'

44 Horton, *John Howe*, 15.

45 Howe, *Delighting in God*, 193.

like one of Baxter's 'Associations') with other local ministers.[46] Importantly, the problems he faced reinforced his concern to avoid the corrosive effects of controversy.

> Great reason I have to repent, that I have not with greater earnestness pressed upon you the known and important things wherein serious Christians do generally agree: but I repent not I have been so little engaged in the hot contests of our age about the things wherein they differ.[47]

In this respect at least, Torrington 'begat its image' upon John Howe.

2.4 Chaplain to Oliver Cromwell

If the first experience of a clerical charge proved a challenge for the confident Magdalen Fellow, the move to London was a near catastrophe. Calamy maintains that Howe was reluctant from the first to take up the Chaplaincy, eventually agreeing only at Cromwell's personal insistence.[48] This may have been the way Howe himself, his memory coloured by later developments, came to recall the transfer. Whatever his initial hopes or fears, within a short time he was looking for a way out of a role he increasingly disliked. The best evidence we have from this period is the correspondence between Howe and Richard Baxter, some of which has already been cited. These letters reveal a young man out of his depth, at times depressed and increasingly desperate to escape a difficult situation. They are also a key early record of Howe's relationship with Baxter.

The first of the series was dated at Whitehall, 12 March 1657/8.[49] In it Howe referred to a meeting with Baxter at Kidderminster 'some years since' and to his admiration of Baxter's publications as reasons for his letter. He sought Baxter's view on whether he should preach publicly against the religious 'neglects' he observed in Cromwell's household. Importantly, though Howe's concern signalled his moral scrupulousness, the expedient of writing to Baxter for advice sug-

---

46 'Some overtures made by me were the occasion of a settled meeting of the neighbouring ministers of different persuasions.. which hath been discontinued and forsaken by one party...Torrington was the place of meeting...which, if not supplied by a person inclined to peace... will not draw in both parties thither.' Howe to Baxter, 1 June, [16]58.

47 Howe, *Delighting in God*, 475.

48 Calamy 16-17.

49 Howe to Baxter, March 12, [16]57, *Baxter Correspondence*, Vol ii, 297, (Rogers, *Life*, 53-7; Keeble, *Calendar*, no. 436). This would have been 1657/8, approximately 15 months after Howe's arrival in London.

gests a diffidence and lack of confidence about the proper course of action.

Baxter's judicious reply of 3 April counsels most definitely against speaking out. 'A time there is for open plain dealing; but as long as the case is not palpable, desperate, and notorious, and you have leave to speak privately, that may suffice you.'[50] Baxter goes on, effectively to recruit Howe as his agent at Whitehall. 'I would awaken your jealousy to a careful (but very secret and silent) observance of the infidels and Papists, who are very high and busy.' With this letter, Baxter sent three enclosures concerning 'healinge principles' for Protestant unity which he wanted Howe to commend to Cromwell. One of these was a plan already submitted by Baxter to the Independent Philip Nye.[51] Such schemes of reconciliation found an enthusiastic supporter in Howe. His speedy reply (13 April) endorsed Baxter's concerns and suggested amendments to the plan.[52] On 8 May, he reported to Baxter on a meeting with Nye about the proposals.[53]

Thus we find Baxter influencing Howe at a crucial period in the younger man's life. Their shared concern for unity would remain constant. However, as will be seen, Howe's vision as to how this unity might be brought about would develop in ways quite different from Baxter's approach.

Howe's next letter (25 May) has already been cited for what it indicates about the rapidly growing (though relative) appeal of Torrington. He was concerned about the futility of his present position.

> My call hither, was a work I thought very considerable; the setting up of the worship and discipline of Christ in this family....But now at once I see the designed work here hopelessly laid aside. We affect here to live in so loose a way...that it were as hopeful a course to preach in a market, or in any assembly met by chance, as here.[54]

Baxter's reply, evidently calling on Howe to stay at Whitehall, was ineffective. Howe's frustration mounted to crisis point. Only one week later he wrote to Baxter again. Torrington was now portrayed as a place in which 'my ministry…was not... altogether in vain'. The

---

50 Baxter to Howe, April 3, 1658, *Baxter Corr.* iii, 200 (Rogers, *Life*, 58-61; Keeble *Calendar*, no. 443).

51 See Keeble, *Calendar*, notes 443:6-8 for details.

52 Howe to Baxter, April 13, 1658, *Baxter Corr*, iii, 198 (Rogers, *Life*, 61-3; Keeble, *Calendar*, no 447).

53 Howe to Baxter May 8 1658, *Baxter Corr* iii, 196 (Rogers, *Life*, 63-65; Keeble, *Calendar*, no. 450).

54 Howe to Baxter, May 25 [1658].

following long extract gives a crucial insight into Howe's perception of himself and his plight.

> Here my influence is not like to be much, (as it is not to be expected a raw young man should be much considerable among grandees;) my work little; my success hitherto little; my hopes, considering the temper of this place, very small; especially coupling it with the temper of my spirit, which did you know it, alone would, I think, greatly alter your judgement of this case. I am naturally bashful, pusillanimous, easily brow-beaten, solicitous about the fitness and unfitness of speech or silence in most cases, afraid...of being counted uncivil etc: and the distemper being natural (most intrinsically) is less curable. You can easily guess how little considerations are like to do in such a case. I did not, I confess, know myself so well as, since my coming up, occasion and reflection have taught me to do. I now find my hopes of doing good, will be among people where I shall not be so liable to be overawed. I might have known this sooner, and have prevented the trouble I am now in. Though the case of my coming up thither, and continuance, differ much, so as that I can't condemn the former, yet I more incline to do that than justify the latter.
>
> I shall beseech you to weigh my case over again.[55]

Howe's admirers have glossed over this telling passage, dismissing it as 'perfectly ludicrous' modesty.[56] Certainly, his painful self-assessment must be interpreted carefully. Intensely introspective breast-beating was typical of divines like Howe. He himself encouraged it. In *The Blessedness of the Righteous* he asked 'what power is there in man, more excellent, more appropriate to reasonable nature, than that of reflecting, of turning his thoughts upon himself?'[57]

The letter may display the exaggerated pleading of one attempting to justify his desire to escape an unhappy situation, but it cannot be ignored. The very fact that Howe felt the need to justify himself to Baxter in this dramatic fashion suggests that his self-accusation of being 'bashful, pusillanimous, easily brow-beaten' was not completely without foundation. He was torn between his own sense of duty, the solicitations of some from Torrington, and pressure from Baxter. He sought, but seemed incapable of finding, a resolution which could satisfy all.

At this very point of despair, Howe found his answer. On 3 June, 1658, just two days after his gloomy letter, he wrote again to Baxter.

---

55 Howe to Baxter, 1 June [16]58.

56 Rogers, *Life*, 72n. See also Horton, *John Howe*, 52.

57 Howe, *Blessedness*, 166. For the introspection of nonconformists see Keeble, *Literary Culture*, 204-214.

> Since my last, something has come into my thoughts which may be a medium betwixt my deserting my present station, etc; i.e. to retain a relation still to Torrington, (which hitherto, for want of a successor, I could not divest myself of,) and get leave to be with them a quarter of a year....[58]

Despite Howe's obvious relief, this was an indecisive compromise. Nevertheless, he negotiated the right to maintain his living at Torrington. The arrangement was for a series of interim ministers, with Howe himself spending three months of each year in Devon.[59] The arrangement may have begun immediately. There is no mention of Howe in the descriptions of Cromwell's death on 3 September 1658. As Household Chaplain he might have been expected to have attended the dying Protector or at least offered prayers, but this appears not to have happened.[60] Howe may have already been in Devon. He was present, however, in the official funeral party on 23 November.[61]

Howe was seemingly incapable of making a clean break from Whitehall. The death of Oliver Cromwell only made resignation more difficult. Howe had a high opinion of Oliver's more obviously devout son, Richard. He retained his post as Household Chaplain but spent much of Richard Cromwell's Protectorate in Torrington.[62] The next extant letter to Baxter is dated 21 May, 1659. By this time the younger Cromwell had been all but deposed. This event, blamed by him squarely on elements in the army, Howe regarded as a disaster.

> Sir, such persons as are now at the head of affairs, will blast religion, if God prevent not. The design you writ me of, some time since, to introduce Infidelity or Popery, they have opportunity enough to effect.

---

58 Howe to Baxter, June 3 [16]58, *Baxter Corr.* iv, 81 (Rogers, *Life*, 74-5; Keeble, *Calendar*, no 457).

59 In the winter of 1658-9, Howe's stand-in was the young Increase Mather (1639-1723) - See M.G. Hall (ed) 'The Autobiography of Increase Mather,' *Proceedings of the American Antiquarian Society*, Oct. 1961, 271-360, 283; M.G. Hall, *The Last American Puritan: The Life of Increase Mather 1639-1723* (Middleton, Conn: Wesleyan University Press, 1988), 44.

60 Godwin records that Cromwell 'was principally attended on his death-bed by the two eminent divines, Goodwin and Owen' - W. Godwin, *History of the Commonwealth of England* (London: 1828), vol. 4, 573.

61 R.F. Sherwood, *The Court of Oliver Cromwell* (London: Croom Helm, 1977), 109.

62 Matthews, in *CR*, 279, suggests that Howe's place at Torrington was taken, by John Bullock on 26 March 1659. If so, this must have lasted only a very short time. Increase Mather had been at Torrington over the winter. He records the reason for *his* departure as Howe's return. Mather took up a chaplaincy on Guernsey in April 1659 - 'Autobiography' 283.

> I know some leading men are not Christians. Religion is lost out of England, farther than as it can creep into corners...I am returning to my old station, being now at liberty beyond dispute.[63]

Howe did return to Torrington, to await developments. He had performed pastoral functions in two settings, Torrington and Whitehall. In the first he appears to have met with some success but at least equal frustration; in the second he had come face to face with his own weaknesses. Still greater trial was to come.

2.5 Ejection in 1662

The course of events which resulted in the re-establishment of the Church of England and culminated in the Act of Uniformity and the great ejection of 1662 has been noted already. During the hiatus before the Act of Uniformity an incident occurred at Torrington which signalled Howe's later concerns. In October 1660, he was accused of preaching sedition. He was acquitted of the charge,[64] but the sermons on which it was based introduced themes which would come to dominate his ecclesiology.

Although the sermons have disappeared the Information and depositions of this case have survived. The accusation was made that Howe, in preaching against ceremony on 30 September and 14 October, 1660, encouraged rebellion against those who would reintroduce such measures as the wearing of surplices and kneeling at communion. In his defence, some twenty Torrington parishioners insisted that Howe's intent was merely to warn them against 'having our hearts more set upon [ceremonies] than upon the substantial duties of God's worship'. Thus, although the tone and intent of the sermon was in doubt, the subject matter was not. The aversion to ritual indicated in these sermon topics links Howe with a long tradition of 'puritan' concerns. Importantly, however, there were also hints of a slightly new path down which Howe would eventually go. His text was taken from Galatians 6: 7-8: 'Be not deceived: God is not mocked. For whatsoever a man soweth, that shall he also reape, for he that soweth to the flesh, shall of the flesh reape corruption; but he that soweth to the Spirit shall of the Spirit reape eternal life.'[65]

---

63 Howe to Baxter, May 21 [1659], *Baxter Corr.* vi, 235 (Rogers, *Life*, 92-5; Keeble, *Calendar*, no. 574).

64 There was controversy over the validity of the hearings by which Howe was acquitted - see Calamy 27-29.

65 British Library Add. MS 11,342 A. 5, 6. Along with the rebellion charge, there was also a suggestion that Howe had refused his Archdeacon entry to his Church and declined infant baptism to those not 'of his congregated Church'.

As will be shown, Howe's theology came to centre on pneumatology. The 1660 sermons may be the first sign of that concentration.

That mature thought was, as yet, some way off. On Bartholomew's Day in 1662 Howe was ejected under the provisions of the Act of Uniformity. Many who were to be ejected spelled out their reasons for nonconformity in farewell sermons. Howe appears to have been no exception. Unfortunately his final sermons in Torrington have not survived. Nevertheless, it is clear that he did not hold all the possible objections. As he appears never to have taken it, the requirement to renounce the Solemn League and Covenant was not an issue. Neither, apparently, was he averse to the requirement to swear loyalty to the King. In 1666 he would be prepared, unlike many others, to take the demanding Oxford Oath.[66]

Why then, did the self-described 'pusillanimous' Howe choose nonconformity and the consequent penalty of ejection? Calamy relates two anecdotes from the 1660s which give insight into Howe's reasons. The first was a meeting with the Bishop of Exeter, Seth Ward (1617-1689), occasioned by proceedings against Howe for unauthorised preaching, at which Howe cited his objection to reordination.[67] The second incident is particularly interesting, given his later concerns. John Wilkins (1614-1672) (who, though married to Cromwell's sister, had conformed and in 1668 was made Bishop of Chester) pressed Howe as to why he, whom Wilkins knew to be a man of latitude, could not accept the settlement. Howe replied that there were many reasons but that, in the face of a settlement which appeared to show none, 'this very latitude, was so far from inducing him to Conformity, that it was the very thing which made him a Non-conformist.'[68]

In the same conversation, Howe specified a lack of true, parochial discipline in the new Church structure as 'a very considerable objection against the Establishment'. The lack of this foundation, he averred, made conformity akin to 'going into a falling house.' Rogers provides the text of a document written by Howe (most likely in the 1650s) on the responsibilities of ministers, which presupposes a local right to exclude unfit parishioners from communion.[69] Later, during comprehension negotiations in 1680, Howe would assure Bishop

---

66 Howe was one of twelve in Devon who signed a memorandum setting out the sense in which they took the oath. Characteristically, he then took further pains to record his personal motivation for this action - see Bodl. Rawl. MS. D. 1350. 329; Calamy 40-43.

67 Calamy 39.

68 Calamy 32-3.

69 Rogers, *Life*, 67-69.

Lloyd of St Asaph that 'a very considerable obstacle [to comprehension] would be removed, if the law were so framed as to enable ministers to attempt parochial reformation.'[70]

Issues of parochial discipline and reordination were of particular concern to conservative nonconformists like Richard Baxter. Geoffrey Nuttall has pointed out how discipline and reordination pivot on views of episcopacy.[71] That Howe shared these concerns in 1662 and articulated them during negotiations with the established Church as late as 1680 is unremarkable. However, it will be shown that discipline would fade as a factor in Howe's ecclesiology. It would be one of the ways in which he would depart from his friend and erstwhile mentor Richard Baxter.

Although he commenced ministry with a profound and comprehensive theological system in place, the years 1654-1662 were difficult ones for John Howe. There are clear grounds for questioning the myth that his ministry at Torrington was tranquil bliss and that his performance at Cromwell's Court was marked for its clear-sighted resolution and integrity.[72] The confidence he acquired at the Universities was seriously challenged by the vicissitudes of church life and the intrigue of the last years of the Interregnum. Far from the serene passage through strife implied by the hagiographers, the 1650s had been exacting. They left their mark. Howe might well have faded into obscurity. That he didn't suggests that he was able somehow to regain a sense of purpose. This is indeed what happened, although the new vision would take more than a decade to materialise.

---

70 Calamy 72.

71 G. Nuttall, 'The First Nonconformists' in G. Nuttall and O. Chadwick (eds). *From Uniformity to Unity 1662-1962* (London: SPCK, 1951), 149-187.

72 The myth endures, most obviously in American historiography. See Hall, *Last American Puritan*, 42, 44. See also Keeble, *Literary Culture*, 19.

CHAPTER 3

'God's Conversableness with Man'

3.1 Dealing with Defeat

It is difficult to comprehend fully the mood of the ejected clergy of 1662. That John Howe was a man of principle cannot be doubted. He remained strong enough in his views to accept the consequences of dissent. Yet he was only thirty-two, an ejected minister, by now with a family to support. He did not have the public profile of such as Baxter and Owen and it is probable that he lacked their assurance and resolution. He certainly had little of their polemical fire. In 1662 he must have faced his temporal future with some disquiet. He had prefigured his own likely feelings about the general crisis in the despondent letter to Baxter which followed the fall of Richard Cromwell: 'religion is lost out of England, farther than as it can creep into corners'.[1]

As events would show, this assessment was too gloomy. Yet Howe himself effectively 'crept into corners' for a decade and a half after his ejection. This is the period about which the least is known of his activities. What is clear is that these were critical years in his theological development. The corners in which he secluded himself apparently received enough light to read by and provided peace sufficient for deep contemplation. When he emerged, on his return to London in 1676, he would rapidly assume a role at the centre of nonconformist affairs. Within two years he would publish or preach ideas which revealed a mature and resilient systematic divinity.

For nine years Howe remained in Devon, probably in Torrington. Although he preached occasionally in the houses of sympathetic gentry, he did not set up conventicles or provoke the authorities. The conversation with Bishop Ward mentioned in the previous chapter resulted from Howe's concern to pre-empt rumoured action against him for his country house activities.[2] In 1665 he was listed in

1 Howe to Baxter, May 21 [1659]

2 Calamy 37.

the episcopal return as living in Great Torrington 'peaceably'.[3] It is therefore most unlikely that Howe was imprisoned in this same year 'for two months in the Isle of St Nicholas' as reported by Calamy.[4] In 1666 he took the Oxford Oath, perhaps to avoid expulsion from Torrington under the provisions of the Five Mile Act.

In 1668 Howe published his first major work: *The Blessedness of the Righteous*.[5] This treatise on personal eschatology (specifically, the Christian's hope of heaven) was based on Torrington sermons. Though turgid in its prose and convoluted in its argument, it was apparently well received.[6] In the prefatory epistle, Howe signalled themes which would become dominant in his thinking. The topic of heaven was chosen carefully. Howe did so firstly because it was 'so little disputable'. He castigated those who divert to 'contentious jangling'.

> When contention becomes a man's element, and he cannot live out of that fire, strains his wit, and racks his invention, to find matter of quarrel...and loves dissension for itself; this is the unnatural humour which hath so unspeakably troubled the church, and dispirited religion, and filled men's souls with wind and vanity; yea with fire and fury. This hath made Christians gladiators, and the Christian world a clamorous theatre, while men have equally affected to contend, and to make ostentation of their ability so to do.[7]

Secondly, heaven appealed precisely because it was 'otherworldly'. Hope of heaven enabled acceptance of present sufferings. In an earlier letter of comfort to his brother-in-law, Obadiah Hughes,

---

3 G.L. Turner (ed), *Original Records of Early Nonconformity under Persecution and Indulgence* (London: Unwin, 1911), vol. 1, 180,189.

4 Calamy 43-5. This suggestion is based upon hearsay and inferred from a letter by Howe to his brother-in-law, Obadiah Hughes (who had been imprisoned in 1665 - *CR*, 281-2) in which Howe gives thanks for mutual 'Occasions of thanksgiving'. Calamy himself expressed some doubt about the report and later biographers have generally discounted its accuracy - see Hewlett, *Memoir*, xxi; Rogers, , *Life*, 121; Horton, *John Howe*, 79.

5 *Works* II, 1-260. In 1659 he had published a sermon (not extant) preached to the House of Commons followed, in 1660, by the sermon *Man's Creation in a Holy but Mutable State* (*Works* I, 462-473).

6 In his prefatory note, Richard Baxter finds it necessary to anticipate that 'plain unlearned readers' may 'blame the accurateness of the style'. Howe, *Works* II, 8. Baxter had some questions about possible antinomian tendencies in Howe's soteriology. In a letter of 2 June 1668 Howe assures him that 'my visible scope and drift in that part of my discourse will vindicate my words from any such meaning' - Howe to Baxter 2 June 1668, *Baxter Corr* ii, 121. (Keeble, *Calendar*, no 753).

7 Howe, *Blessedness*, 5.

he had referred to 'the unkindness and instability of a surly, treacherous world' concluding 'if we cannot, God will outwit it and carry us, I trust, safe thro to a better World, upon which we may terminate Hopes that may never make us ashamed.'[8] Moreover, confidence in the spiritual reality of the 'last end' is 'the very soul of religion'. Without it 'religion were the vainest, most irrational, and most unsavoury thing in the world.'[9]

Important epistemological themes were emerging in this early work. The essential component of 'blessedness' was intense divine-human meeting, or a 'vision of God'. This encounter attended a personal, heart conversion. As Spurr has detailed, personal conversion lies at the heart of the 'puritan experience'.[10] Howe certainly rejected any suggestion of the efficacy of right belief or sacraments. He anticipated the response of those who did not accept the need for a 'heart-change'.

> They are (they say) orthodox Christians; they believe all the articles of the Christian creed; they detest all heresy and false doctrine; they are no strangers to the house of God, but diligently attend the enjoined solemnities of public worship...they have been baptised, and therein regenerate, and would we have more?[11]

The true 'vision of God' was an immediate, intuitive encounter, the excellence of which exceeded sensual experience, intellectual activity and even faith, which Howe defined as 'taking a thing upon report'.[12] Howe's relegation of faith and right belief is particularly interesting, as it prefigures the scepticism which will be seen to lie behind his irenic ecclesiology.

> Is it not possible thou mayest be a Christian for the same reasons for which one may be a Jew, or a Mahometan, or a mere pagan? as, *viz.* education, custom, law, example, outward advantage, &c...and what then is become of thy orthodoxy, when, as to the formal object of thy faith, thou believest but as Mahometans and pagans do...?[13]

3.2 Reconstruction in Antrim

Howe's next publication, *The Vanity of Man as Mortal* (1671) continued the theme of heaven-oriented faith. Again the prefatory epistle

---

8 Cited by Calamy 43-45.

9 Howe, *Blessedness*, 5.

10 Spurr, *English Puritanism*, 159-162.

11 Howe, *Blessedness*, 125.

12 Howe, *Blessedness*, 63-5.

13 Howe, *Blessedness*, 137.

is revealing, but in this case the interest lies in the biographical information which may be gleaned.

The epistle is dated April 12, 1671 at Antrim, Ireland. Howe had just arrived in Antrim as Chaplain to Lord Massarene. The decision to take the position was probably not difficult. Calamy asserts that Howe was 'reduc'd to straits' financially.[14] This would not be surprising, as 1670 saw considerable pressure on nonconformity in England, following upon the second Conventicles Act.[15] The epistle was principally addressed to John Upton, the head of a Parliamentarian, Devon family. The main branch of this family was based at Lupton, near Dartmouth. Another had settled in Ireland in the 1590s and was related to the same Lord Massarene whom Howe was serving by 1671. George Hughes, Howe's father-in-law and close friend, had, in his second marriage, wed Rebecca Upton, the daughter of John Upton. Her brother, Ambrose Upton, had been Canon of Christ Church, Oxford, until 1660. The occasion of the writing of *The Vanity of Man as Mortal* was the death (in Spain) of another brother, Anthony Upton.[16]

Howe was an intimate of this family group. In letters to Baxter he referred to Ambrose Upton as his 'uncle'.[17] In the 'Epistle Dedicatory' to *Vanity* he recounted the funeral gathering at which, including himself, there were present 'no less than twenty, the brothers and sisters of the deceased, or their consorts, besides his many nieces and nephews and other relations.'[18] Although the rest of the party cannot be reconstructed with any confidence, the possi-

---

14 Calamy 50.

15 Howe's brother-in-law John Hickes recounts some of this harassment in *A True and faithful Narrative of the Unjust and Illegal Sufferings, and Oppressions of Many Christians...in Devon*, (1671).

16 Tracing the connections of the Uptons is complicated by the fact that there were two John Uptons, uncle and nephew, who were both married to daughters of Sir John Lytcott and were thus both connected by marriage to Cromwell's Secretary, John Thurloe. The younger John Upton was a member of Parliament for Dartmouth in 1679 and 1681. See W.H. Upton, *Upton Family Records, being Genealogical Collections for an Upton Family History* (London: 1893), 105-128. Also B.D. Henning (ed) *The House of Commons 1660-1690* (The History of Parliament) (London: Secker & Warburg, 1983), Vol. III, 621; G.R. Aylmer, *The State's Servants: The Civil Servants of the English Republic, 1649-1660* (London: Routledge & Kegan Paul), 1973, 220-221 & 402 n.26 and various 'Upton' entries in Venn (ed) *Alumni Cantabrigienses* and the *DNB*.

17 See Howe to Baxter, March 12, [1658] (Keeble, *Calendar* 436, n.2.); Baxter's reply April 3, 1658, *Baxter Corr.* iii, 200, (Keeble, *Calendar*, no. 443); Howe to Baxter, May 21 [1659].

18 J. Howe, *The Vanity of Man as Mortal*, [London, 1671], *Works*, II, 261-315, 262.

bilities are intriguing. The family network was extensive. Cromwell's Secretary of State, John Thurloe, was a close connection.[19] Relations by marriage included George and Obadiah Hughes, Thomas and Samuel Martyn and Howe's brother-in-law, the radical John Hickes.[20] All of these were nonconformists, active in or around Plymouth in the 1660s and 1670s. Thomas Martyn and Hickes would present to Charles II the 'grateful acknowledgement' of Devon ministers for the 1672 Indulgence. All were imprisoned at some time. Hickes was to be executed in 1685 for his part in the Monmouth rebellion. To these Devon activists may be added Richard Baxter, who was the brother-in-law of Ambrose Upton. Such clerical personnel, together with the politically active Upton branches and Lord Massarene, constituted a significant nonconformist nexus. The family links explain Howe's appointment to Antrim.

It is not particularly surprising that Howe should figure near the centre of such a circle. Yet it is notable that, of the nonconformist clergy in this assembly, Howe was the least active, the least notorious in episcopal eyes, the most desirous of a quiet life. Not that he was unaware of the struggles which dissenters faced. He called on his associates to oppose with 'heroic vigour' the 'prosperous wickedness' of the time. Yet the opposition was to be pacific and the 'vigour' to be for holiness. Howe's eschatological framework was again evident.

> Let us (my worthy friends) be provoked, in our several capacities, to do our parts herein; and, at least, so to live and converse in this world, that the course and tenor of our lives may import an open asserting of our hopes in another.[21]

Though he published a major work and consolidated a place in a significant network, Howe's career from ejection to his departure for Ireland must have been personally frustrating. Apart from occasional excursions to country houses, he was seldom able to preach. He appears to have relished long afterwards the one public preaching engagement that is known. In a second-hand account, Calamy records 'providential' circumstances which surrounded Howe's embarkation for Ireland. His ship being delayed for some time (probably in Bristol) due to unfavourable winds, he was pressed into preaching in a local church on three occasions to a 'prodigious multi-

19 See Aubrey, *Mr Secretary Thurloe: Cromwell's Secretary of State 1652-1660* (London: Althone Press, 1990), 205-212.

20 The Uptons' clerical connections were mostly by marriage, sometimes through a second spouse. The network may be tracked through the entries for these nonconformists in *CR*.

21 Howe, *Vanity of Man*, 264.

tude'. Howe's own evaluation of this incident suggests such opportunities were rare: 'if my ministry was ever of any use, I think it must have been then.'[22]

This sanguine recollection may have been fuelled by the symbolic importance of his last week in England and the new beginning in prospect. If he sought opportunity for quiet reflection, he was to find it at Antrim. If there remained outstanding questions in his theology, these would be met. If he craved preaching and teaching, he was to find opportunity for both. The years in Ireland would complete the shaping of John Howe.

Life for dissenters was very different in Ireland from what it was in England.[23] The weaker position of the established Church meant that tight restrictions on nonconformists were impossible. Howe was given a remarkable latitude by the established Church authorities. The light duties of private chaplain allowed him time for regular preaching. Calamy records that Howe was not only tolerated but welcomed at the Parish church in Antrim. Both the Bishop and Archbishop endorsed his ministry. He actively entered the small but widespread English Presbyterian community. The Antrim Presbytery minutes for the period reveal Howe to have been an busy and respected member. In 1672 a divinity school was established in Antrim, run by Howe and the local Presbyterian incumbent. Howe was given additional responsibility for coaching candidates for ordination held to lack sufficient training. His ministry, though, extended further and included frequent preaching in Dublin.[24]

That none of this activity can be described as spectacular does not lessen its importance. Though little more than mundane ministry in normal times it was, for Howe, a season of consistent, recognised results. The boost to his confidence must have been considerable. Moreover the atmosphere of co-operation and greater freedom powerfully cohered with Howe's own inclinations. His employer, Massarene, was noted for his efforts towards securing better relations differing between parties. In this context Howe refined his distinctively irenic ecclesiology.[25]

---

22 Calamy 51.

23 On this see P. Kilroy, *Protestant Dissent and Controversy in Ireland 1660-1714* (Cork: Cork University Press, 1994) and R.L. Greaves, *God's Other Children' Protestant Nonconformists and the Emergence of Denominational Churches in Ireland, 1660-1700* (Stanford: Stanford University Press, California) 1997.

24 Calamy 53-4; Carson, 'John Howe', *passim;* Kilroy, *Protestant Dissent* 27, 40.

25 On Massarene's activities see Greaves, *God's Other Children*, 199-201, 377. Howe had little taste for sectarian polemics. In 1673 he was invited by the Antrim Presbytery to contribute to a refutation of the Quakers. He accepted

A new note of emerging assurance was indicated and further stimulated by Howe's writing. It was through this activity, above all, that his maturity and reputation grew. In 1674 a second volume based on themes from Torrington sermons appeared. In *Delighting in God,* motifs found in earlier writings were continued. Though the collection manifested a concern for serious, personal piety, the other-worldliness already observed in *The Blessedness of the Righteous* lay at the heart of the treatise. The plight of the nonconformist was to be alleviated by exultant contemplation of God. In many ways it was a volume complementary to the first. 'Delight in God' was the presently available foretaste of the heavenly experience of 'Blessedness'.

Yet there was another note being played. It was the second part of the treatise, that which explored practical divinity, which related most closely to earlier sermons. The first half of *Delighting,* a theoretical foundation for the second, was new. Howe's Platonic background was once more evident in his religious epistemology. 'Delight in God' presupposed a communication from God which consisted of 'an inwardly enlightening revelation of himself'. This is the same 'intuition' which had been placed above faith and knowledge in the earlier *Blessedness*. This time, however, it was carefully distinguished from 'an enthusiastical assurance' which declined to be tested against external revelation.[26] Platonism was tempered by evangelical orthodoxy.

The extended attention to the possibility of God's communication with individual humans is indicative of the direction of Howe's thought. Mediation was not required; direct connection was possible - indeed, it was the ideal. This confidence in the potential for immediate relationship would be fully explored in Howe's next work, *The Living Temple*. It would become the foundation for his invisiblist ecclesiology.

By 1675 Howe was being noticed. He was invited by some in the congregation of the recently deceased Lazarus Seaman to take up the resultant vacancy in the Presbyterian chapel at Haberdashers' Hall, London. The call was not unanimous; another party preferred Stephen Charnock (1628-1680). In December, Howe undertook the journey mentioned at the start of the last chapter. He travelled to London to ascertain the details of the position and to assess the level of his support. His 'Considerations and Communings with my Self concerning my present Journey, Dec. 20. 75. By night, on my Bed' was no hasty note. In typical fashion Howe penned a long missive,

---

the commission but appears to have dropped out of the project early. The pamphlet never appeared. See Greaves, *God's Other Children*, 204-5.

26 Howe, *Delighting in God*, 487, 530.

examining his motives and the possible ramifications of a shift to the capital. He recorded a debilitating illness which appears to have affected him during 1675. 'I am now sensibly under great decays, and not likely to continue long...What a Summer had I of the last? Seldom able to walk the Streets; and not only often disabled by Pain, but Weakness.'[27]

If Howe himself contemplated the prospect of returning to London with some trepidation, Lord Massarene was even more concerned. Indeed, he hoped Howe would not take up the position. In a letter to the Presbyterian M.P. John Swynfen, Massarene reported that he had been warned that 'Mr How will be wheedled from ye', though he declined to believe his informant.[28] Nevertheless, when Howe was eventually appointed, his Antrim patron was philosophical. Massarene appears to have written again to Swynfen seeking his help in finding a replacement as 'you found so good success in the choice of the last'. His assessment of the potential value of his chaplain in ecclesiastical affairs is significant: 'no man can be better fitted to steer between the two extremes'.[29]

It is difficult to judge whether Massarene's opinion of Howe was shared by others in dissent. However, Howe's own 'Considerations' give some support and suggest the likely ground for the high regard in which he was increasingly held. The conventional note of humility and self-doubt was still present, but it is clear that Howe had achieved some notoriety.

> I have carefully examined what selfish respects I can have in this matter. Is it worldly Emolument? In this my Heart acquits me in the

---

27 Calamy 65. The nature of this illness is impossible to identify with absolute assurance. But it may have been a variety of gout. Howe was in Bath in 1668 'for the benefit of his health' (Rogers, *Life*, 125). He was ill again in 1682, requiring 'a course, for the repairing of languishing health, which required some weeks' attendance abroad' - Howe, *The Faithful Servant Applauded and Rewarded* (funeral sermon for Richard Fairclough) *Works* III, 388-411, 391. The intimation of illness during the year militates against Horton's suggestion that Howe was in London in Feb/Mar 1675. This assertion is based on three recorded sermons dated in those months. It is more likely that these were delivered in the early part of 1676 by the amended calendar, after Howe had moved permanently to London.

28 Letter, Lord Massarene to John Swynfen, Feb 10th 75/6 - William Salt Library, Swynfen Letters MSS 454. no 24, 1.

29 The provenance of this quotation is uncertain. Lacey (*Dissent*, 445-6) cites William Salt Library MSS 254, Swynfen Letters, No. 24, 1-2. This appears to be an inaccurate reference. Lacey possibly refers here to the letter of Feb. 10 1675/6 (already cited, note 101 above), though this predates Howe's decision to go to London and does not contain the words Lacey quotes. The other letter cannot now be traced among the Salt manuscripts.

> sight of God. Is it that I affect to be upon a publick Stage, to be popular and applauded by Men? To this I say…That I do verily believe, that I shall be lower in the Eye and Esteem of the People in London, when I come under their nearer view. I know my self incapable of pleasing their Genius. I cannot contrive nor endure to preach with elaborate Artifice. They will soon be weary, when they hear nothing but plain Discourses of such matters as are not new to them. Yea and Ministers that now judge of me by what I have written, (when Matter and Words were in some measure weigh'd) will find me when I converse with them, slow to apprehend things, slow to express my own Apprehensions, unready, entangled and obscure in my Apprehensions and Expressions: so that they will soon say, this is not the man we took him for.[30]

Howe had not been a notable leader during the Interregnum. He had taken no major public role since the Restoration. At least in private he could express a lack of confidence. His fame in England in 1675 rested solely on a small number of publications. Nevertheless it is clear that these works signalled an emerging theological force. The troubles and setbacks of the fifties and sixties had given Howe significant material for reflection; the years at Antrim completed the process. Here was an authentic new voice.

3.3 The 'Puritan Impulse'

Although *The Living Temple* was not published until 1676, it was written during Howe's stay at Antrim. The work which appeared as he arrived in London was in fact merely the first instalment of a projected two-part treatise. Interestingly, this first part was a work of natural theology. Howe argued against the notion that 'glorious apparitions', 'terrible voices' and 'surprising transformations' (i.e. miraculous interventions) were necessary for God to make himself known to humans.[31] Further, he refuted arguments which would limit the 'immensity' of God. God is truly everywhere, and has 'converse with all men.'[32] In terms of the categories employed in this study, these arguments might suggest that Howe's theological emphasis had swung to the immanence of God. If so, it would appear to run counter to the 'other-worldliness' of his earlier works. Yet this openness to the divine presence must be understood as an examples

---

30 Cited by Calamy 61.

31 J. Howe, *The Living Temple or, A Designed Improvement of that Notion that A Good Man is the Temple of God,* [London, 1676] (pt I), *Works* I, 1-163, 108-131 esp. 111-118.

32 Howe, *Living Temple,* I, 132-163, esp. 132-3 & 160-63.

of the puritan 'sense of the holy' discussed in chapter one. Howe certainly valued the immanent activity of God.[33] The key, however, lay in the right sequence. *The Living Temple,* among his most rationalistic works, nevertheless gave priority to immediate, transcendent divine contact. It was, in fact, the most complete example to that date of Howe's ability to integrate his philosophical training with his religious orthodoxy, and to incorporate both into a distinctively 'puritan' piety.

The term 'puritan' is a troublesome one. The complex and not always profitable debate over its definition has spawned a truly daunting literature.[34] I do not intend to rake over the coals in detail yet again. Suffice it to say that the approaches which have proved most consistently useful are those which seek to identify some common element in the *piety* of those called 'puritan.' The two most

---

33 Indeed, he was capable of eloquent expression of his conviction that 'nature is nothing else but divine art.' See Keeble, *Literary Culture*, 257-60.

34 The material written on the issue of the definition of puritanism is substantial. The notable contributions in the past thirty or so years are: C. Hill, *Society and Puritanism in Pre-Revolutionary England,* (London: Secker & Warburg), 1964, Ch 1, 13-29; B. Hall, 'Puritanism: the Problem of Definition' in C.J. Cuming (ed), *Studies in Church History,* II, (London: Nelson, 1965), 283-296; McGrath, *Papists and Puritans Under Elizabeth I* (London: Blandford Press, 1967), 27-46; C.H. George, 'Puritanism as History and Historiography', *P&P,* No. 41, Dec. 1968, 77-104; W. Lamont, 'Puritanism as History and Historiography: Some Further Thoughts', *P&P,* No. 44, Aug. 1969. 133-146; D. Little, *Religion, Order and Law: A Study in Pre-Revolutionary England* (Oxford: B. Blackwell, 1970), 250-259; H.C. Porter (ed), *Puritanism in Tudor England* (London: Macmillan, 1970), 1-14; I. Breward, 'The Abolition of Puritanism', *JRH,* Vol 7, No. 4, Dec. 1973, 20-34; M.G. Finlayson, 'Puritanism and Puritans: Labels or Libels?', *Canadian Journal of History,* Vol. VIII, No. 3, Dec. 1973, 201-223; R.L. Greaves, 'The Nature of the Puritan Tradition' in R.B. Know (ed), *Reformation Conformity and dissent: Essays in honour of Geoffrey Nuttall* (London: Epworth, 1977), 255-273; P. Christianson, 'Reformers and the Church of England under Elizabeth I and the Early Stuarts', *JEH,* vol. 31, No. 4. October 1980, 463-482; P. Collinson, 'A Comment: Concerning the Name Puritan', *JEH,* Vol. 3, No. 4, October 1980, 483-488; Finlayson, *Historians, Puritanism and the English Revolution* esp. chs 3 & 6; J. Morgan, *Godly Learning: Puritan Attitudes towards Reason, Learning and Education* (Cambridge: CUP, 1986), 9-22; M.B. Endy Jr., 'Puritanism, Spiritualism, and Quakerism'; T.D. Bozeman, *To Live Ancient Lives: The Primitivist Dimension in Puritanism* (Chapel Hill, NC: University of North Carolina Press, 1988), 3-12); L.A. Sasek (ed), *Images of English Puritanism: A Collection of Contemporary Sources 1589-1646* (Baton Rouge: Louisianna State Univeristy Press, 1989), 1-27; P. Lake, 'Defining Puritanism - again?' in F.J. Bremer (ed), *Puritanism: Transatlantic Perspectives on a Seventeenth-Century Anglo-American Faith* (Boston: Massachusetts Historical Society, 1993), 3-29; Spurr, *English Puritanism,* 3-8.

prominent proponents of piety as the key to English puritanism have been Geoffrey Nuttall and Richard Greaves. Greaves succinctly puts the case.

> At the heart of the puritan experience is an evangelical piety dominated by an essentially emotional searching for a spiritual communion with God, made possible by the inner workings of the Holy Spirit, and achieved with an immediacy that sets it apart from traditional Anglican modes of worship, which are fundamentally sacerdotal in nature.[35]

Greaves' approach is clearly valuable, in that it can both incorporate the controversial concerns of 'puritans' and cope with the way in which the appellation crosses boundaries and time frames. Yet it has limitations. As Lake notes, 'what it gains in subtlety it loses in precision'.[36] The distinctive effects of piety must be explored. Here theology is crucial. As Spurr, in the best recent account of the 'puritan impulse,' notes, 'theology connects an objective account of how God operates, with the Christian's own subjective experience of God's dealing with them.'[37] Howe was one who was very concerned with 'how God operates'. At many points in the present study his theology will be shown to cohere with, indeed promote, the puritan religious style. Such linkages are essential if the characteristics identified by Nuttall and Greaves are to be anchored in the debates and controversies of a specific period.

The Living Temple is an important example. In it, Howe's philosophy, orthodoxy and piety came together in mature expression. Though less consistently so than in the earlier works, the deductive method used in Howe's argument was typically Platonic. Though he eschewed the temptation to attempt a proof of God from the very notion of divinity, he proceeded to do so from the idea of infinity. Further, from the attributes of God he 'disproved' the 'deistic' view

---

35 R.L. Greaves, 'The Nature of the Puritan Tradition', 258. See also Nuttall, *The Holy Spirit in Puritan Faith and Experience* (Oxford: B. Blackwell, 1947), *passim;* R.L. Greaves, *Society and Religion in Elizabethan England* (Minneapolis: University of Minnesota Press, 1981), 3-14; S. Ahlstrom, *Theology in America: The Major Protestant Voices from Puritanism to Neo-Orthodoxy* (New York: Bobbs Merrill, 1967), 27.

36 P. Lake, *Anglicans and Puritans?: Presbyterianism and English Conformist Thought from Whitgift to Hooker* (London: Unwin Hyman, 1988), 5. Greaves too is aware of the difficulty. 'What this means for the historian...is that the nature of Puritanism is elusive....Certain fundamental characteristics may be delineated, but in the end there can be no substitute for a careful immersing in Puritan literature in a quest to grasp what is at root experiential in nature.' - 'The Nature of the Puritan Tradition', 257-258.

37 Spurr, *English Puritanism*, 153.

that God cannot be known directly.[38] However, the Platonic element is clearly incidental to this work. Howe drew on a wide range of classical authorities, notably Cicero and (in one place) the Stoics.[39] As would be expected, he cited the Cambridge men, especially 'the incomparable Mr More,'[40] but also scholastic theology, employing forcefully the argument from design (in the process, anticipating Paley's example of the watch).[41] Even so, the significance of this work does not lie in the breadth of its sources. (*The Blessedness of the Righteous* had displayed similar erudition.) What distinguishes *The Living Temple* is its sharpness and immediacy. Whereas, in *Blessedness,* Howe deliberately chose a non-controversial topic, with *The Living Temple* he entered contested ground.

3.4 *The Living Temple* in Context

The intellectual history of the seventeenth century has been primarily interested in questions of epistemology and political theory. Yet, there was another debate which consumed enormous energy in England during Howe's career. This turned on metaphysical issues, primarily the question of substance. What is the nature of 'spirit' and 'matter'? How do the two relate? This was far more than an esoteric controversy. Churchmen and nonconformists alike recognised the risks for orthodox theology. This threat could take a number of forms. The materialism of Descartes and Hobbes implied atheism. The response of the Cambridge Platonists suggested an incorporeal monism. More disturbing still was the corporeal monism which appeared in explicit form in Spinoza. John Pocock has shown how these apparently diverse ideas could alike be perceived as dangerous by orthodox thinkers.[42] *The Living Temple* must be read in terms of this debate.[43]

---

38 Howe, *Living Temple* I, 28, 84-91, 145.

39 See e.g. Howe, *Living Temple* I, 21, 24, 35; II, 216-217.

40 See e.g. Howe, *Living Temple* I, 34, 35, 59, 63, 169 .

41 Howe, *Living Temple* I, 42-44.

42 See Pocock, 'Thomas Hobbes: Atheist or Enthusiast?, *passim* and J.G.A. Pocock, 'Enthusiasm: The Antiself of the Enlightenment', in M. Fairburn and B. Oliver (eds), *The Certainty of Doubt: Tributes to Peter Munz,* (Wellington: Victoria University Press, 1996), 117-139.

43 The debate over substance in the seventeenth century was complex. My summary is taken from the overviews in S.M. Fallon, *Milton among the Philosophers: Poetry and Materialism in Seventeenth-Century England* (Ithaca, NY: Cornell University Press, 1991), 1-78 and in L.E. Loeb, *From Descartes to Hume: Continental Metaphysics and the Development of Modern Philosophy* (Ithaca, NY: Cornell University Press, 1981), esp. 76-110. See also E. Cassirer, *The Platonic Renaissance in*

The decline of Aristotelian science was, in part, matched by the repristination of Epicurean atomism. This approach rapidly attained a vogue in the 'new philosophy' of the seventeenth century. Elements of it were picked up by Descartes and Hobbes. Epicurus held that visible phenomena, even the formation of the universe, could be explained as the result of collisions between the minute particles of which matter is constructed. Such a view presented theological difficulties. Whilst not necessarily excluding the existence of God, Epicurean atomism was a mechanical metaphysic which did not require any continuous divine input. In the eyes of wary orthodox thinkers, this amounted to atheism.

The dangers were not lost on the Cambridge Platonists. Henry More is an interesting case in point. More was initially impressed with Descartes' attempt to reconcile mechanistic physics with theism. Descartes posited a dualistic framework of two, independent types of substance: 'thinking' (*res cogitans*) and 'extended' (*res extensa*). Mechanical explanations could suffice for *res extensa* but not for the incorporeal *res cogitans*. The appeal of this to More was its preservation of a sphere (*res cogitans*) into which theistic concepts of God might fit. However, he came to regard Cartesian ontology to be flawed in its rigid dualism. In particular, Descartes failed satisfactorily to account for any interaction between *cogitans* and *extensa*.

More's disillusionment with Descartes was fuelled by Hobbes' more thoroughgoing materialism. Unlike Descartes, Hobbes did not exclude reason and thinking from his description of matter as motion. Life itself 'is but a motion of the limbs'.[44] Even God was conceived in material terms, as an incomprehensible 'spirit corporeal'.[45] Orthodox concepts of God were clearly compromised by this view.

The Platonists' response was itself extra-orthodox. In contrast to the mechanical physics of both Descartes and Hobbes, the Platonists had an ontological vision of corporeal matter infused with spirit. Instead of the dualism of Descartes, both Cudworth and More described a hierarchy of being from terrestrial, physical matter up to the Divine. Between these extremes were humans souls, demons and angels. Against the mechanical determinism of Hobbes, the Plato-

England (ET Edinburgh: Nelson, 1953), 137-156; E. Lichtenstien, *Henry More: The Rational Theology of a Cambridge Platonist* (Cambridge, MA: Harvard University Press, 1962) 10-11 & *passim*; R.L. Colie, *Light and Enlightenment: A Study of the Cambridge Platonists and the Dutch Arminians* (Cambridge: CUP, 1957), 49-65.

44 T. Hobbes, *Leviathan*, (1651) (Cambridge: CUP, 1990), 9.

45 Cited Fallon, *Milton*, 40. See Hobbes *Leviathan*, 76-78

nists held that it was this intermediate spirit realm which interacted with and motivated corporeal matter.[46]

John Howe entered the metaphysical debate over substance with the first part of *The Living Temple*. Its sub-title declared it to be 'Against Atheism , or the Epicurean Deism'. That the significance of this has been lost on some commentators provides a useful study in misinterpretation. Howe's biographer, Robert Horton is an example. Although claiming a great admiration for this work, Horton completely misses the metaphysical context. He took 'Epicurean Atheism' to refer merely to the low morality of Restoration England (picking up the seeking of pleasure associated with Epicurus). Horton's misinterpretation might indicate that he had read only the first chapter of *'The Living Temple'* (in which Howe linked atheism with licentiousness). However, it is more likely that, seduced as he was by the Howe myth, Horton found Howe's philosophical arguments unattractive and was happier associating him with such a typically 'puritan' concern as morality.[47] Yet, *The Living Temple* was much more than a moral treatise. In fact it was the foremost nonconformist contribution to the debate over substance.

Howe shared the Platonists' concern to preserve an active role for the spiritual. Like them, he rejected the atomistic explanations of the Epicureans and recognised the dangers in the ideas of both Descartes and Hobbes. However, he did not incorporate the neoplatonic emanationist features of More and Cudworth's 'plastic' hierarchy. Howe's response depended on a framework which was more clearly dualistic and, most importantly, aggressively orthodox.

Much of the first part of *The Living Temple* was taken up with what appear to be standard arguments for the existence of God, from 'first cause' and 'design'. Noting these, Horton lamented that Howe 'still dwelt in the cobwebs of scholastic reasoning'.[48] This badly misconstrues Howe's intent. The mere existence of God was assumed, based on the 'common assent' of all nations, in all times. As will be shown in chapter four, this consensual argument was a feature of Howe's mitigated scepticism. In *The Living Temple* the arguments from first cause and design were employed primarily to establish the nature of God as 'eternal, uncaused, independent, and necessary'. Once established, these divine qualities provided a foundation essential to the arguments which addressed Howe's real concerns.

46 Fallon, *Milton*, 50-78. See also F.J. Powicke, *The Cambridge Platonists, a Study* (London: Dent, 1926), 110-129, 150-173.

47 See Horton, *John Howe*, 104-122; Rogers, *Life*, 363-391.

48 Horton, *John Howe*, 108.

First, almost as an aside, Howe dismissed the pure Epicurean model, asserting that the posited primordial atoms in free fall themselves required a divine 'first cause'. The very movement of the atoms offended a true notion of eternity. In a typically dense passage, Howe argued that the divine quality of 'eternal necessity' precluded the motion and change which lay at the heart of Epicurus's model.

> For let it be considered, if every part and particle that makes up the matter of this universe were itself a necessary being, and of itself from all eternity, it must have not only its simple being, but its being as such, of itself necessarily, or rather everything of it, or any way belonging to it, must have its very simple being itself. For whence should it receive any accession to itself, when it is supposed equally independent upon its fellows, as any of them upon it?... Or suppose no alteration of figure (as Epicurus admits not) were necessary, but of situation, and motion till it become conveniently situate. Even this change also will be simply impossible. Because you can frame no imagination of the existence of this or that particle, but you must suppose it in some or other *ubi,* or point of space, and if it be necessarily, it is here; for what is simply nowhere is nothing. But if it be here necessarily...it must be here eternally, and can never not be here. Therefore we can have no notion of necessary alterable or moveable matter, which is not inconsistent and repugnant to itself; therefore also motion must proceed from an immoveable mover.[49]

Breathtaking as this logic is, it was merely an opening shot. The principal aim of the work was to provide a secure philosophical and theological base to puritan piety: to establish the 'Conversableness of God with Man'. Howe's target was what he perceived as the tendency of materialism to quarantine God; to exclude the spiritual from the material. His very title, *The Living Temple,* implied that 'a good man is a temple of God' signalling Howe's concern with the intimate relation of the Divine to the human. He identified in the Epicurean concept an agenda contrived to isolate God.

> Great care was taken, that he be set at a distance remote enough; that he be complimented out of this world, as a place too mean for his reception, and unworthy such a presence; they being indeed unconcerned *where* he had his residence, so it were not *too near them.* So that a confinement of him somewhere, was thought altogether necessary.[50]

---

49 Howe, *Living Temple,* I, 32-33n.

50 Howe, *Living Temple,* I, 134.

This 'confinement' led to the crucial problem as Howe perceived it: that the Epicurean God 'is altogether unconversable with men'.[51] It was therefore first necessary to demonstrate that God was more than merely a 'first cause' or 'prime mover'. His continued and constant activity in the world must be shown. Anticipating the laws of thermodynamics Howe argued not only for a *constant* mover but a persistent, wise and infinitely *responsive* one. A mere force, constantly applied but unintelligent and unresponsive, would lead to chaos.

> For, not to insist that nothing of impressed motion is ever lost, but only imparted to other things,...we will admit that there is a *continual decrease* or loss, but never to the degree of its *continual increase* [from the prime source]. For we see when we throw a stone out of our hand, whatever of the impressed force it do impart to the air, through which it makes its way...yet it retains a part [of the force] a considerable time, that carries it all the length of the journey, and all does not vanish and die away on the sudden. Therefore, when we here consider the continual momently renewal of the same force, always necessarily going forth from the same mighty Agent, without any moderation or restraint; every following *impetus* doth so immediately overtake the former, that whatever we can suppose lost, is yet so abundantly oversupplied, that, upon the whole, it cannot fail to be ever growing, and to have grown to...all-destroying excess.[52]

In the face of this problem even Descartes acknowledged 'that God himself is the universal and primary cause of all the motions that are in the world.'[53] Howe demanded more: 'that what men commonly call *universal nature,...*they must confess is nothing else but *common providence*.'[54]

Howe, then, insisted on a God who is not excluded from the material sphere. However, his was not a repeat of the Platonists' response. Howe's description of God required a definite duality - a transcendence of the divine from creation. In the first part of *The Living Temple* Howe addressed this issue obliquely, in response to an objection to the notion of the 'immensity' of God.

> *First, That no difference can be conceived between God and creatures, if God, as they commonly speak be wholly, in every point, or do fill all the points of the universe with his whole essence: for so whatsoever at all is, will be God himself.*

---

51 Howe, *Living Temple,* I, 136.

52 Howe, *Living Temple,* I, 38-39.

53 Cited by Howe, *Living Temple,* I, 39.

54 Howe, *Living Temple,* I, 40-41.

> *Answ.* And that is most marvellous, that the *in-being* of one thing in another must needs take away *all their difference*, and confound them each with other; which sure would much rather argue them distinct. For certainly it cannot, without great impropriety, be said that any thing is in itself; and is both the container and contained.[55] (original emphasis)

Spirit was distinct from matter. Howe eschewed the infinite gradation of being found in More and Cudworth. The divine was necessarily 'over against' the material. It was transcendent. If God was to reach out to his creation, he must first be at arm's length.

Howe next turned to the mechanical tendency of the new philosophy. Hobbes regarded all living beings as machines; Descartes allowed to humans the additional, distinguishing quality of 'mind', sourced in God. Howe made conventional criticisms of Descartes' mind/matter duality, picking up the usual problems of how to distinguish between the two and how they relate one to another. His real concern lay, however, with the thoroughgoing mechanism manifested in such as Hobbes but regarded by Howe as being sourced ultimately in Epicurus. In a lengthy discussion, Howe asserted the absurdity of attempting to explain the source of rationality and other human qualities by means of atoms. These unique human characteristics implied, indeed required, the existence of a soul, the powers of which 'are so much above the natural capacity of matter' that 'it is plain it must have a cause diverse from matter.'[56]

That 'cause' was God, the transcendent God, not to be confused with matter. God put the spark of himself in the human soul. Here was the nub of the argument. The presence of this 'spark', this 'image,' distinguished the human soul as the site of Howe's 'Living Temple' and exploded the Epicurean vision of a remote divinity. The essential point was made that God, though transcendent, 'converses' with humans. Moreover the conversation was immediate - bypassing tradition, sacrament and authority, even the mind.

By means of logical argument and in the terms of a live philosophical debate, Howe had established the validity of the puritan expectation of immediate encounter with God. However, he had achieved only half of his design. 'Conversableness' had been established by the lights of sound reasoning, liberally 'tinacktured' (to use Calamy's word) with Platonic discourse. (The 'spark' of divinity conjures a favourite theme in Platonic epistemology.) But this could never be sufficient to provide a foundation for the religion of ortho-

55 Howe, *Living Temple*, I, 161-2.

56 Howe, *Living Temple*, I, 77-8

dox dissent, which relied heavily on revelation. Part One of *The Living Temple* was but prolegomena.

The central themes which flowed from this introduction would be expounded in a series of sermons preached in the winter of 1677-8, but not published until after Howe's death. These provide an essential contemporary counterpoint to the first part of *The Living Temple*. They reveal Howe's mature theology to be one which placed considerable emphasis on the spiritual and immediate, the transcendent activity of God. In the first nineteen sermons Howe employed ideas which would later appear in systematic form in the second part of *The Living Temple*. In them, he described the operations of the Holy Spirit

> as relating to particular persons, in a single or private capacity; for the regenerating of souls, or implanting in them the principles of the divine and spiritual life; the maintaining of that life [and] the causing and ordering [of] all the motions that are proper thereunto.[57]

The sermons on the Holy Spirit signalled an intended and necessary expansion of Howe's vision of God's dealings with his creatures into the discourse of orthodox religious experience. An authentic basis for nonconformist piety required more than clever philosophy. Howe's systematic articulation of the theological aspects of *The Living Temple* would not appear for another 26 years, but it is clear that he had it in mind from the beginning. The 1676 edition of Part One ends with Howe's summary and prospect. His arguments, he suggests,

> may render us assuredly certain, that we shall find him a *conversable Being*, if we seriously apply ourselves to converse with him, and will but allow him the liberty of that temple within us, whereof we are hereafter (with his leave and help) to treat more distinctly, and at large.[58]

In the event, the second part of *The Living Temple* would not be published until 1702. The quarter-century hiatus undoubtedly had its effect. The terms of the debate has shifted somewhat. Nevertheless, Part Two depended on Part One throughout, just as Part One anticipated its sequel. The vision was conceived and planned in the 1670s and the two sections are properly considered together. This is

57 *Whole Works*, V, 215. A second group comprises fifteen sermons covering the Spirit's influence on 'the felicity and prosperous state of the church in general.' In these, Howe outlines a comprehensive pneumatological eschatology. The importance of this aspect of his thought will be discussed more fully in chapter seven.

58 Howe, *Living Temple*, I, 163.

significant, as it is in Part Two that the full orthodoxy of Howe's design becomes evident.

In the opening chapters of the 1702 publication, the essentially transcendent nature of God was further emphasised. Now, however, the target was not the materialism of Descartes and Hobbes but the equally objectionable monism of Spinoza. This scheme destroyed true religion, for

> it is all one whether we make *nothing to be God*, or *every thing*; whether we allow of no God to be worshipped, or leave none to worship him. [Spinoza's] portentous attempt to identify and deify all substance...hath a manifest design to throw religion out of the world that way.[59]

Howe's conception of immediate, personal communion with the Divine was threatened by 'Epicurean Atheism' in all its forms. Not burdened with mechanistic notions, he had avoided some of the questions on how spirit interacted with matter. Nevertheless, he was careful to define his view of the Holy Spirit's 'indwelling' of Christians. Even here he predicated his response by emphasising 'otherness'.

> It will not be inconvenient to say somewhat of the true import of the phrase *giving the Spirit*. It is evident, that whereas giving imports some sort of communication, there is yet a sense wherein that blessed Spirit is, to any creature, simply incommunicable. There is a περιξωρησιζ, or mutual *in-being*, of the sacred persons in the Godhead, which is most peculiar to themselves, not communicable to creatures with them.[60]

Properly conceived, the idea of the 'giving of the Spirit' thus excluded notions such as being 'godded with God' or 'christed with Christ'. The phrase was rather to be understood in two senses.

> [1.] Somewhat *real*, when he vouchsafes to be in us, as the spring and fountain of gracious communications, influences, and effects which are most distinct from himself.
>
> and
>
> [2.] Somewhat *relative*, the *collation of a right* to such a presence....God gives Himself, his Son, his Spirit, to them that covenant with him....And when we so covenant, then hath this *giving* its full and complete sense.[61]

The individual thus had immediate *relationship*, but not *identity* with the divine. By this understanding, Howe attempted to steer be-

---

59 Howe, *Living Temple*, II, 175.

60 Howe, *Living Temple*, II, 296.

61 Howe, *Living Temple*, II, 298-9.

tween the Scilla of Cartesian 'confinement' of God and the Charybdis of monist assimilation.

Howe's aggressive orthodoxy came to the fore at this point. He lamented the ruination of the temple designed by God as his dwelling place within humans. Since the fall God '*hath withdrawn himself* and *left this temple desolate*.'[62] Consistent with his drive for immediacy, Howe dismissed the physical temple in Jerusalem as merely prefiguring the 'Immanuel'.[63] It was thus to the incarnate Christ that humans must look as both model and seed of the true relationship between creature and creator.

> When...God...at length sends down his Son: He puts on man; becomes Immanuel; an incarnate God among men; and a man inhabited by all the fullness of God. This man was, therefore, a most perfect Temple; *the original one*: *i.e.* not only a single one himself, but an *exemplary* Temple, to which all others were to be conformed...whereby he was also a *virtual one*, from which life and influence were to be transfused to raise and form all others. But in order to its being so, this very temple must become a sacrifice, and by dying, multiply; a *seminal* temple....Behold then the wonderful conjunction of both in the one Immanuel! Who was by his very constitution an *actual Temple*; God with us: the habitation of the deity returned...and fitted to be (what it must be also) a most acceptable sacrifice.[64]

The second part of *The Living Temple* thus added an essential component to Howe's vision. If the possibility of converse with God was shown philosophically in Part One, the actuality of this divine-human intercourse was established theologically (specifically, Christologically) in Part Two. In the completed work, Howe laid out the foundations for a piety which both took seriously the wider debates of the day and simultaneously satisfied the 'puritan' requirement of a grounding in revelation and experience. Crucially, credibility was lent to the quest for immediate encounter with a transcendent God. Within this theoretical scaffold a new ecclesiology could be built.

In philosophical terms, Howe broke little new ground in the controversy dominated by Descartes, Hobbes, Spinoza and More, but that was scarcely a failure. Howe's object went beyond metaphysics. His concerns were religious; he sought to identify and explain divine activity in the world. At stake was the soteriological question of how God might be met. Immanentalist theologians like Parker and Thorndike had emphasised that God's work was mediated through

62 Howe, *Living Temple* II, 225.
63 Howe, *Living Temple* II, 230.
64 Howe, *Living Temple* II, 231.

nature. They did not, however, join Spinoza in holding God to be identified with nature. Like them, Howe accepted the immanent presence of God but rejected any suggestion of immanence of substance. Yet immanence in whatever form played only a small role in Howe's system. In *The Living Temple* he sought a metaphysical foundation for immediate, spiritual communion.

Howe did not reject the 'new philosophy' wholesale. Indeed he was in tune with important members of the emerging scientific community. Oakley has shown how the early modern move away from immanence made space for the development of scientific method. Theologically orthodox apologists for the new philosophy (such as Howe's friend, Robert Boyle) eschewed the medieval notion that the order of nature was an immanent 'participation in a divine reason'. Rather

> the tendency...was to set God over against the world he had created and which was constantly dependent upon him, to view that world as an aggregate of particular entities linked solely by external relations, each comprehensible in isolation from the others and open to investigation only by empirical endeavour.[65]

This too was atomisation, though a form which avoided the obvious theological pitfalls of the Epicurean variety. Howe represented a religious version of this shift. His emphasis on the creation of a 'Living Temple' in the souls of 'Good Men' was inherently individualistic. These may be individuals 'linked by external relations' but Howe was sowing the seeds of an ecclesiology which would ultimately have to justify church as 'an aggregate of particular entities'. In this very tendency, although it was arguably suited to the times, Howe's strategy was replete with dangers. To those dangers, his own dreams of pacific unity would ultimately fall prey.

65 Oakley, *Omnipotence*, 81.

CHAPTER 4

Signs of Fresh Thinking in Dissent

On 20 October, 1676 one John Bigrig wrote to the Secretary of State, Sir Joseph Williamson, seeking an appointment. As a reference he claimed to be 'well known to Mr Howe, a very learned man in London and a great friend of Mr Boyle'.[1] Bigrig's name-dropping is interesting on two counts. It indicates, first, how securely Howe had established himself by 1676. His links were not limited to the intellectual elite. He maintained close contact with dissenters in Parliament such as John Swynfen and Philip, Lord Wharton. He became an intimate of the family of Lord Russell[2] and was a personal friend of both Edward Stillingfleet, Dean of St Paul's, and John Tillotson , Dean of Canterbury.

These contacts matched a growing confidence in his role as a leader in dissent. Calamy records an encounter between Howe and 'a certain Nobleman, who was at that time great at court' who offered to champion the nonconformist cause. Howe rebuffed the advance, stating

> that the dissenters being a Religious People, he thought it highly concern'd 'em, if they fix'd upon any particular Person for that purpose, to make the choice of one that would not be asham'd of them, and whom at the same time they might have no occasion to be asham'd of: And that a Person in whom there was a concurrence of these two Qualifications was very difficult to find. And he heard no more of him.[3]

Calamy gives no date for this meeting, other than that it took place 'during Charles's reign' but it could have been as early as 1676. Both Shaftesbury and Buckingham were 'aggressive in seeking nonconformist support' at this time. Howe's response suggests that, of

1 See S.P. Dom. Car II 386, no 80 (C.S.P.D. Vol 18, 377).

2 On Swynfen see Lacey, *Dissent*, 445-6. Howe would travel to Holland with Wharton in 1685. He was consulted with a view to arranging marriages within the Russell family - see Rogers, *Life* 234-237.

3 Calamy 240-241.

these two, George Villiers (1628-1687), the 2nd Duke of Buckingham, is the more likely. By November 1676 Buckingham was seeking to introduce a 'bill for the ease and security of all Protestant dissenters'.[4] Whatever the actual details, the story indicates that the John Howe who took up the pastoral charge at Silver Street was a different person from the one who shuddered at his own 'pusillanimity' in 1658.

Bigrig confirms a more specific connection: between Howe and the most important English chemist of the age, Robert Boyle (1627-1691). The origin and nature of Howe's relationship with Boyle is obscure. They had mutual friends in Joseph Glanvill (1636-1680) and Edward Stillingfleet.[5] The link may have been established during Howe's period in Antrim, where Bishop Roger Boyle (Robert's cousin) approved Howe to preach in the parish church.[6] It is even possible the connection goes back as far as the Howe family's 1630s exile in Ireland.[7] What is certain, however, is that Robert Boyle had a hand in Howe's first controversial work. Boyle, himself wrestling with the relationship between faith and reason, appears to have requested Howe to write on a particular aspect of the problem.[8] The result was Howe's *The Reconcilableness of God's Prescience* (1677).[9]

---

4 See Calamy 240-1; Lacey, *Dissent*, 40-44, 79-80; T. Harris, 'Introduction: Revising the Restoration', 11.

5 Around this time Howe was apparently serving as an intermediary between Boyle and Glanvill - see letters, Glanvill to Boyle in T. Birch (ed) *The Works of the Honourable Robert Boyle*[1772] (Hildesheim: Gg. Olms, 1965-6), Vol. 6, 631-3. On Stillingfleet's connection with Boyle see M. Hunter, 'Casuistry in Action: Robert Boyle's Confessional Interviews with Gilbert Burnet and Edward Stillingfleet, 1691.', *JEH*, 44 (1993), 80-98.

6 On the Boyle family's relations with nonconformists in Ireland see Greaves, *God's Other Children, passim*

7 Calamy records that, during the Irish rebellion 'both Father and Son were ...exposed to very threatning (sic) danger, the place to which they had retired being for several weeks together beseig'd and assaulted by the Rebels, tho without success.' Lismore Castle the seat of the Earl of Cork (Robert Boyle's father) held out famously against a siege during the rebellion. Any link remains speculative. The indexes to the Lismore Castle Muniments contain no reference to Howe's family.

8 See J.W. Wojcik, *Robert Boyle and the Limits of Reason* (Cambridge: CUP, 1997).

9 J. Howe, *The Reconcilableness of God's Prescience of the Sins of Men with the Wisdom and Sincerity of his Counsels...to Prevent Them*, [London, 1677], *Works*, II, 474-513.

4.1 The Sincerity of God

Reconcilableness tackled the classic theological problem of the relationship between the power of God and the free will of humans. Howe did not address the familiar question of predestination directly. At stake, rather, was the perfect divine knowledge, juxtaposed with human freedom to disobey - both to be reconciled with God's 'counsels and exhortations' not to sin.

> So that...there seems to be committed together, - either, first God's wisdom with this part of his knowledge; for we judge it not to consist with the wisdom of a man, to design and pursue an end which he foreknows he shall never attain: - or, secondly, the same foreknowledge with his sincerity and uprightness; that he seems intent upon an end, which indeed he intends not. The matter then shortly comes to this sum:- Either the holy God seriously intends the prevention of such foreseen sinful actions and omissions or he does not intend it. If he do, his *wisdom* seems liable to be impleaded, as above. If he do not his *uprightness* and *truth*.[10]

Howe was not too confident about this treatise. Rather than the product of long research and careful polishing it had been 'mostly, huddled up in the intervals of a troublesome, long journey' (possibly during his move from Antrim to London). It was issued pseudonymously. Not until he published a *Postscript,* in answer to the controversy which ensued, did Howe reveal his authorship. The response was certainly strong. The undeniable Arminianism of Howe's tract provoked an answer from Theophilus Gale, to which Howe replied in the *Postscript,* and a vituperative outburst from Howe's Magdalen College contemporary, Thomas Danson (1629-1694), against whom Andrew Marvell wrote in Howe's defence.[11]

Subsequent interpretation has taken its cue from these responses, assuming that Howe's concern was to stake out a position on the disputed ground between predestination and free will. In his first letter to Richard Baxter, Howe had noted approvingly the modified Calvinism of Baxter's 1649 work *Aphorisms of Justification.*[12] The ar-

---

10 Howe, *Reconcilableness,* 475.

11 T. Gale, *The Court of the Gentiles,* 1678; Howe's reply was issued in a 1678 *Postscript* to his initial publication (*Works* II, 514-526). T.D[anson], *De Causa Dei; or a Vindication of the Common Doctrine of Protestant Divines concerning Predestination,* 1678 prompted Marvell's, *Remarks on a Late Disingenuous Discourse*; a third reply, both to Howe's initial publication and his answer to Gale was *A Letter to a Friend, touching God's Prescience about Sinful Actions* by J. Troughton (1678). No response was made by Howe to this work - see Wallace, *Puritans and Predestination,* 179-80.

12 Howe to Baxter, March 12, 1657, Baxter Correspondence, Vol II, 297.

gument of *Reconcilableness* certainly coheres with that early position, but it was not intended to rake over those coals. Only in the *Postscript* was Howe reluctantly forced onto that battle ground.

The 1677 *Reconcilableness* was aimed at two audiences, neither of them hard line Calvinists. It was intended both as apologetic and polemic. Its immediate apologetic context was the response to Socinianism, a debate with which Robert Boyle was particularly concerned. Howe's acquaintance Joseph Glanvill had argued that orthodoxy was reasonable and open to rational enquiry.[13] Howe agreed with this position, and noted in the *Postscript* that the original tract was written in sympathy with Boyle's quest to reconcile religion and reason.

> I wrote it upon the motion of that honourable gentleman to whom it is inscribed: who apprehended somewhat of that kind might be of use, to render our religion less exceptionable to some persons of inquiring disposition, that might, perhaps, be too sceptical and pendulous, if not prejudiced.[14]

However, the debate was complicated by the ongoing polemical dispute between Churchmen and dissenters. Glanvill was a Churchman who had argued strongly against nonconformity. This wider polemical context is important. The nonconformist, Robert Ferguson, had attacked Glanville, relegating the claims of reason and insisting that some doctrines must be accepted as mysterious and held by faith.[15] But similar arguments had been put forward by William Sherlock (1641-1707) who had insisted that the believer's union with Christ must be mediated through the church and that therefore conformity to the authorities of the established Church was

---

13 J. Glanvill, *A Seasonable Recommendation and Defence of Reason, in the Affairs of Religion; Against Infidelity, Scepticism and Fanaticisms of all sorts* (London: 1670). On Glanvill see *DNB.*; J.I. Cope, *Joseph Glanvill, Anglican Apologist* (St Louis: Washington University Press, 1956); R.H. Popkin, 'Introduction' to (R.H. Popkin, ed) J. Glanvill, *Essays on Several Important Subjects in Philosophy and Religion*, (New York: Johnson Reprint, 1970), v-xxxiii; N.H. Steneck, ''The Ballad of Robert Grosse and Joseph Glanvill' and the Background to *Plus Ultra*', *The British Journal of the History of Science*, XIV, 1981, 59-74; R.H. Popkin, *The Third Force in Seventeenth-Century Thought* (Leiden: Brill, 1992), 246-253.

14 Howe, *Postscript*, 514. This was later partially recognised by the prominent Baptist Robert Hall (1764-1831) who described *Reconcilableness* as 'the most profound, the most philosophical, and the most valuable of all Howe's writings.' R. Hall, *The Works of Robert Hall A.M.* (London: nd), vol. 1, 164.

15 R. Ferguson, *The Interest of Reason in Religion with the Import & Use of Scripture-Metaphors; and the Nature of the Union Betwixt Christ and Believers* (London: 1675).

necessary.[16] Thus Ferguson was forced to hold off the claims of reason on the one hand and arguments for conformity, based on the mystical authority of the visible church, on the other.

Howe was similarly concerned to maintain a distance from conformist views. In particular he needed to keep open the expectation of God's 'conversableness' with individuals, which he had argued philosophically in the *Living Temple*. *Reconcilableness* made no concessions to those, like Ferguson, who would limit (and therefore disarm) reason. Yet neither did Howe accept the criticism of the sceptics who claimed to identify inconsistencies in theological statements. Apparently conflicting doctrines need not be a threat to reason or religion. If there was a problem, it lay with the 'scantiness' of the human mind. Nevertheless,

> though the comprehension of our minds be not infinite, it might be extended much further than usually it is, if we would allow ourselves with patient diligence to consider things at leisure, and so gradually to stretch and enlarge our own understandings.[17]

This relative confidence in the reach of reason flows directly from Howe's common-sense Platonism. The genesis of true reason lies not in humanly derived first principles but in divinely (and universally) granted intuition. There are some attributes of God (e.g. moral goodness) which 'commonly…approve themselves to every man's understanding' and about which we may be entirely confident.

> For it is at first sight evident, since God is most certainly willing to be known of them that are sincerely willing to know him; that what is a natural impression stamped by his own hand on every man's mind, hath more of absolute certainty, than what depends on metaphysical subtlety.[18]

Because of their divine origins, the axioms of faith were entirely trustworthy and therefore able to be employed reasonably. Indeed Howe argued that not to employ them confidently was itself unreasonable. The effects of the fall were not to be ignored but, unlike Ferguson, Howe did not regard depravity as fatal to the powers of reason. Rather it caused the lesser risk 'of mistaking a dictate of depraved nature for an authentic common notion.'[19] The safeguard against this danger was scripture. Howe conceded that this argument only worked for those who accepted scripture as God's 'own word'. This was perhaps a questionable assumption of at least some

---

16 W. Sherlock, *A Discourse Concerning the knowledge of Jesus Christ, and Our Union and Communion with Him* (London: 1674).

17 Howe, *Reconcilableness*, 477.

18 Howe, *Reconcilableness*, 478.

19 Howe, *Reconcilableness*, 479.

of the Socinians, but it was a smart apologetic ploy and one which fitted well with his common sense approach.

In common sense, verified by scripture, Howe had what he regarded as a sure foundation for theological method. By these lights he mapped out a logical argument on the issue at hand. His apologetic approach was two-pronged: first to establish that it was not unreasonable to hold the positions he defended and, secondly, to anticipate objections and show these to be themselves unreasonable.

The central problem at stake was the apparent contradiction between God's integrity and his prescience. How could God exhort humans not to sin when he knew they were going to? Was he unwise, insincere, or did he in fact not know what the outcomes would be? The frame of the argument was swiftly set. Citing 'the natural complexion of our minds' in tandem with 'the report which his word makes of him', Howe asserted it was impossible - unreasonable - to question either the honesty or wisdom of God. God's prescience was also beyond doubt. Common sense testified that all God's attributes were perfect. Scripture confirmed the perfection of God's knowledge; reason demanded that it is 'a higher perfection to know all things at once, than gradually to arrive at the knowledge of one thing after another'.[20]

To this point Howe had done no more than confirm that his presenting problem was indeed a reasonable one. The bulk of the remainder of the treatise is taken up with argument to show that the apparent inconsistency was neither logical nor real. Howe pursued every ramification of the question until each petered out. Amidst this detail, his principal argument may be identified as follows.

There is no inherent logical contradiction between knowing someone will do something and telling them not to do it. The issue was whether it is reasonable to call for an end known to be unattainable. At this point Howe insisted on the indivisibility of God's ends. God, unlike humans, is an end in himself. Therefore his purpose in relation to humans may be summed up as 'that he may be found in everything to have done as became him, and was most worthy of himself.'[21] It fits with God's wisdom that his laws and standards be promulgated and that obedience be demanded of all his creatures. If not, then his kingdom would be innately anarchic, not reflecting his own character. Thus, in the very act of exhorting to holiness, God is actually achieving his end (properly understood) and the question 'is it reasonable?' becomes ridiculous.

---

20 Howe, *Reconcilableness,* 481.

21 Howe, *Reconcilableness,* 491.

But what of God's *sincerity* in relation to his creatures? Can he be said to be genuine in offering a reward for obedience to those he knows will not obey? To this Howe responded that God never indicated an intent to save all, no matter what. He rejected the notion that God's offer was unconditional. Rather, God was willing 'to pardon, save and restore them to a blessed state, upon such terms as shall be agreeable.'[22] Here Howe depended on the picture of God at arms-length which he set up in *The Living Temple.* This was a creator who dealt in genuine relationship with his creatures - declining, in general, to force himself upon them.[23]

Here Howe created a problem for himself. In his apologetic purpose, he had been moderately successful. He had considered in turn all the logical issues which might be said to attend his central problem. By his lights, God's prescience of the sins of men was indeed reconcilable with the wisdom and sincerity of his exhortations against those sins. However, for his polemical concern not to undermine nonconformity, a clear difficulty had arisen.

In order to establish the sincerity of God, Howe had to show that the offer of salvation and the warning of punishment were both universally made. To do so he had cited general revelation, together with the laws and precepts of special revelation, as the principal means by which God had communicated. Immediate divine contact with individuals would not help his case, as such contact could not, by nature, be held to be universal. Yet individual encounter was what Howe had argued for in *The Living Temple* and it was the very privilege which fellow nonconformist Ferguson maintained against Sherlock. It was, moreover, essential to the claim to follow individual conscience. Howe was in danger of weakening the basis for the right to dissent.

He added further difficulty with a lengthy refutation of the notion that a sincere God must overwhelm his creatures to ensure an obedient response. Here too, he was exposed. Howe readily agreed that God could break in to the private, internal world of the soul and effect change. Yet how was he to avert the charge of unfairness in that, in the majority of cases, God did not break in in this way? All Howe had to offer was a feeble resort to the sovereign right of God to do as he pleases. He ran a huge polemical risk in order to further his

22 Howe, *Reconcilableness,* 497.

23 Howe insisted that divine prescience did not exclude free will. This is in contrast to Peter Sterry, another Platonist and one-time Chaplain to the Cromwells who concluded that free-will must be sacrificed – Sterry, *A Discourse on the Freedom of the Will* (London: 1675).

apologetic purpose, which was best served by emphasising the external, ordinary means by which God deals with humans.

> [It is] manifest, to any sober reason, that it were very incongruous…that a whole order of intelligent creatures should be moved by inward impulses; that God's precepts, promises, and communications, whereof their nature is capable, should be all made impertinencies, through his constant overpowering of those that should neglect them; that the faculties, whereby men are capable of moral government, should be rendered, to this purpose, useless and vain; and that they should be tempted to expect to be constantly managed as mere machines, that know not their own use.[24]

In thus appearing to down-play the potential for individuals to gain direct leading from God, Howe's argument might have delivered dissent to the visible church. Samuel Parker could have readily endorsed such sentiments. Howe had opened a window to spread apologetic light but knew he must swiftly close it to shut out polemical danger. This he did, in the next paragraph.

> Nor is it less apprehensible, how incongruous it were also, to suppose…God should have barred out himself from all inward access to the spirits of men, or commerce with them….It is manifestly congruous that the divine government over man should be (as it is) mixed or composed of an external frame of laws, with their proper sanctions and enforcements, and an internal effusion of power and vital influence, correspondent to the several parts of that frame; and which might animate the whole….[25]

The intended focus of *The Reconcilableness of God's Prescience* was swamped in a reaction which concentrated instead on the implications for the doctrines of grace. Howe's Platonic approach to the narrow question he addressed was unlikely in any event to make much impact on the wider debates which exercised Boyle. As an apologetic work it was no more than adequate. Moreover, Howe came close to handing a significant argument to the Church party. As has been noted already, he would give considerable attention to the issue of the Spirit's interaction with individuals in his first years in London. When he returned to nonconformist polemics in 1680 he would be much more sure-footed.

4.2 Conformist Attacks on Dissent in 1680

Howe would wait two years before publishing another work. In 1680, dissent was challenged by two Churchmen who had been re-

---

24 Howe, *Reconcilableness,* 511.
25 Howe, *Reconcilableness,* 511

garded as its friends. John Tillotson and Edward Stillingfleet were moderates - conformists who nonetheless maintained warm relations with nonconformist leaders. Howe knew both well and their provocative statements would force him to refine his view of authority in a direction which would have significant implications for the ecclesiology of dissent.

On 2 April, 1680, apparently at short notice, John Tillotson preached before the King at Whitehall. This sermon was subsequently published as *The Protestant Religion Vindicated from the Charge of Singularity and Novelty.* [26] Although the sermon as a whole was directed against Rome, it contained a clear censure of 'enthusiasts' who might resist the religious structures established by the magistrate. Indeed, Tillotson's was a modified form of the Constantinian ecclesiology already observed in Samuel Parker.[27] To this stance, nonconformists took exception. Calamy records that Howe remonstrated privately with Tillotson on the matter, with some success.[28] However, a further attack from an unexpected quarter would soon demand a more public response.

Little more than a month after Tillotson's effort before the King, Edward Stillingfleet preached a sermon before the Lord Mayor which was immediately published as *The Mischief of Separation*.[29] If John Tillotson had attacked nonconformity in passing, Stillingfleet addressed the issue head on. The reaction was instantaneous. A multitude of responses and defences appeared. In 1681 Stillingfleet would publish a long treatise, greatly extending his arguments and answering his critics, entitled *The Unreasonableness of Separation*.[30]

Stillingfleet had much in common with Tillotson. He too was a naturally irenic person, a friend of many of the moderate dissenters and was several times involved in discussions towards comprehen-

---

26 Tillotson, *The Protestant Religion Vindicated from the Charge of Singularity and Novelty* (London: 1680).

27 For a detailed consideration of Tillotson's argument and its relation to that of Parker and Hobbes see J. Marshall, 'The Ecclesiology of the Latitude-men 1660-1689: Stillingfleet, Tillotson and "Hobbism"', *JEH*, Vol. 36, No 3, July 1985, 407-427, esp. 421-425 and M.P. Sutherland, 'Protestant Divergence in the Restoration Crisis'.

28 Calamy 76.

29 E. Stillingfleet, *The Mischief of Separation: A Sermon Preached at Guild-Hall Chapel, May 11. MDCLXXX... Before the Lord Mayor, &c.* (London, 1680).

30 E. Stillingfleet, *The Unreasonableness of Separation: or An Impartial Account of the History, Nature, and Pleas of the Present Separation from the Communion of the Church of England...* (London, 1681). For a discussion of John Locke's unpublished response to both of Stillingfleet's pamphlets on separation see J. Marshall, *John Locke: Resistance, Religion and Responsibility* (Cambridge: CUP, 1994), 95-110.

sion. Yet Stillingfleet operated an ecclesiology significantly different from that of Tillotson. He was an example of how, in the seventeenth century, irenicism did not necessarily equate to toleration, especially when the Church appeared threatened. It was just such a perceived threat which provided the context of *Mischief*. The sermon did not appear out of thin air in 1680. In the same year, Stillingfleet made an important contribution to the apology for episcopal power in Parliament, against the onslaught of Shaftesbury and others.[31]

Stillingfleet demonstrated a clear concern for the visible church. His definition of the church was institutional and echoed Richard Hooker's concern for order.[32] Hammond's development of the concept of the 'national Church' had provided a defence against accusations of schism from outside (Rome) and against justifications of separation within.[33] Stillingfleet, though rather weakly, sought to align his visible society with this model.

> [I]f there be one Catholick Church consisting of particular Churches consenting to one Faith; then why may there not be one national Church from the consent in the same articles of Religion, and the same Rules of Government and Order of Worship?[34]

Unity and order were crucial markers, Stillingfleet asserted the necessity for a church to be encompassing, monolithic and uniform. It was not for nothing that he took as his text Philippians 3:26: 'let us walk by the same rule, let us mind the same things.'[35] Just as the body of Christ was not divided, neither was a true church. Stillingfleet adopted the common argument that, if diversity were allowed, it would feed on itself, leading to fragmentation and schism. The result would be catastrophic. Such was the 'mischief of separation' that the religious security of the nation would be at risk. He warned:

---

31 E. Stillingfleet, *The Grand Question, Concerning the Bishops' Right to Vote in Parliament in Cases Capital*, (1680). For a discussion of this and the entire controversy see the articles by M. Goldie: 'John Locke and Anglican Royalism', *Political Studies*, XXXI, (1983), 61-85; 'Danby, the Bishops and the Whigs' in Harris, Seaward and Goldie (eds.), *The Politics of Religion in Restoration England*, 75-105; 'Priestcraft and the birth of Whiggism' in Phillipson and Skinner (eds.), *Political Discourse in Early Modern Britain*, 209-231. See also R.T. Carrol, *The Common-Sense Philosophy of Religion of Bishop Edward Stillingfleet 1635-1699* (The Hague: Nijhoff, 1975), 25.

32 Stillingfleet, *Mischief*, 17.

33 Howe recognised that Stillingfleet's defence of the national Church was in part aimed to 'acquit us from the imputation of schism' - Howe, *Letter*, 520. Spurr in *Restoration Church*, 155, dismisses this comment as a 'jaundiced aside'. In fact it was a perceptive recognition of the concerns of Church of England visiblists.

34 Stillingfleet, *Mischief*, 17-18.

35 Stillingfleet, *Mischief*, 10-11.

I never expect to see [the Protestant Religion among us] survive the destruction of the Church of England.[36] Toleration would be but the thin end of the wedge.

> An *universal Toleration* is that *Trojan Horse*, which brings in our enemies without being seen, and which after a long Siege they hope to bring in at last under the pretence of setting our Gates wide enough open, to let in all our friends.[37]

The only defence against those 'enemies' (namely: popery) was unanimity. The best means of achieving this was uniformity of practice.

> Men may please themselves in talking of preserving *Peace and Love* under separate Communions; but our own sad experience shews the contrary; for...nothing tends more to unite mens hearts than joyning together in the same prayers and sacraments....[38]

Stillingfleet's case pointed in a direction quite different from that of Tillotson. His definition of the church, his paramount concern for its institutional unity, the dire consequences of division that he predicted and the remedy he prescribed show that the visible church took priority in his ecclesiology. This was a version of the high church position exemplified by Herbert Thorndike. If the national Church of England - personified in its bishops, both proclaimed and made whole in its rituals - was weakened, Christianity itself was threatened. If dissenters would but realise the damage they were causing, they would desist.[39]

Leading dissenters, Howe included, disagreed.[40] This time, a private chat would not suffice as an answer. A careful examination of

---

36 Stillingfleet, *Mischief*, 23.

37 Stillingfleet, *Mischief*, 58.

38 Stillingfleet, *Mischief*, 32. There is a clear echo here of Laud's view that 'unity cannot long continue in the Church where uniformity is shut out at the church door' - W. Laud, *Works*, (Oxford: LACT, 1854) IV, 60.

39 In the 'Epistle Dedicatory' to *Mischief*, Stillingfleet declared his desire to find 'a certain foundation for a lasting UNION among our selves. Which is impossible to be attained, till men are convinced of the EVIL and DANGER of the present SEPARATION.'

40 The most significant public responses were: R. Baxter, *Richard Baxters Answer to Dr Stillingfleet's Charge of Separation...*, (London: 1680); J. Owen, *A Brief Vindication of the Nonconformists from the Charge of Schism...* (London, 1680) in W.H. Goold (ed) *The Works of John Owen, D.D.* (London: 1850-3), Vol. XIII, 305-342; [J. Humfrey and S. Lobb], *An Answer to Dr Stillingfleet's Sermon, by Some Nonconformists, Being the Peaceable Design Renewed* (London: 1680); T.P. [V. Alsop], *The Mischief of Impositions or, A Soveraign Antidote Against a Late Discourse Called the Mischief of Separation* (London: 1680); J. Howe, *A Letter Written out of the Country to a Person of Quality in the City who took offence at the*

their replies does more than identify the key issues in the dispute between dissent and the established Church. Also uncovered are significant differences within dissent itself. A clear divergence of nonconformist views was emerging.[41] This is worth examining, as Howe's position is clarified when set against those of his older contemporaries, especially Owen and Baxter. Indeed, in Howe's contribution (his most successful venture into polemical debate) the seeds of a new ecclesiology of dissent may be observed.

4.3 Responses of Conservative Dissent

Richard Baxter's *Answer* was compromised by his apparent determination to take Stillingfleet's attack personally. Baxter had sought clarification on several points because 'you have told the Magistrates and the World what you think of me as guilty of sinful separation.'[42] Unhappy with the Dean's reply, Baxter wrote a lengthy disputation which, Stillingfleet suggested, appeared to have been 'written...in one continued fit of anger'.[43]

On the crucial question of the true church, Baxter rejected Stillingfleet's definition as inexact and misleading.

> This definition...maketh an Army, a Navy, a Ship, a company of Christian Merchants, or Corporation, &c. to be a Church: For all these may be 'Societies of Men united together for their Order and Government, according to the Rules of the Christian Religion': For the Christian Religion giveth Rules to all sorts of Christian Societies.[44]

To be of any use, 'church' must be distinguished from such general societies. Baxter did this in two ways. Firstly, he asserted that the proper notion of church could only refer to a religious body instituted by God. Baxter rhetorically asked for proof of the divine institution of 'National Regent Churches', implying that none could be produced.

> God made the Form of the *Universal Church*, of which the particular are parts; whose Form also is of his making: And if God hath made *National Regent Churches* as distinct from *Christian Kingdoms* and *Commonwealths*, we will obey them; if not, we must know what Men

---

Sermon of Dr Stillingfleet, Dean of St Paul's, Before the Lord Mayor (London: 1680).

41 For further detail on the significance of this debate see M.P. Sutherland, 'Protestant Divergence in the Restoration Crisis'.

42 Baxter, *Answer*, 8.

43 Stillingfleet, *Unreasonableness*, lx.

44 Baxter, *Answer*, 36.

made them, and by what authority, and whether God authorized them thereto[45]

In the universal church, authority resided in Christ himself. In the local body this was exercised through the pastor. Indeed, the relation of pastor to flock was constitutive of this manifestation of the church.[46] Any other medium of authority was either invalid or suspect. The episcopal authority which Stillingfleet had sought to establish failed, along with the national Church. If Stillingfleet's definition was followed, secular 'Christian Kingdoms' (the divine institution of which Baxter accepted[47]) might possibly rank as 'Churches', but this did not justify civil authority over the true church. The authority of the magistrate was 'accidental', rather than 'constitutive'.[48]

Baxter's theological development has been plotted by William Lamont.[49] For most of his career he gave a high place to both the magistrate and a national church. Though never a true Erastian, he accorded an important spiritual role to civil authority. This was limited to a carefully defined sphere – supporting, rather than directing the discipline of the pastor in the local congregation. The national church he envisaged subsisted within this magisterial zone. Significantly, Baxter's *Answer* to Stillingfleet was written in the period (c. 1678-1683) in which Baxter appeared to lose faith in magistracy. Yet, even in 1680, though distanced from direct authority over the congregation, the magistrate did not disappear altogether.

Another feature of Baxter's *Answer* was more consistent with his life-long concerns: conscience was allowed only a very circumscribed role. In *Mischief*, Stillingfleet had been hard on any resort to conscience.

Men ought not to rest satisfied with the present dictates of their *Consciences*, for notwithstanding them, they may commit very great sins. I am afraid, the common mistating (sic) the *Case* of an *Erroneous Conscience* hath done a great deal of Mischief to conscientious men, and betrayed them into great security, while they are assured they do act according to their Consciences.[50]

He went on to distinguish between 'Errors of Conscience' of two types. Those caused by 'invincible Ignorance' will not be 'imputed as

45 Baxter, *Answer*, 39.
46 Baxter, *Answer*, 35.
47 Baxter, *Answer*, 42.
48 Baxter, *Answer*, 43-44.
49 Lamont, *Richard Baxter and the Millennium*, 210-284, see esp. 243-256.
50 Stillingfleet, *Mischief*, 43.

Sin' but 'if men fall into *Wilful Errors of Conscience*...they may be in...great danger of committing heinous sins.'[51]

In what was otherwise a point for point, often pedantic, rebuttal of Stillingfleet's sermon, Baxter takes no issue with this section. His only comment was to agree that 'if we make not Gods Laws the Rule of Conscience, no wonder if we err: God preserve us from all corrupting prejudice, passions, interest and Canons.'[52] The inclusion of 'Canons' in the list of undesirable influences was a polemical sting in the tail. Nevertheless, on this issue, Baxter, always suspicious of unbridled conscience, was in substantial agreement with Stillingfleet.

The response by John Owen was a more measured work than Baxter's *Answer*. As might be expected from a redoubtable Congregationalist, Owen's ecclesiology centred on 'particular or congregational' Churches, which 'stated with their officers according to the power of the gospel, are entire churches, that have just right and power to reform themselves.'[53] In agreement with Baxter, Owen held that this right derived from Christ's own institution of these bodies. The 'right and power to reform themselves' was crucial. Baxter was prepared to accept parochial churches as 'true'. Owen, however, cast doubt on this, because these bodies lacked the essential capacity for local reform. Owen thus made a stronger case for separation from parish churches than did Baxter, who preferred to argue merely against coercion into them. Nevertheless, both men agreed in their rejection of the national church as lacking Christ's institution and true communion.[54]

Owen, like Baxter, had an invisiblist ecclesiology. True communion was not a matter of uniformity but of 'faith and love, and all the fruits of them, unto the glory of God.'[55] His fundamental orientation was made starkly obvious in his assertion that Churches did not exist for themselves.

> Let none mistake themselves herein; believers are not made for churches, but churches are appointed for believers. Their edification, their guidance and direction...is their use and end; without which they are of no signification.[56]

---

51 Stillingfleet, *Mischief*, 44-5. For the importance of a properly informed conscience to ideas of intolerance see M. Goldie, 'The Theory of Religious Intolerance in Restoration England'.

52 Baxter, *Answer*, 91.

53 Owen, *Brief Vindication*, 315.

54 Owen, *Brief Vindication*, 316, 318.

55 Owen, *Brief Vindication*, 314.

56 Owen, *Brief Vindication*, 317.

That, without such benefit to believers, churches 'are of no signification' was a conclusion which Stillingfleet could never contemplate.

If they shared this basic ecclesiology, Baxter and Owen also had similar views regarding authority. For both, the mind of Christ was all. However, Owen relegated the magistrate further than Baxter. He might intrude on outward matters, but these were of no account in the real business of religion.

> In what kings, potentates and other supreme magistrates, might do to accommodate the outward profession of religion unto their rule and the interest thereof, we are not at all concerned...whilst they impose not the religious observation of their constitutions unto that end upon our consciences and practice.[57]

This reference to conscience was not absolute. Like Baxter, like Stillingfleet, Owen wrote only of *enlightened* conscience. His response to the Dean's section on erroneous conscience was to eschew any disagreement.

> We seek no shelter nor countenance from what is pleaded by any concerning the obliging power of an 'erroneous conscience,'...for we acknowledge no rule of conscience in those things which concern churches..., but divine revelation [scripture] only...This rule we attend unto, and enquire into the mind of God in it, with all the diligence we are able.[58]

Baxter's *Answer* and Owen's *Brief Vindication* reflected similar underlying ecclesiologies. The focus was almost entirely on the local congregation as a manifestation of the invisible body. The wider, visible, church, with its inevitable concern for hierarchies and structure, had next to no place. Nevertheless, this was a tempered invisiblism. The individual was suspect and conscience valid only if strictly hedged and channelled. This was a conventional view of conscience, one they shared with Stillingfleet.[59] A concession was in fact made to the need for a visible authority (the pastor for Baxter, the congregation as a whole for Owen). In the three remaining responses to Stillingfleet, a subtle shift is evident. The specific doctrine

57 Owen, *Brief Vindication*, 316.

58 Owen, *Brief Vindication*, 339-340.

59 For an insightful description of how conscience operated in the cases of two Englishman, a century apart, see A. Kenny, 'The Conscience of Sir Thomas More' in *idem*, *The Heritage of Wisdom: Essays in the History of Philosophy*, (Oxford: B. Blackwell, 1987), 108-115 and D. Woolf, 'Conscience, Constancy and Ambition in the Career and Writings of James Howell' in J. Morrill, P. Slack and D. Woolf (eds.), *Public Duty and Private Conscience in Seventeenth-Century England: Essays Presented to G.E. Aylmer* (Oxford: Clarendon Press, 1993), 243-278.

of the church was similar but, to quite different effects, conscience and the individual were of far greater importance.

The most unusual of the answers to Stillingfleet is *An Answer to Dr Stillingfleet's Sermon*, attributed to John Humfrey (1621-1719) and Stephen Lobb (1647?-1699). This was largely a republication of a 1675 treatise which had made detailed proposals to resolve the problem of nonconformity.[60] Both authors began their clerical careers as Presbyterians. By 1680, although careful to eschew extreme separatism, they were aligned with Congregationalists.[61] As might be expected from a reissued work, the *Answer* made little attempt to meet Stillingfleet's arguments directly. It is most interesting as a general apology for nonconformity.

Humphrey and Lobb laid great stress on the duty of ministers to preach the gospel. Tensions, they asserted, arose when the imperative to promote union and prosperity conflicted with the duty to preach. Answering their own question: 'Which is the greater matter?', Humfrey and Lobb confirmed an ecclesiology radically different from that of Stillingfleet.

> What is *Parochial Union* in comparison?...The preaching of the Gospel, and *Particular Assemblies*, are of *Divine*, *Parochial Churches* are of *Human* Institution. That which is of Divine, is undeniably to be prefer'd before that which is of Human appointment.[62]

'Parish Churches' were indeed true churches but only by virtue of being examples of 'particular assemblies'. The parochial structure of the established Church was not crucial. Humfrey and Lobb relegated as of human institution what Stillingfleet held to be of divine provenance. Where, to them, separation was justified if it meant saving men's souls, to Stillingfleet it could lead only to destruction. Whereas *Mischief* called for submission to episcopal authority, Humfrey and Lobb asserted 'there is no burden whereof we ought to be more sensible, than that which lies upon our Consciences'.[63]

Here Humfrey and Lobb departed somewhat from Baxter and Owen. Though they all espoused similar formulations of the doctrine of the church, Humfrey and Lobb took a different path on the question of authority. There were two manifestations of this shift. The first was the apparently Erastian flavour of the solution Hum-

---

60 J. Humphrey and S. Lobb, *The Peaceable Design* (London: 1675).

61 Humfrey and Lobb, *Answer*, 3-4. See entries in DNB and CR for Humfrey and in the annotated index to A. Gordon, (ed) *Freedom After Ejection: A Review (1690-1692) of Presbyterian and Congregational Nonconformity in England and Wales*, (Manchester: Manchester University Press 1917), for Lobb.

62 Humfrey and Lobb, *Answer*, 5-6.

63 Humfrey and Lobb, *Answer*, 3.

frey and Lobb proposed to the problem of nonconformity. In the national church, authority was devolved on the monarch.[64] However, this 'Erastianism' was more apparent than real. National structures were merely accidental, external institutions. Ultimately they mattered little. They might be safely left to the secular authority ordained by God for such mundane matters. In the meantime, individuals guided by their conscience and pastors responsible for discipline, could get on with the job of true religion.[65]

The second shift related to the role of conscience. In part of their *Answer* which repeated the 1675 treatise, individual scruple provided the framework for a justification of nonconformity. The case depended on a notion which may be styled as 'constructive separation'.

> If there be but one Particular imposed on us as a condition of Conformity, which we prove to be sinful...*it is not the Refuser, but the Imposer is guilty of the Schism.*[66]

This was a direct contradiction of Thorndike's formula for allocating the blame for schism. Humfrey and Lobb proceeded to delineate reasons why nonconformists found conditions relating to reordination, the declaration of assent to the Prayer Book, and subscription to the oaths in the Act of Uniformity and the 'Oxford' Act to be a 'Hazard of some sprain to their Consciences'.[67]

4.4 The Sincerity of the Believer

An important role for the strictures of conscience is also a feature of a fourth response to Stillingfleet: *The Mischief of Impositions*, by Vincent Alsop (1630-1703). Alsop was born in the same year as John Howe and the two had remarkably parallel careers. Both matriculated at Cambridge as sizars in 1647, both were ejected in 1662, both took up important pastorates in London in the late 1670s, both were instrumental in the 'Happy Union' of the 1690s. Yet Alsop and Howe would take quite different stances on the plight of dissent

---

64 In another passage, the Government of the Church is declared to be part of the Administrative Law, under the Monarch, rather than of the inviolable Constitution - see Humfrey and Lobb, *Answer*, 19.

65 Gary De Krey has identified this distinction between public and private spheres in earlier writings by Humfrey, Owen and Nye. See G.S. De Krey, 'Rethinking the Restoration: Dissenting Cases for Conscience, 1667-1672', *HJ*, 38, I, (1995), 53-83, 60.

66 Humfrey and Lobb, *Answer*, 7.

67 Humfrey and Lobb, *Answer*, 9.

during James' reign.[68] These factors make a comparison of their respective contributions to the Stillingfleet controversy of considerable interest.

Alsop's work was a sharp, sometimes satirical, refutation of Stillingfleet's points. The Dean was highly indignant at the treatment he received.[69] On the face of it, Alsop's view of the church seemed close to that of Owen. National Churches were discounted as 'prudential contrivances for common security' to which 'the Scriptures are perfect strangers'. The 'particular', local church, responsible for its own Government, was what mattered.[70]

As the title of his work suggested, Alsop's stance on nonconformity picked up the 'constructive separation' line of Humfrey and Lobb. The fault lay not with dissenters but with those demanding a narrow uniformity.[71] However, there was no pseudo-Erastianism in *The Mischief of Impositions*. The focus was very much on conscience. In a lengthy 'Epistle Dedicatory' Alsop set out 'the principles upon which the present Separation is carried on'. These related primarily to authority. Although scripture and Christ's ordinances were accorded objective priority, the role of the individual was crucial. Just as a particular church might choose its own pastor, so

> every particular Christian [has] the same power to chuse his own Church...I will thank my friends that will recommend to my choice an able Physician, a faithful Lawyer but I am sure I love my health, my life, my estate so well as not to put the Election out of my own hands into theirs, who are not likely to love me better than my self: and if I chuse amiss, the greatest wrong will be my own.[72]

The diversity which arose from individual choice was to be accepted, not ridiculed.

> [L}et him [Stillingfleet] not always miscall *Conscience* by the scandalous name of *Fancy!* The very truth is we have no Mathematical certainty in these matters [of worship and liturgy and]...from some little trouble that arises in a Church from the levity and volubility of men's minds, to bring in that enormous, monstrous principle, of enslaving all mens judgments and conscience...is a medicine worse than Poyson.[73]

---

68 Alsop's writings and 1680s career are covered by Beddard in 'Vincent Alsop and the Emancipation of Restoration Dissent'. See also Gordon, *Freedom After Ejection*, 199.

69 Stillingfleet, *Unreasonableness*, lxii-lxv.

70 [Alsop], *Mischief of Impositions*, 28, 30.

71 [Alsop], *Mischief of Impositions*, [iv].

72 [Alsop], *Mischief of Impositions*, [ix].

73 [Alsop], *Mischief of Impositions*, [xxvii-xxviii].

Importantly, unlike Baxter or Owen, Alsop took Stillingfleet to task over his statements on conscience. Whilst in full agreement that wilful error does not excuse sin, he rejected the inference that 'men ought not to rest satisfied with the present dictates of their consciences'.[74]

> Conscience is more my rule than the dictate of any Church: and if I ought not to rest satisfied with that which God has made my *next and immediate* guide, I may the more lawfully examine their commands, which are more remotely such.[75]

This confidence in direct, divine ministration allowed Alsop to 'take the voice and countermand of Conscience to be God's voice'.[76]

Alsop departed markedly from Stillingfleet (and Baxter and Owen) in introducing sincerity as a factor. In the case of a soul which sins out of genuine error,

> God may pity it, though erroneous, if sincere; for sincerity is more in the sight of him who desires truth in the inward parts than Orthodoxy: and he sees the general frame of the heart to be upright...though in the application of the general frame of heart to this or that particular practice it may be out most wretchedly.[77]

Alsop was no Quaker; he did not propose a fully competent 'inner light'. Like his fellows, he stressed the need for conscience to be informed and attuned to God. Nevertheless, the mere employment of sincerity was significant in that it signalled a movement to a more pronounced individualism.

A complex picture emerges. Unsurprisingly, the nonconformist respondents to Stillingfleet agreed in rejecting the notion of a divinely instituted national church. Structure and hierarchy were discounted in favour of local or 'particular' congregations, in which the true saints might become evident. This is as near as it is possible to come to an 'orthodoxy of dissent'. Restoration nonconformity was characterised by a fundamental bias towards the invisible church. Ecclesiology, however, is more than discrete formulations of the doctrine of the church. When related factors are examined, differences of degree emerge within this basic orientation. Baxter and Owen were more cautious about the role of individual conscience than were Humfrey and Lobb. Vincent Alsop went in the opposite direction, making conscience more central. That Alsop, a 'Presbyterian', embraced what appears to be the most extreme position defies simplistic party analysis. This challenge to conventional expectations is

---

74 Stillingfleet, *Mischief*, 43.

75 [Alsop], *Mischief of Impositions*, 74.

76 [Alsop], *Mischief of Impositions*, 75.

77 [Alsop], *Mischief of Impositions*, 77.

strengthened by a consideration of the response to Stillingfleet by John Howe.

Howe adopted a style unlike any other respondent. Rather than a head-on attack, his answer to Stillingfleet was cast in the form of a mildly censorious letter to a third party. It was the shortest and most pacific of nonconformist responses to *Mischief*. Though clearly the product of a theologian, Howe's *Letter Written Out of the Country* was written as if by one layman to another. He reproved the passion of his notional correspondent's reaction to Stillingfleet's sermon, taking as his text Galatians 6:1: 'Considering thyself, lest thou also be tempted'. The Dean acknowledged the tone:

> he discourses Gravely and Proudly, without Bitterness and Rancor, or any sharp Reflections, and sometimes with a great mixture of Kindness towards me; for which, and his Prayers for me, I do heartily Thank him.[78]

The distress of the 'Person of Quality', Howe believed, arose from his fear of the possible impact of the sermon on the nonconformist cause, and his anger at Stillingfleet's action. Howe's stated aim in the *Letter* was to 'first defend the cause against Dr Stillingfleet, and then add somewhat in the defence of Dr Stillingfleet against you.'[79] Howe undertook this double task with some humour and considerable skill. Importantly, his rhetoric revealed an individualism even more extreme than Alsop's and a thoroughgoing rejection of the visible church. He carried the 'constructive separation' argument further than the responses already considered. Like them, he adopted the theme of conscientious objection but, more thoroughly than had the others, Howe centred his argument on the religious consequences for the believer.

Howe elevated the role of the individual conscience still further. This is evident in three features of his *Letter*. The first was structural. Humfrey and Lobb took the importance of conscience as axiomatic and concentrated their arguments on specific points of objection to uniformity. Alsop made more direct use of conscience but, in his engagement with Stillingfleet, followed a method similar to that of Humfrey and Lobb. Howe, by contrast, adopted conscientious scruple as his central argument. Merely by the space he accorded this underlying problem, he magnified its importance.

Second, and more important, was the treatment of conscience in the argument itself. Howe cited two apparently conflicting elements in Stillingfleet's *Mischief*. The first was the dominant argument that it was sinful to worship in separation from the established Church.

---

78 Stillingfleet, *Unreasonableness*, lxi-lxii.

79 Howe, *Letter*, 508.

The second lay in Stillingfleet's acknowledgement that a genuinely erroneous conscience could create 'a necessity of sinning, if he acts with it or against it.'[80] Howe argued that Stillingfleet had placed nonconformists in an impossible predicament. They were unable to hear the word or receive the sacraments without committing either the sin of separation (by attending conventicles) or the sin of offending against their conscience (by submitting to the Church). Nonconformists were thus 'damned if they did, and damned if they didn't'.

> We are indeed satisfied that our sin...would contribute little to our salvation. But when also we are satisfied that we cannot enjoy the means of salvation in his way without sin; and he tells us, we cannot without sin enjoy them in our own: we hope every door is not shut up against us, and cannot think the merciful and holy God hath so stated our case, as to reduce us to a necessity of sinning to get out of a state of damnation.[81]

By this understanding, one part of Stillingfleet's case must fail. To Howe there was no doubt as to which: Stillingfleet's insistence on uniformity was invalid. The rule of conscience was part of God's order; the rituals and external form of the Church of England were not.

> For any divine law that can be supposed to oblige us to the use of the things we scruple, or else to live without the worship and ordinances of God, not knowing of any ourselves, we must wait until we be informed of it.[82]

In proposing an irreconcilable tension in Stillingfleet's case, Howe either misunderstood or misused the Dean's concession on conscience. Stillingfleet acknowledged that to breach conscience was sinful but he did so grudgingly and in passing. His real point was that the *consequences* of sinful action might be avoided, if the error was genuine. Even this was a straw position, admitted in order to set up his intended characterisation of the nonconformists' error as 'wilful', rather than merely the product of 'invincible ignorance'.[83] Importantly, Stillingfleet never conceded that truth was other than objective (and accessible, by implication, through the Church). He did no more than acknowledge genuine error as a plea in mitigation, where God's ordinances had been broken. Sin, like truth, remained external.

---

80 Stillingfleet, *Mischief*, 44.

81 Howe, *Letter*, 514.

82 Howe, *Letter*, 514.

83 Stillingfleet, *Mischief*, 44-45.

By contrast, Howe argued that the individual conscience could, on its own, define sin - 'those things be sinful to us which our consciences judge to be so'.[84] In this, as had Alsop, Howe was amplifying the subjective element of sincerity and relegating objective standards. It was a theme of huge significance in Howe's own religious sense. On the December night in 1675 when he reflected on his journey to London, he identified sincerity as the key criterion of his fitness to take up the post in Silver Street.

> Tho I have earnestly beg'd Light to guide me therein, so as that I might do that herein which in the Substance of the thing is agreeable to the holy Will of God, yet I have much more importunately pray'd that I might be sincere in what I do, not only because I know God will pardon ignorance…where he beholds Sincerity...; but also from the higher Esteem I have of sincerity, above all Light and Knowledge without it, and the greater Excellence of the thing it self.[85]

Keith Thomas has noted a transition in the seventeenth century from 'a conception of morality as the application of divine laws to human affairs to the idea of it as the simple love of God and pursuit of goodness.'[86] John Howe, in the importance he placed on the self-reliance of the individual before God, was part of this trend.

The third strand of Howe's subjective individualism came out in his 'defence' of Stillingfleet against the passion of Howe's fictitious correspondent. Stillingfleet had been known for moderate and irenic views. His apparent *volte face* since his 1661 work *Irenicum* had received unfavourable comment. Howe sought to temper the hostility of this reaction with a significant insight into the formation of opinions. As this passage signals ideas which become important in later works, it is quoted at length.

> Believe him [Stillingfleet], in the substance of what he said, to speak according to his present judgment. Think how gradually and insensibly men's judgements alter, and are formed by their converse: that his circumstances have made it necessary to him to converse most, for a long time, with those who are fully of that mind which he here discovers...and who, therefore must have the more power and influence upon him, to conform his sentiments to their own.
>
> We ourselves do not know, had we been, by our circumstances, led to associate and converse mostly with men of another judgement, what our own would have been. And they that are wont to discover most confidence of themselves, do usually but discover most igno-

84 Howe, *Letter*, 517.

85 Cited by Calamy 60.

86 K. Thomas, 'Cases of Conscience in Seventeenth-Century England' in Morrill *et al*, *Public Duty and Private Conscience in Seventeenth-Century England*, 29-56, 51.

rance of the nature of man: and how little do they consider the power of external objects and inducements to draw men's minds this way or that. Nor, indeed, as to matters of this nature, can any man be confident that the grace of God shall certainly incline him to be of this or another opinion or practice in these matters; because we find that those we have reason to believe have great assistances of divine grace are divided about them, and go not all one way.[87]

Howe echoes here Alsop's acknowledgement that 'mathematical certainty' is impossible. As has been noted already, a degree of scepticism fed Howe's irenic approach to controversy. Despite his high place for sincere conscience, Howe was cautious about the fallen human capacity to hear God correctly. This was, however, a limited rather than a thoroughgoing scepticism. As was evident in *Reconcilableness*, Howe's platonic common sense gave him confidence in the key truths of Christian faith. His doubts related to 'these matters' - issues of form and ritual, the points on which he engaged Stillingfleet. Howe's brand of scepticism will be examined more closely in the next chapter. At this point it is enough to note that his method and epistemology reinforced, rather than weakened, his individualism. On all but the core doctrines of the faith, conscientious believers were to be given space.

Stillingfleet saw in the enforcement of uniformity a means of leading people to the truth. By contrast, Howe's very recognition of the shaping power of 'external objects and inducements' led him to reject the claims of the visible Church. Near the close of his *Letter* Howe lampooned exclusivity based merely on form.

They have least reason to expect much compliance from others, who bind themselves up within their own party, are as enwrapt as leviathan in his scales, call themselves the church, and call all men separatists that will not be of their church. And perhaps they assume and appropriate the name with no more pretence or colour, and with no better sense, than if a humoursome company of men should distinguish themselves from others by wearing a blue or yellow girdle, and call themselves mankind.[88]

All the nonconformist respondents to Stillingfleet displayed a fundamental orientation towards the invisible church. Yet, when crucial related variants are introduced, a simple Church/dissent, visible/invisible dichotomy becomes untenable. There was a spectrum of ecclesiological views in dissent, driven by different degrees of bias towards the invisible. Howe's 1680 *Letter* suggests he was more concerned with conscience and individualism than some oth-

87 Howe, *Letter*, 530.

88 Howe, *Letter*, 534.

ers. In this controversy at least, Howe and Alsop took positions which accorded a greater role to typically invisiblist concerns than did Baxter and Owen, with Humfrey and Lobb occupying a middle ground. All rejected the claims made by Stillingfleet for the visible Church of England. All sought the immediate, rather than mediated authority of God. However, for Baxter and Owen, the principal scene of this encounter was the particular congregation. For Alsop and Howe it was the individual conscience. By this interpretation, Howe must be ranked among the more radically invisiblist writers in mainstream nonconformity. This is a departure from earlier assessments. Geoffrey Nuttall's placement of him among the theologically 'conservative' or 'middle' parties must be questioned, as must Field's close identification of Howe with Baxter throughout his career.[89] By 1680 Howe was among the innovators, preparing a new ecclesiology of dissent. Yet, if Howe's ecclesiology is to be identified with feisty advocates of toleration and independency like Alsop, how are we to account for his own consistently irenic efforts towards comprehension? Some clues will emerge as we examine his later ecclesiological writings.

By 1680 significant ecclesiological fault lines were becoming evident. In the Church of England, the much vaunted unity was beginning to fray.[90] Even among moderates like Stillingfleet and Tillotson, quite different theological paths were evident. Within dissent, a new approach was gaining ground. Owen would soon be dead. Baxter would retreat to an earlier, more isolated position. Determined to burst the 'scales of leviathan', Alsop and Howe would pursue invisiblist ideas which would assume greater significance as the decade progressed.

---

89 Nuttall, *The Holy Spirit*, 6-19, 33, 49; Field, 'Rigide Calvinism in a Softer Dresse,' 155-6 and *passim*.

90 On the concern for visible unity within the Church of England, and the ecclesiological tensions which it sought to contain, see Spurr, *Restoration Church*, 105-165.

CHAPTER 5

A New Basis for Unity

The provocative statements in 1680 by the relative moderates Tillotson and Stillingfleet were portents of a more general hardening of attitudes towards dissent. Significantly, the end to Church overtures to dissent coincided exactly with the resolution of the 'exclusion' issue. This was a crisis precipitated by attempts to exclude the King's brother, James, from possible succession to the throne on the grounds of his Catholicism. A complex web of political and religious interests was at work, one result of which was a series of approaches from leaders in the established Church to dissenters. These moves dissolved once parliamentary moves to exclusion failed and the Church once more found it necessary to maintain a strong connection to the Crown. John Howe was directly involved in these discussions. On 14 November, 1680 he was called to a meeting with Bishop Lloyd of St Asaph at Tillotson's home. There they discussed 'what [Howe] thought would satisfy the nonconformists, that so they might be taken into the Church'. Calamy records that they agreed to meet again the following night, this time at Stillingfleet's residence. Howe suggested bringing Baxter along, but Lloyd strongly preferred Bates. However, no negotiations were to take place.

> They waited until eight, till nine, till near ten a Clock; but the Bishop neither came, nor sent, nor took any notice of the matter afterwards. And that very Night, as they heard the next Morning, the Bill of Exclusion was thrown out of the House of Peers, by a majority of thirty Voices, fourteen of which were Bishops. And after this, there was no farther occasion for any talk about a Comprehension.[1]

---

1 Calamy 71-3. Thomas, 'Comprehension', 226, suggests that the debates on Comprehension and Toleration did not begin until after the rejection of the Exclusion Bill. However, Horwitz's account in 'Protestant Reconciliation' shows that behind-the-scenes activity had been going on for some time. Moreover, the debates Thomas cites were very much limited to the Com-

What backing for compromise which might have existed in the Church hierarchy dissipated when the bid for exclusion failed. The preservation of the succession may have convinced Churchmen that their constitutional position too was safe and that they need no longer court nonconformists.[2]

In the event, the resolution of what Jonathan Scott has termed the 'Restoration Crisis' proved temporary.[3] In 1683, by now firmly established in nonconformist affairs in London, John Howe warned the young Earl of Kildare of the risks of the public sphere. 'It is a slippery stage; it is a divided time, wherein there is interest against interest, party against party.'[4] Tensions remained unresolved, leading some to seek violent solutions. Plots and rumours of plots would become open rebellion in the Monmouth uprising.[5] The shifts and reverses of policy under James II could not prevent the glorious revolution of 1688/9. With the subsequent passage of the 'Toleration Act', the alienation of nonconformists from the Church of England was more or less completed.

For most of this period, John Howe remained in London, an active preacher, writer and advocate for dissent. The notable exception was a two-year sojourn in the Netherlands, which commenced with a mysterious decampment in 1685. The reasons for this journey have not previously been satisfactorily explained. Both the writings of this decade and the Netherlands interlude are crucial to our understanding of Howe and, consequently, the fate of later Stuart dissent.

In the previous chapter, Howe's vision of the church was considered in a spectrum of views which ran from the visiblist ecclesiology of the Churchman Edward Stillingfleet through the plainly invisiblist views of fellow nonconformist Vincent Alsop. The structure and roots of Howe's arguments were shown to differ at important points from those of other leading nonconformists.

The diversity of views within broad dissent is further traced in this chapter. Attention shifts from specific controversies to the

---

mons. They were not sponsored by the Church. Calamy was quite correct to mark an end to discussions between leading divines on 15 November 1680.

2 For an examination of the implications of the 1680 controversies for the exclusion debate see Sutherland 'Protestant Divergence in the Restoration Crisis'.

3 Scott's analysis has been the subject of considerable debate. See J. Scott, *Algernon Sidney and the Restoration Crisis, 1677-1683* (Cambridge: CUP, 1991). See also the debate in *Albion*, vol. 25, No 4, 1993 and Scott's more recent *England's Troubles*, esp. 182-204.

4 J. Howe, *Self-Dedication...*, (1683) *Works*, I, 345-378, 377.

5 See R.L. Greaves, *Secrets of the Kingdom: British Radicals from the Popish Plot to the Revolution of 1688-1689* (Stanford: Stanford University Press, 1992).

events and thought of a tumultuous decade. Between 1681 and 1683 Howe published a series of works on tolerance and Christian unity. In this most difficult of times for Restoration dissent, he articulated more clearly and intentionally than ever before his uniquely irenic ecclesiology. The emphasis on the transcendent activity of God we have already observed continued, but with a new sharpness and urgency. Yet, paradoxically, in this decade Howe came closer to active political dissent than his doctrinal position might suggest was likely. In particular, the significance of his activities early in James II's reign has never fully been appreciated.

The mature writings of the 1680s and his political connections provide a framework for the comparison in this chapter between Howe's thought and that of John Locke. Differences will be noted which call into question Locke's intellectual continuity with orthodox dissent. The analysis informs more than just our understanding of the two men. When set in the tense and changing circumstances of later Stuart dissent, it sheds fresh light on the theological dynamics of the period.

5.1 The Dynamics of Christian Charity

Three works published by Howe in the early 1680s stand out. The first, *Thoughtfulness for the Morrow* (1681)[6] clearly revealed the transcendentalist direction of Howe's thought. In the second, *Of Charity in Reference to Other Men's Sins*[7] (also published in 1681) Howe first employed Christian love as a dynamic integrating principle. This theme was fully developed in the third treatise from this period, *Union Among Protestants* (1683).[8] More than any other work, this last revealed the sophistication of Howe's irenic approach to ecclesiastical disputes.

Of Thoughtfulness for the Morrow was a reflection on Matthew 6:34: 'Take no thought for the morrow: for the morrow shall take thought for the things of itself: sufficient for the day is the evil thereof.' It was dedicated to Ann, Lady Wharton, third wife of 'Saw-Pit' Wharton,

---

6 J. Howe, *Of Thoughtfulness for the Morrow: with an appendix; Concerning the Immoderate Desire of Foreknowing Things to Come* [London, 1681], *Works* II, 391-450.

7 J. Howe, *Of Charity in Reference of Other Men's Sins*, [London, 1681], *Works*, II, 453-473.

8 J. Howe, *A Sermon Concerning Union Among Protestants; A discourse Answering the Following Question, 'What May Most Hopefully Be Attempted to Allay Animosities Among Protestants, That Our Divisions May Not Be Our Ruin?'* [London, 1683], *Works*, III, 156-188.

later to be Howe's sponsor and companion on a 1685 flight to the Netherlands. Continuing an earlier theme, Howe placed detachment from the pressures of the world in the centre of his argument in *Thoughtfulness*. The work is particularly interesting as it reveals further the complexity of Howe's philosophical influences. There is a clear note of Stoicism in this treatise, never more so than in a passage in which Howe pauses to summarise his case, before expounding its application.

> All thinking is not caring. This is one special sort of care, not about duty but event, and about event wherein it does not depend upon our duty, that is, considered abstractly from it; and so the thing intended is, that doing all that lies within the compass of our duty to promote any good event, or to hinder bad, that then we should cease from solicitude about the success....[9]

Howe was not promoting a naïve quietism. He did not suggest that prudent recognition of future duties or preparation for approaching trials be abandoned.[10] Caution over the practical arrangements of life was not the problem. It was 'care, not about duty but about event' which was at issue. The Stoics argued that the happiness of the virtuous person was not dependant on outcomes, but on having done all that could rationally be expected. Howe employed a distinctly Christian version of this view. Concerns and fears, either for ourselves or for the success of Christianity, were held to reflect a poor understanding of the faith. Outcomes belonged to God, not the believer.

Yet more than Stoicism sustains Howe's case in *Thoughtfulness*. The treatise was directed against unwarranted attention to complex eschatological schemes. Howe's warning was that by 'undue excursions into futurity...we can but bewilder and lose ourselves to no purpose'.[11] He perceived that the error of such endeavours lay not in being too *detached* from worldly reality, but in being too *concerned* for it. Here, rather than Stoicism, Howe's Platonism is evident. Efforts to predict the future through interpretations of signs and prophecies revealed an infatuation with what was 'temporary and terrene'. Even if utopian, such visions remained worldly.

> To think of a state approaching, wherein all things shall be perfectly and unexpectedly well for ever, is but cold comfort. Blessed God! what a mortal token is this! Do we understand nothing of distemper in it? Do we see ourselves as *men of time*...and do not our hearts misgive at the thought?...Can the felicity of heaven belong to them that

9 Howe, *Thoughtfulness*, 416.
10 Howe, *Thoughtfulness*, 397-401.
11 Howe, *Thoughtfulness*, 395.

> value it not as their best good, but count a terrestrial paradise of their own devising better?[12]

Throughout *Thoughtfulness* Howe relegated the natural and sensual in favour of the heavenly and spiritual. Accordingly, the alternative to the 'distemper of futurity' was not for Christians to live only for the present. 'Surely no worse thing can rule over me, than a sensual spirit; that binds me down, and limits me to this spot on earth, and point of time.[13] Time itself was a trap, a problem to be dealt with. As it was naturally both limited and limiting, it provided an inadequate context for the Christian and was to be eschewed as an ultimate reference point. 'Neither our present duty or peace, nor our future safety or felicity, can be provided for as they ought, till our minds be more abstracted from time, and taken up about the unseen, eternal world.'[14]

Whether it drew on Stoic or Platonic categories, Howe's rejection of time was more than a philosophical nicety. It was an aspect of his understanding of the truly religious life as an unmediated, spiritual relationship with God. This was further emphasised when he listed the roots of 'undue thoughtfulness' for the future. One was an expectation that God's blessing will include material comfort (a false hope, according to Howe). In a crucial passage he effectively limited God's interest to the Christian's spiritual welfare.

> 'Shall we not be subject to the Father of spirits, and live?' Heb. xii. 9... The title which the sacred penman there fixes on God, 'the Father of spirits'...ought to be both instructive, and grateful to us. He is the great Paternal Spirit. We (in respect to our spirits) are his offspring... In this context, the fathers of our flesh, and the Father of spirits are studiously contradistinguished to one another. *The relation God bears to us as our Father terminates on our spirits.* And his paternal care and love cannot help but follow the relation, and principally terminate there too. He must be chiefly concerned about our spirits, that they be preserved in a good and healthful state.[15] (emphasis added)

The emphasised sentence is telling. Here, Howe starkly exposed his bias towards encounter with the transcendent God. The result was an overwhelmingly 'inward' faith. Concluding the first section of *Thoughtfulness,* he recommended two endeavours. The first was the submission of 'our thoughts and the inwards workings of our spirits', for 'do not all the laws of God that enjoin us any duty, lay

---

12 Howe, *Thoughtfulness*, 437.
13 Howe, *Thoughtfulness*, 429.
14 Howe, *Thoughtfulness*, 391.
15 Howe, *Thoughtfulness*, 406.

their first obligation upon our inward man?'[16] The second called for a concomitant indifference to outward events. Nature (the realm of time) had no role in faith or salvation.

> One that fears God and...believes in a world to come...hath little cause to concern himself about interveniences, which, as to his part in that world, will not alter his case. We are not the surer of heaven, if the sun shine out to-morrow; nor the less sure, if it shine not.[17]

Thoughtfulness was not a work of ecclesiology, in that Howe did not present a specific picture of the church. Nevertheless, this work demonstrated how committed he was to building a foundation for the Christian life which escaped the shifting sands of time and material existence. His relegation of nature in favour of an unmediated, spiritual experience of divine grace clearly points to a theology constructed on the radical transcendence of God. The essay thus articulated a foundation for the profoundly invisiblist ecclesiology Howe was coming to espouse. Yet, as will be seen, this commitment to detachment, to eschewing 'a terrestrial paradise of [human] devising,' stands in paradoxical contrast to his developing links with political dissent.

In the same year that *Thoughtfulness* appeared, Howe's assistant minister, Daniel Bull, was discovered to have committed adultery. This lapse necessitated Bull's removal from office[18] but more important for our purposes than the fate of the unfortunate Bull is the fact that his fall prompted Howe's work *Of Charity in Reference to Other Men's Sins*.

Howe took his text from 1 Corinthians 13:6, '[charity] rejoiceth not in iniquity'. In a model of puritan exposition, he examined in detail the context, tenses and likely meanings of the words of his text. The work is more, though, than an occasional sermon. Howe was groping towards something bigger than a palliatory call for generosity towards Bull.

Charity established a crucial element in Howe's irenic approach to church disputes. In this sermon, Christian love emerged as a philosophical force. Assuming the role of an integrative principle, it was identified with the very nature of God and was essential to all other virtues.[19] As the defining characteristic of Christians, charity was by nature inconsistent with iniquity or any rejoicing thereat. True charity may require the godly to 'decline the society' of those who sin in order to vindicate 'the Honour of the Christian religion', but it pre-

16 Howe, *Thoughtfulness*, 426.
17 Howe, *Thoughtfulness*, 427.
18 For Bull see Rogers, *Life*, 196; *CR* 85.
19 Howe, *Charity*, 460-461.

cluded any satisfaction at this outcome. 'It ought to be very grievous to us, when the reproach of our religion cannot be rolled away without being rolled upon this or that man; if especially, [he is] otherwise valuable.'[20]

Moreover, the regrettable necessity of shunning the sinful provided no excuse for the bitterness between Churchmen and dissenters. Most importantly, no-one had the option to excuse themselves from the church as a whole.

> When wickedness breaks forth...is this no matter of lamentation to you?...Will you say you are unrelated to him...or have no concern with him? Can any party be united within itself, by so sacred ties as all true Christians are with the whole body of Christ?[21]

Of those 'sacred ties', charity was the foremost - 'the eternal bond of living union'[22] among the saints in heaven. By extension from its function in this invisible body, charity also must guide the church on earth.

Howe was explicit about the connection between charity and the church disputes of the 1680s. In his preface (which, in the nature of these things, was really an afterword) he identified charity as the solution to those problems. 'We vainly expect, from either eloquence, or disputation, the good effects, which charity alone (could it take place) would easily bring about without them.'[23] The source of unity was found in this Christian virtue and not in authority or structure. That Howe should conceive of the issues in this way is no surprise. An invisiblist ecclesiology naturally seeks and accepts a unity expressed through such an immaterial quality as charity. Concrete expressions such as uniformity or hierarchical institutions, by contrast, characterise visiblist concepts of the church.

Howe did not exclude all indirect operation of God's will. In one place in *Charity* he acknowledged God's action through natural endowments and providence, in addition to unmediated grace.[24] However this sermon confirmed the transcendentalist orientation encountered in *Thoughtfulness*. Howe's bias to the invisible church was nowhere more apparent than in the following passage from the preface, which is important enough to be quoted at length.

> What piety is to our union with God, that is charity to our union with one another. But we are too apt, as to both, to expect from the outward form, what only the internal, living principle can give; to covet

20 Howe, *Charity*, 468.
21 Howe, *Charity*, 471-2.
22 Howe, *Charity*, 473.
23 Howe, *Charity*, 451.
24 Howe, *Charity*, 466-467.

the one with a sort of fondness, and deny the other. One common external form in the Church of God, wherein all good men could agree, were a most amiable thing, very useful to its comely, better being; and the want of it hath inferred, and doth threaten, evils much to be deplored, and deprecated. But this divine principle [charity] is most simply necessary to its *very being*. Whatsoever violates it is the most destructive, mortal schism; as much worse than an unwilling breach of outward order, as the malicious tearing in pieces a man's living body, is worse than the accidental rending of his clothes.[25] (original emphasis).

Christian love had, of course, featured in Howe's earlier works and is obviously a common theme in Christian discourse. However, by 1681 it had assumed a role in Howe's thinking which went far beyond the regulation of human relationships. It would continue in this place through the rest of his career. The sentiments expressed in the preface to *Charity* were to set Howe's theological agenda for the next two decades.

A clue as to why charity emerged as a dominant principle in Howe's thought at this time may be found in his scholarly interests. In 1679, Matthew Poole had died, with his master work *English Annotations on Holy Scripture* unfinished.[26] Howe was one of many who assisted with a posthumous completion of the commentary. His project was the Epistles of John, published in a volume which appeared in 1682, the year following *Charity*. Significantly, love is the major theme of the longest of the letters: I John. Howe cited this book several times in *Charity* and it is highly likely that the epistle's radical promotion of love as the basis of faith and communion had a great impact on his thinking during the early 1680s.

There were other influences, besides his own study. Howe's intellectual circle may be partially reconstructed. Richard Baxter and the Platonist, Henry More, have already been identified. As will be seen, Howe appears to have known John Locke. Another contact of interest was Joseph Glanvill. Rector of Bath from 1666 and advocate for the Royal Society, Glanvill (1636-1680) was an admirer of Baxter and mutual friend of Boyle and Howe. In 1669 Glanvill published a sermon called *Catholic Charity Recommended*[27] in which he set out

25 Howe, *Charity*, 452.

26 For Poole see *CR* 394-5. For the history of the completion of the *Annotations* see Wood, *Athenae Oxonienses*, Vol. 4, Col. 112-3.

27 J. Glanvill, *Catholic Charity Recommended in a Sermon, before the Right Honourable the Lord Mayor and Aldermen of London: In order to the abating the Animosities among Christians that have been occasion'd by Differences in Religion*, (London: 1669).

themes which Howe developed in his own *Charity* and subsequent works. Glanvill will be seen to have anticipated Howe's arguments in at least two other instances.

The most important work on ecclesiological issues that Howe published in the early 1680s was *Union Among Protestants*. This treatise addressed the question 'What may most hopefully be attempted to allay animosities among protestants, that our divisions may not be our ruin?' Howe eschewed any comment on 'laws and constitutions' (the province only of rulers) or controversies between ecclesiastical parties (which he regarded as fruitless). Instead the emphasis was on what Christians may do in their 'private capacities'.[28]

Once again, the dominant concept was charity. This time the text was Colossians 2:2: 'That their hearts may be comforted, being knit together in love, and unto all riches of the full assurance of understanding, to the acknowledgement of the mystery of God.' But Howe had developed his ideas. Simple, unqualified charity was not sufficient. Charity would bring about unity only within the context of 'a clear, certain, efficacious faith of the Gospel'.[29] In other words, it must be a distinctly *Christian* charity. In *Union Among Protestants,* Howe discoursed on the dynamic interplay between charity and 'full assurance of understanding'. A proper understanding of the gospel (the 'mystery of God') would lead naturally to a unifying love. In turn, when exercised, this love would allow yet further insight into the gospel. Charity and assurance would thus build on each other to create a natural unity among Christians.

Here, charity was functioning on a grander scale than in the 1681 sermon. It was now a key factor, not only in unity, but in the epistemology of faith. Howe was proposing a theory of knowledge in which love was a principal, active component. I will draw out the importance of this and other features of *Union Among Protestants* by comparing its arguments with those of John Locke's *Letter Concerning Toleration*, published in 1689. First, however, we must acknowledge the personal and political context in which Howe wrote his treatise.

5.2 Radical Politics

The importance of John Locke (1632-1704) in intellectual histories of the later Stuart period is enormous. There is much current attention to Locke's social and intellectual links with the divines of the day.

28 Howe, *Union*, 156-7.
29 Howe, *Union*, 160.

Some historians, notably Richard Ashcraft, seek to associate Locke closely with nonconformity.[30] Others find continuities with 'latitude men' such as Stillingfleet and Tillotson.[31] This fascination with Locke is alone a sufficient reason to use his ideas on toleration as a control, alongside which to place Howe's views. There are, however, other reasons to link the two men. It is clear that they were acquainted with each other.[32] As noted in the previous chapter, Locke took an interest in the Stillingfleet controversy (he owned a copy of Howe's *Letter Written Out of the Country*).[33] His own influential *Letter Concerning Toleration*, although not published until 1689, was written in 1685, only two years after Howe's *Union Among Protestants*.

The connections between the two men go beyond their intellectual interests. Whilst Locke's political associations have been long recognised, Howe's have not been fully appreciated. Despite Howe's strictures in *Thoughtfulness for the Morrow*, he seems to have been an intimate in circles of political dissent.

The principal evidence for Howe's political connections comes from an enigmatic incident which occurred two years after *Union Among Protestants* appeared. In August 1685 he abruptly left London to travel to Europe with Philip, Lord Wharton. Having told few of his decision to go, he had to write a letter back to his congregation to account for his disappearance.[34] He would not return until 1687. Although Howe's behaviour in this instance has caused some puzzlement to his hagiographers, they have proved equal to the task

---

30 See Ashcraft, *Revolutionary Politics, passim* and 'John Locke, Religious Dissent, and The Origins of Liberalism' in G.J. Schochet (ed) *Restoration, Ideology, and Revolution* (Washington: Folger Institute, 1990), 149-167; 'Latitudinarianism and toleration: historical myth versus political history' in R. Kroll, R. Ashcraft, and P. Zagorin (eds.) *Philosophy, science, and religion in England 1640-1700* (Cambridge: CUP, 1992), 151-177. A similar connection is attempted, unconvincingly, by J.W. Baker, 'Church, State, and Toleration: John Locke and Calvin's Heirs in England', in W.F. Graham (ed.), *Later Calvinism: International Perspectives* (Kirksville: Sixteenth Century Journal Publishers, 1994), 525-543.

31 E.g. G.A.J. Rogers, 'Locke and the latitude-men: ignorance as a ground for toleration', in Kroll *et al* (eds.) *Philosophy, science, and religion in England 1640-1700*, 230-252 and, in the same volume of essays, J. Marshall, 'John Locke and Latitudinarianism', 253-282.

32 See the reference to Howe in a letter from Isabella Duke to Locke, 21 October, 1686 in E.S. De Beer (ed.), *The Correspondence of John Locke*, 8 vols., (Oxford: 1976), vol. 3, letter 873, 58.

33 Harrison and Laslett, *The Library of John Locke*, 159.

34 J. Howe, *Letter to His Congregation and Friends*, [London, 1685], *Works*, III, 556-560.

of reconciling it to their view of him. His failure to give advance warning they blame on the short notice Howe himself received of the offer to accompany Wharton.[35] By casting Howe as one caught up in the plans of others, they have sought to preserve intact his unblemished honour and integrity.

This explanation will not do. It does not even fit with Howe's public admissions. Final preparations were certainly rushed,[36] but the secrecy surrounding the journey did not arise merely from a lack of notice. Howe may have been given little warning of the precise timing of his departure, but he made it clear in his letter that the concept of the trip had an earlier provenance. Even so, he

> could not so much as bid farewell to [you], the solemnity whereof you know our circumstances would not admit. Nor could I have opportunity to communicate to you the grounds of my taking this long journey, being under promise while the matter was under consideration, not to speak of it to anyone that was not concerned immediately about it.[37]

The larger question of the trip itself has been equally poorly explained. Why did Howe choose exile, when others (such as Alsop, Bates and Humphrey) remained in London? In his letter, he cited the effects of the ongoing persecution and his preference for an untroubled existence. 'It...has been my settled habitual sense and sentiment a long time, to value and desire…peace and quiet, with some tolerable health, more than life.'[38] Howe's biographers have uncritically accepted his need to escape the general pressure on dissent. The account at least fits with what we know of Howe's personal diffidence and desire to avoid controversy. Yet, if a pathological aversion to strife was indeed all that lay behind Howe's departure, this alone would challenge the later portrayals of him as a fearless champion of nonconformity. Fortunately (perhaps) for that memory, the evidence suggests there was more, much more, at stake than Howe's emotional security. He himself hinted at other reasons but declined to detail them, as the exercise 'would lose time that I may more prof-

---

35 See Calamy 113; Rogers, *Life*, 223; Horton, *John Howe*, 159-160.

36 Wharton had been granted a passport on 7 August and was in Dover expecting to travel within five days. Unfavourable winds delayed the actual departure until 18 August. See J.K. Clark, *Goodwin Wharton* (Oxford: OUP, 1984), 139-40. This chronology corrects G.F.T. Jones' suggestion that the party did not leave England until December 1685 (see G.F.T. Jones, *Saw-Pit Wharton: The Political Career from 1640-1691 of Philip, fourth Lord Wharton* (Sydney: Sydney University Press, 1967), 254.

37 Howe, *Letter to His Congregation*, 556.

38 Howe, *Letter to His Congregation*, 556.

itably employ, for both you and myself'. By this he meant writing, but the excuse was probably convenient. There is evidence to suggest that Howe's decision to leave related more to specific, immediate danger than to mere timidity or general discomfiture.

The timing of Howe's decampment, in August 1685, is important. Monmouth's rebellion had been crushed only one month previously. The arrests and trials of those implicated were still in train. Howe's abrupt migration must be understood in the context of Monmouth's failed cause. One who would be executed for his part in the uprising was John Hickes, Howe's former brother-in-law.[39] Another friend, Matthew Mead, had been implicated in the 1683 Rye House plot and was a principal figure in the Monmouth conspiracy. Like Howe, he fled to the Netherlands in 1685.[40] In the early 1680s Howe had had contact with the conspirator Robert Ferguson.[41] Along with several who would be subsequently implicated, Howe had met with Monmouth in the autumn of 1682.[42]

Of the conspirators not caught in 1685, Greaves points out that 'a surprising number...made their way to the continent.'[43] There is no reliable evidence to implicate either Howe or Wharton in the rebellion itself.[44] Nevertheless, Wharton feared increased persecution of dissenters and the associations of both men with many of those involved undoubtedly placed them at risk.[45] Wharton, who arranged and financed Howe's trip, had disingenuously obtained leave from

39 Howe's sister, Hickes' first wife, Abigail, had died in 1675. By 1685 Hickes had remarried. For Hickes see entries in *DNB*, *CR* and R.L. Greaves and R. Zaller, *Biographical Dictionary of British Radicals in the Seventeenth Century*, 3 vols. (Brighton: Harvester Press, 1982).

40 On Mead's radical involvement see R.L. Greaves, *Secrets of the Kingdom*, 286-289 and 'The Rye House Plotting, Nonconformist Clergy, and Calvin's Resistance Theory' in Graham (ed.) *Later Calvinism: International Perspectives*, 1994, 505-520 esp. 517-519. The same age as Howe, Mead was a contemporary at Cambridge (although Howe dates their first meeting to about 1656). When Mead died in 1699, Howe preached the funeral sermon - J. Howe, *A Funeral Sermon for the Reverend Matthew Mead* [London, 1699], *Works* III, 458-481, 477.

41 Letter from Ferguson to his wife, July 1680, S.P. Dom. Car. II, 414, No. 5 (*CSPD* Charles II, Vol. 19, 1679/80, 541).

42 Memo of Sergeant Ramsay, Sept. 17-25, S.P. Dom. Car. II, 420, No. 116 (*CSPD* Charles V 21, 429-30).

43 Greaves, *Secrets of the Kingdom*, 295.

44 Goodwin Wharton recorded in his autobiography that his father was a conspirator but Goodwin is an unreliable witness and there is no support for his suggestion in any other record - see J.K. Clark 343 n. 5.

45 Jones, *Saw- Pit Wharton*, 253; Clark, *Goodwin Wharton*, 140.

the King on the basis of a journey to France.[46] The actual destinations were first Emmerich and then Utrecht - both in the Netherlands and both continental refuges for nonconformist and political exiles.

For the period of his own exile, Howe settled in Utrecht. He preached regularly in the English church and assisted in the training of young men for ministry. He had contact with such rebels or sympathisers as Locke, Mead, Sir John Thompson (and his chaplain Walter Cross) and Sir Patience Ward.[47] He was also reported to have met again with the now fugitive Robert Ferguson. This Howe strenuously denied, in a letter to the English Consul in which he protested his 'detestation of any practices against Government'.[48] Despite this avowal, Howe did have contact with the court of William of Orange. He discussed the future of nonconformity with Gilbert Burnet (1643-1715), a confidant of both William and Mary and later Bishop of Salisbury.[49] He had at least one audience, on the eve of his return to England, with the couple themselves.[50]

There can be little doubt where Howe's sympathies lay in the mid-1680s, nor that his movements brought him into orbits very close to those of John Locke. His surprise departure for Holland may not have been as a fugitive, but it was almost certainly prompted by his connections with those who were. In August 1685, the 'solemnity of [Howe's] circumstances' was greater than has hitherto been recognised.

5.3 Howe and Locke: Two Views of Conscience

There were, then, significant links and shared experiences between Howe and Locke. Howe's *Union Among Protestants* and Locke's *Letter Concerning Toleration* were products of the same difficult period. There were differences between the two works. Whereas Howe restricted his comments to the private sphere, Locke addressed the

---

46 S.P. Dom Jac. II, Entry Book 336, 197, Aug 7 1685 (*CSPD* James II, vol. 1, 441). See also BL Add. MSS 41,818, fol. 106v.

47 Calamy 126-127; G.F. Nuttall, 'English Dissenters in the Netherlands 1640-1689' in *Nederlands Archief voor Kerkgschiedenis*, 59, 1978, 37-54; Ashcraft, *Revolutionary Politics*, 471-2.

48 Letter from John Howe, Utrecht, July 15/25 [16]86 - British Library Add Ms 41819 fol. 213r. In this letter Howe makes another mention of poor health. On Ferguson see Greaves and Zaller, *Dictionary*,Vol. I, 276-7.

49 Calamy 127-8. Like Howe, Burnet was an intimate of the Wharton family – Jones, *Saw-Pit Wharton*, 255; Clark, *Goodwin Wharton*, 332 n. 32.

50 On the basis of Howe's own report, Calamy (130-1) asserts there were several meetings with William. Details are given of only this one. See also Lacey, *Dissent*, 186, 199-200, 343 n. 41.

role of the civil magistrate.[51] Howe's arguments called for unity among Christians, based on tolerant acceptance of difference; Locke pursued the related but different cause of toleration within the state. This difference of focus reflects significant departures at a fundamental level. Nevertheless there remain considerable points of overlap, which must first be noted.

Both Howe and Locke built their cases on the cruciality of charity. Mirroring Howe's own intellectual path, Locke opened with an allusion to Johannine themes. Charity was essential both to Christianity and toleration. 'If the Gospel and the apostle may be credited, no man can claim to be a Christian without charity, and without that faith which works, not by force, but by love.'[52]

Their joint dependence on charity was matched by an inwardly oriented view of religion. This has been noted several times in Howe's writing. For Howe, the value of full assurance was that it produced 'an inward vital owning' of the truth.[53] Locke appeared equally certain: 'all the life and power of true religion consists in the inward and full persuasion of the mind.'[54]

For both writers, individual conscience was central. Howe's declaration: 'to do anything against the preponderating inclination of my judgement and conscience were great wickedness[55] appeared to find an echo in Locke. 'No way whatsoever that I shall walk in against the dictates of my conscience, will ever bring me to the mansions of the blessed.'[56]

If the comparison was halted at this superficial level, Howe and Locke might seem very close on the ecclesiological spectrum. Their shared emphases on charity, inward religion and individual conscience would suggest that both were invisiblists, differing only in degree from such as Owen and Baxter. But would such an interpretation be valid? A closer analysis reveals fundamental theological differences between Locke and Howe. Gary Remer has pointed out that Locke's case for toleration had two major strands. One highlighted the individual's right to conscience, the other was a version of what Remer calls 'the sceptical case for toleration' and what G.A.J.

---

51 J. Locke, *A Letter Concerning Toleration* (1689) reprinted in J. Horton and S. Mendus (eds.) *John Locke: A Letter Concerning Toleration in Focus*, London, 1991, 12-56, 17.

52 Locke, *Letter*, 14.

53 Howe, *Union*, 162.

54 Locke, *Letter*, 18.

55 Howe, *Union*, 180.

56 Locke, *Letter*, 32.

Rogers terms 'the argument from ignorance'.[57] Both conscience and scepticism were also important to John Howe, but he conceived of them and employed them in a fashion fundamentally different from that of Locke. I shall discuss the two arguments separately.

Though both proclaimed its importance, Howe and Locke had different understandings of the nature of conscience. For Locke, conscience was reduced to judgment. This would be explicitly stated in his *Essay Upon Human Understanding*. Conscience 'is nothing else, but our own Opinion or Judgment of the Moral rectitude or pravity of our own actions.'[58] The individual must 'by meditation, study, search, and his own endeavours'[59] attain the 'full persuasion of the mind' which lay at the heart of true religion. Locke's conscience thus essentially had only one constructive input and that was human. Its output was similarly terrestrial, focused on 'actions'.

Howe, by contrast, did not so confine conscience. It was not merely a matter of individual decision, rational or otherwise. Rather, conscience was one end of a relationship - 'conscience towards God'.[60] More than mere 'action' it produced the richer idea of obedience. It must lead to 'an "acknowledgement", an inward, vital owning, a cordial embrace'.[61] Whereas Locke spoke of a unifocal ethical judgement, Howe's 'conscience' had a twin focus: first on God and secondly, dependent on that encounter, on compliant behaviour.

This distinction between Locke's and Howe's understandings of conscience is crucial, as it reflects related differences in their ecclesiologies. Locke regarded the church simply as 'a voluntary society of men'.[62] Individuals were free to pursue their salvation in whichever of these societies they chose. As importantly, they were just as free to leave, if they perceived their salvific interests were not being promoted.

Howe too acknowledged the responsibility and right of the individual to seek God's favour for himself. 'Who can doubt but I ought to use for my soul...the aptest means that I can ordinarily have for the promoting its edification and salvation?'[63] He would not, how-

---

57 G. Remer, 'Humanism, Liberalism, & the Sceptical Case for Religious Toleration', *Polity*, Vol. XXV, No. 1, Fall, 1992, 21-43; Rogers, 'Locke', *passim*.

58 J. Locke, *Essay Concerning Human Understanding*, [London, 1689] ed H. Nidditch (Oxford: 1975) 70.

59 Locke, *Letter*, 29-30.

60 Howe, *Union*, 175.

61 Howe, *Union*, 161-2.

62 Locke, *Letter*, 20.

63 Howe, *Union*, 174.

ever, accept Locke's pragmatic reduction of the church to a society for public worship. The church transcended any one given group. *Union Among Protestants* was not a call to the Church of England to leave dissenters alone. It was a plea to all parties to recognise and promote their oneness.

> [Charity is not] a love to Christians of this or that party or denomination only. That were as much unduly to straighten and confine it. The love that is owing to Christians as such, as it belongs to them only, belongs to *all* them who, in profession and practice, do own sincere and incorrupt Christianity. To limit our Christian love to a party of Christians, truly so called, is so far from serving the purpose now to be aimed at [unity], that it resists and defeats it.[64]

There was a considerable distance between Howe and Locke on this point. To Howe, 'society', no matter how big and whatever its purpose, was an inadequate description of the people of God. Just as conscience had a divine ingredient, so did the church. It was a spiritual organism - the body of Christ. Joining it may have had an inevitable voluntary component but *leaving* it was not so simple. Locke suggested that, if the Christian discovered error or incongruity he was 'as free to go out as...to enter'.[65] To Howe this was unacceptably casual. Even in 'cases of great wickedness' no member could break 'from the body of other Christians in the world, so as not to be concerned in the affairs of the body.'[66]

In all the writings examined in this chapter, Howe placed great importance on the individual but always it was the individual before God, the recipient of divine grace or inspiration. Howe's ideal was the individual, shorn of mediating structures and forms, wholly open to the divine. By contrast, Locke was able to discuss conscience and the church almost entirely in terms of the human alone, reliant only upon native capacity to choose and judge. As Nicholas Wolterstorff describes it, in Locke's schema 'God is never present to the mind'.[67] Locke's was the individual effectively shorn of God. To Howe that was not only undesirable, it was inconceivable. The Divine was always an active partner. Though both writers described religion as 'inward', their concepts of 'inwardness' differed markedly. Locke's inner world was the semi-autonomous world of the mind. Howe used 'inner' as a cypher for 'spiritual'. His inward realm was the scene of encounter with the transcendent God.

---

64 Howe, *Union*, 165.

65 Locke, *Letter*, 20.

66 Howe, *Charity*, 471.

67 N. Wolterstorff, 'Locke's Philosophy of Religion' in V. Chappell (ed), *The Cambridge Companion to Locke* (Cambridge: CUP, 1994), 172-198, 186.

5.4 Howe and Locke: Two Types of Scepticism

Differences of a similar nature are found in the second strand of the argument for toleration. Remer traces the roots of the 'sceptical case' for toleration to the Greek 'New Academy' philosophers. Cicero was an important exponent and authority.[68] The argument depended upon a 'mitigated scepticism' which, whilst acknowledging that absolute *certainty* is not available, nevertheless found enough *probability* on crucial issues to act *as if* certainty were possible on those matters. The test of that probability was the consensus of the community. Although this placed a natural limit on freedom of opinion, only those things on which the community as a whole agreed could be insisted upon.

In the sixteenth century the sceptical case was picked up by humanist thinkers, notably Erasmus. Once again the community determined essential ideas. There was, however, an important difference. The 'community' was held to be coterminous with the institutional church. Indeed it was the church, guided as it was by the Holy Spirit, which formed the consensus. Because it was forged with the benefit of divine input, this consensus could be held to be truly certain, not merely probable. The humanist case was that toleration was advisable on matters indifferent, but was to be denied on the essentials.[69]

Like Chillingworth before him, Locke's scepticism ran deeper than that of the humanists. He preferred something closer to the Academician's version. Not even things essential could be treated as certain. Faith, by its very nature, depended upon probability.[70] Locke held back, however, from complete religious toleration on this ground. It was an unresolved tension in his case that conscience could not be exercised without a belief in God. In addition, as all Christians agreed that Jesus was the Messiah, this doctrine too must be maintained. Although these basic doctrines were, in theory, themselves matters only of probability, disagreement on them was not countenanced. Conveniently for Locke, any practical problems which might have arisen out of this logical inconsistency were evaded because actual disputes almost invariably turned on matters on which Locke held there to be no consensus. On such, not even probability was possible and, accordingly, toleration must be extended.[71]

---

68 Remer, 'Humanism', 25.

69 Remer, 'Humanism', 26-30.

70 Locke, *Essay*, 654-655.

71 See Remer, 'Humanism', 36-37. Wootton points out that, in the first *Letter*, the principal argument is that letting either Civil or Ecclesial authorities deter-

Howe too employed a form of mitigated scepticism. G.A.J. Rogers has shown the 'argument from ignorance' to be characteristic of other Platonists, notably More and Glanvill.[72] By the 1680s, Howe had integrated his Platonist epistemology with charity and his faith in the immediate relation of God to the human conscience. His structure was therefore a variant of the humanist sceptical case. On matters indifferent, no-one could be certain. On these, Howe agreed with Locke that no Christian could judge another. However, although the two men cited the same biblical text, their disparate conceptions of conscience produced parallel differences on forbearance. Locke, following through on his sceptical epistemology, refused the right to judge *error* in another.[73] Howe's concern was with relationship: 'the posture of his heart Godward'. *Sincerity*, rather than error, was the crucial issue in assessing the actions of another.

> I can at least refrain from censuring my fellow Christians...most of all when the matter wherein I presume to sit in judgment upon another is of so high a nature as the posture of his heart Godward: a matter peculiarly belonging to another tribunal, of divine cognizance, and which we all confess to be only known to God himself. And if I would take upon me to conclude a man insincere, and a hypocrite, only because he is not of my mind in these smaller things that are controverted among us, how would I form my argument? No one can, with sincerity, differ from that man whose understanding is so good and clear, as to apprehend all things with absolute certainty, just as they are; and then go on to assume 'But my understanding is as good and clear as,' &c. It is hard to say whether the uncharitableness of the one assertion, or the arrogance of the other is greater; and whether both be more immoral or absurd. But the impiety is worst of all...'Who art thou that judgest another man's servant? to his own master he standeth or falleth' Rom. xiv. 4.[74]

Operating on this subjective level, Howe was even wary of persuasion.

---

mine one's religion is an irrational abdication. It is irrational because, in matters of religion, these authorities are no better able to discern the truth than the individual - see D. Wootton, 'Introduction' in D. Wootton (ed) *John Locke: Political Writings* (Harmondsworth: Penguin, 1993), 7-122, 94-110.

72 Rogers, 'Locke', 235-242. See also A. Gabbey, ''A disease incurable': scepticism and the Cambridge Platonists' in R.H. Popkin and A. Vanderjagt (eds.) *Scepticism and Irreligion in the Seventeenth and Eighteenth Centuries* (Leiden: Brill, 1993), 71-91.

73 Locke, *Letter*, 24-5.

74 Howe, *Union*, 177-8.

> Men of...reason and conscience...bend themselves by argument to convince the reason, and satisfy the consciences of such as differ from them. But herein also there may be an excess that is unprofitable and grievous to those they would work upon by this course[75]

Howe's caution sprang from a distinctive form of the argument from ignorance, one which acknowledged 'idiosyncrasy'. The notion of peculiar attributes or 'constitutional inclinations' of understanding in individuals did not have a long history in 1683. Interestingly, the earliest identified use of 'idiosyncrasy' in this sense was by the ubiquitous Joseph Glanvill in 1665. The title of Glanvill's work is instructive: *Scepsis Scientifica: or, Confest Ignorance the way to science in an essay of the vanity of dogmatizing, and confident opinions*.[76] Glanvill identified idiosyncrasy as a major factor in error,

> For in a sense the *complexion* of the *mind*, as well as *manners*, follows the *Temperament* of the Body. On this account some men are genially disposed to some *Opinions*, and naturally as averse to others.[77]

Howe made much of this idea but, rather than using it to explain error, he cited it as a further reason for tolerance. On the matters in dispute between Church and dissent, he called for caution before imposing any one interpretation.

> What is another man's opinion to signify against my sense and constant experience? Is there not such a thing as a mental *idiosyncrasy* (or peculiarity of temper) as well as a bodily? and whereto what is most agreeable, any man that is not destitute of the ordinary understanding is the fittest judge himself....[78]

Once these 'peculiarities of temper' were acknowledged, the exercise of forbearance became the more essential.

> While there is any thing colourable to be alleged for this or that way, true Christian love, compassion of human frailty, and a duly humble sense of a man's own, would oblige him to think, that conscience towards God may have a greater hand (though, with some, misguided itself) in guiding men the different ways they take, than is commonly thought: and to consider, though such and such reasons seem not weighty to me, they may to some others, who are as much afraid of sinning against God as I; and perhaps their understandings as good in other matters as mine.[79]

---

75 Howe, *Union*, 180. Compare Locke on the duty of persuasion - *Letter*, 19.

76 (London: 1665).

77 Glanvill, *Scepsis Scientifica*, 89. Nevertheless, Glanvill appears to have been very wary of any wider scepticism - see Gabbey, 'A Disease Incurable' 71-2.

78 Howe, *Union*, 174.

79 Howe, *Union*, 175.

Moreover, idiosyncrasy was encountered as much in emotional preference, or taste, as in understanding. These affections, though not rational, were not to be despised. They too could help build faith.

> Though it be true, that our spiritual edification lies more in the informing of our judgements, and confirming our resolutions, than in the gusts and relishes of affection, yet who sees not that these are of great use even to the other...? And they that think all this alleged difference is but fancy show they understand little of human nature, and less of religion.[80]

Latitude was thus necessary 'in these smaller things that are controverted among us'. However, the same arguments did not apply to the essentials of the faith. Howe was not a thoroughgoing sceptic. Like the Academicians, he found crucial matters to be established in the consensus of the community. In *The Living Temple* he argued for the existence of God on the ground of 'common assent'. Significantly he quoted Cicero as a principal authority.[81] In the preface to the 1681 *Thoughtfulness*, he was quite explicit.

> As was said by one that was a great and early light in the Christian Church; 'That is not philosophy which is professed by this or that sect, but that which is true of all sects.' So nor do I take that to be religion, which is peculiar to this or that party of Christians...but that which is according to the mind of God among them all.[82]

Unlike the Academicians, Howe did not reduce truth discerned in this manner to mere probability. In this respect he was in line with the humanists, but with one essential departure. Erasmus allowed only the authorities of the Church to draw from the well of consensus. Howe gave a bucket to each individual. Here his invisiblist ecclesiology intruded. The activity of the Spirit was not limited to the visible hierarchy. Whilst individuals did not *determine* essentials, Howe, in keeping with his elevation of conscience, allowed that they may *recognise* them.

> All good men, in all times and ages of the Christian church, have a constant value and love for the great substantials of religion, which have in them that inward evidence and excellency as command a rectified mind and heart.[83]

Howe's scepticism about inessentials was mitigated by a positive affirmation of religious knowledge about those things which are essential to salvation. These were delineated by consensus, but

---

80 Howe, *Union*, 176-77.

81 Howe, *Living Temple*, I, 21-36.

82 Howe, *Thoughtfulness*, 392. The quote is unattributed.

83 Howe, *Union*, 176.

confirmed to the individual by the inward certainty which arose from the soul's communication with God.

Howe was here building upon the religious epistemology he first articulated in *Delighting in God*. The regenerate were blessed with a special communication of 'the mind of God.' 'Wherefore there is somewhat to be apprehended by God's representation of himself to the minds of this regenerate people, at least *more clearly* than by other men.'[84] By 1683 Howe had developed his ideas much further. Consensus, certainty, unmediated contact with God - all these were held together by a uniquely Christian force: charity. Howe's was a case of impressive symmetry and coherence. As noted above, *Union Among Protestants* described a complex interaction between charity and assurance. This same interaction was emphasised in the Johannine letters on which Howe had been working early in the eighties.

> Beloved, let us love one another; for love is of God, and he who loves is born of God and knows God. He who does not love does not know God, for God is Love. - I John 4:7-8

Howe did not cite this verse in *Union Among Protestants,* but it contains the pith of his argument: by loving we know God.[85] This knowledge in turn allows Christians better to discern the essential from the indifferent, making them thus able to love all the more.

Union Among Protestants confirmed Howe's radical emphasis on the immediate, transcendent activity of God. His case must be distinguished from Locke's. Although both employed individual conscience and the argument from ignorance, Locke and Howe placed these arguments in quite different contexts. At the very heart of Howe's approach was a confidence in direct contact between the divine and the human. Locke had no such positive role for revelation. His arguments depended almost entirely upon human capacity. God had slipped from the picture in any active sense.[86]

---

84 Howe, *Delighting in God*, 492.

85 Interestingly, the passage was cited by Glanvill, *Catholick Charity*, 3.

86 Nicholas Jolley argues that Leibniz' principal objection to Locke's philosophy was Locke's materialism - N. Jolley, *Leibniz and Locke: A Study of the New Essays on Human Understanding* (Oxford: Clarendon Press, 1984), esp. 1-34. Stillingfleet identified atheism lurking behind Locke's protested theism - see S. Hutton, 'Science, philosophy, and atheism: Edward Stillingfleet's defence of religion' in R.H. Popkin and A. Vanderjagt (eds) *Scepticism and Irreligion in the Seventeenth and Eighteenth Centuries* (Leiden: Brill, 1993), 102-120, 118-19. Marshall argues that Locke is best understood in the context of socinianism - 'John Locke and Latitudinarianism,' 269-73.

5.5 Locke and Religious Dissent

There are important ramifications of Locke's relegation of God.. A number of models have been identified in later Stuart ecclesiological discourse. These may be plotted on a spectrum of emphasis on either the visible or the invisible church, on the immanent or the transcendent activity of God. Though the models differed markedly in many respects, they shared a common framework. However much the stress on the immanent or the transcendent varied in degree, divine activity itself was presupposed. Locke effectively excluded himself from this schema. His picture was drawn so as virtually to leave God out. Though he shared an interest in the related issue of authority, Locke's case did not truly depend on Christian ecclesiology at all. He was arguing on a different plane.

This analysis may help us pick our way through recent, conflicting interpretations of Locke. Richard Ashcraft has examined the rationalism of Restoration divines. He has argued persuasively that 'there was not one, but two 'rational theologies', propounded during this period; one by the latitudinarians, and the other by the dissenters.'[87] Citing Howe as one example, he describes dissenting rationalism. 'For nonconformists, 'rational theology' meant that the linkage between divine reason and human reason is an essential precept of religion.'[88] By this interpretation, dissenters emphasised the continuity of their reason and conscience with the mind of God. Howe's approach clearly fits this model. 'Anglicans', by contrast, breached the divine-human continuity by 'interposing the arbitrary will of the magistrate.' Freedom of individual conscience is heavily circumscribed, as it must be subject to this civil authority.

Ashcraft contends that Locke's rationality was in sympathy with the dissenting position. Yet, God was notably absent from Locke's view of reason and conscience, rendering his approach unpalatable to orthodox dissenters. Ashcraft also overstates the difference between Anglicans and dissenters. Both groups linked human rationality to God's mind. Though Ashcraft rightly finds that Anglicans saw this link as indirect and mediated, he is incorrect in suggesting that they regarded the magistrate's will as 'arbitrary'. The immanentalists in the Church saw civil authority as a medium through which God worked, not as a barrier to his will and certainly not as capricious or arbitrary. Ashcroft's 'Anglicans' too held there to be 'a linkage between divine wisdom and human wisdom'. In this they were not as far from the dissenters as Ashcraft suggests.

87 Ashcraft, 'Latitudinarianism', 155.
88 Ashcraft, 'Latitudinarianism', 162.

Though they differed from Howe and others in accepting mediation as natural, even desirable, they did not consider that this hindered the operation of the divine will. For the 'Anglicans' the magistrate was more like a gatekeeper than a highwayman.

It was Locke who departed from this common confidence in God's intervention, be it direct or indirect. I have suggested that it is on this very question of divine-human encounter that Locke must be distinguished from Howe. Ashcraft attempts to associate Locke with dissent by talking up the distinction between dissent and the Church. He overplays the difference, and fails to recognise Locke's discontinuity with both.

Taking a markedly different view, G.A.J. Rogers endeavours to trace a line between Locke and the latitude-men. This he finds in their common use of the very argument from ignorance which has been discussed above. Even on this ground Rogers is cautious, recognising that the line between Locke and such as Tillotson and Stillingfleet is not unbroken. After noting certain parallels, John Marshall judiciously concludes that 'on many issues Locke differed substantially from the latitudinarians'.[89] For one thing, it is clearly problematical to locate the tolerationist Locke among the authoritarian 'Anglicans' Ashcraft describes. Even the friendly 'latitude-men' did not reach a policy of toleration from their use of the argument from ignorance. Rogers concedes the point, suggesting that 'it is only with Locke that this more radical stage of the implications of the argument is reached.'[90]

Rogers' concession, however, highlights a weakness in his analysis which is more serious than he acknowledges. Like Locke, both Alsop and Howe employed forms of the argument from ignorance in favour of toleration. Only by ignoring these dissenters can it be maintained that Locke alone realised the implications of mitigated scepticism for toleration. Moreover, the thread Rogers draws between Locke and the latitude-men is very thin - indeed, more hopeful than real. Locke has been shown to be fundamentally out of

---

89 Marshall, 'John Locke and Latitudinarianism', esp. 273-4.

90 Rogers, 'Locke', 241-2. It is interesting to reflect that, for Joseph Glanvill, the concept of idiosyncrasy did not translate into toleration. Instead he took the view that 'the *Form* and *Circumstances* of *Government* was to be left to the *Ruling Powers* in the Church.' Glanvill's writings in support of the 'new philosophy' are replete with allusions to the immanent work of God. He rejected, for instance, the accusation that the new way encouraged unbelief. Properly understood, nature is 'but his instrument, and works nothing but as empowered from him.'(cited by H.R. McAdoo, *The Spirit of Anglicanism* (London: SCM, 1965), 166). See also Glanvill, *Essays*, Essays IV and V.

step with Howe, a dissenter who used similar arguments and favoured a similar degree of toleration. If this analysis is accepted, it is highly questionable to claim substantial continuity between Locke's ideas and those of Churchmen who, though they appear to have employed one argument in common, came to a different conclusion altogether on the principal issue.

Success in placing Locke among either the dissenters or the Churchmen is improbable. Ironically, if links are to be sought, continuities between Church and dissent are more likely. Both Churchmen and dissenters accepted the active role of God in the human sphere. Where they differed was in the *way* they understood God to work. Only for Locke does God become largely irrelevant altogether. His leap was radical indeed.

Probably too radical. In his analysis of political thinking, Jonathan Scott identifies a decisive burst of innovation during the exclusion crisis. It was this form of 'restoration radicalism' which would ultimately supply the theoretical framework for sustained reconstruction following the glorious revolution. John Locke was a key contributor to that political innovation.[91] For dissent, it was in the years after the exclusion crisis, when renewed pressure was applied, that new thinking emerged. But this nonconformist innovation would need to reflect the essentially religious nature of the movement. John Locke was certainly radical, but his heterodoxy would limit his influence.

Howe, too, was an innovator. The turmoil in the 1680s forced him to refine and articulate his ideas on toleration and unity. Concerned lest 'our divisions be our ruin', he developed a complex amalgam of Christian charity and mitigated scepticism. In contrast to Locke, Howe's arguments ultimately depended on his confidence in the possibility of unmediated intercourse with God. The result was a uniquely irenic ecclesiology which called at once for both tolerance and unity and which, most significantly, connected with the heart of nonconformist piety. From 1690 he would be the most prominent individual in a newly tolerated dissent. The next chapter traces the decidedly mixed outcomes of that leadership.

91 Scott, *England's Troubles*, 37-8.

Chapter 6

Resorting to Hope in the 1690s

6.1 Dissent and James II

The interval on the continent was a turning point in John Howe's career. Howe's congregation, perhaps aware of how truly precarious his situation had been in August 1685, appears to have welcomed him back. With Owen dead and Baxter failing, he assumed a major role in nonconformist leadership. He also reached the peak of his influence in public affairs. The five years following his return in 1687 would be the most politically active of his life. His importance was realised by James II and when, later, the ministers of London gathered to welcome William of Orange, it was John Howe who presented the address.[1] As the 1690s progressed things became more difficult. The fragmentation of nonconformity would affect him deeply, leading him to abandon the efforts towards formal reconciliation which had engaged him since 1680. His preaching and writing continued unabated, but the emphasis shifted. Though unity remained paramount, by the end of the century Howe was disillusioned with debate and negotiation, indeed any endeavours which depended upon human, time-bound methods. His focus turned to ultimate Christian hope. Unity became an eschatological, rather than a present vision.

There was, however, little sign of this in the hectic final years of James II's reign. The mixed reaction of nonconformist clerics to the Declaration of Indulgence on 4 April, 1687 has been noted already. Nevertheless, the Catholic James, by now clearly estranged from the Church of England, continued to build alliances among 'whig collaborators'. Clerical dissent was wooed from all sides. James renewed his Indulgence in 1688 and actively sought nonconformist support. He already had significant allies among the Quakers and Baptists, but had made little headway among the more cautious Presbyterians and Independents. Twice, during the final months of

1 Calamy 139-142; Lacey, *Dissent*, 222-3.

his reign, James made direct approaches to Howe and others but failed to convince them to back his cause.[2]

These holdouts had other commitments. Negotiations with the Church on terms for comprehension were apparently enjoying a renaissance. The Petition of the Seven Bishops (presented in May against the King's direction to read the second Indulgence in the churches) raised the prospect of some willingness to seek an acceptable settlement. Detailed discussions were held during July but nothing resulted.[3] James and the Church were not the only suitors. In 1687 there were secret discussions with an envoy of William of Orange.[4] The complexity of the situation led many to be wary of all overtures. When William eventually landed, nonconformist leaders were reluctant to endorse him before his victory seemed certain.[5]

The turmoil of the times produced strange bed-fellows. Mark Goldie has noted apparent contradictions between the theoretical positions of John Locke and the pragmatic collaboration with James II of some of Locke's friends.[6] Similar issues are presented when Howe's activities in this period are compared with those of Vincent Alsop. Of the respondents to Edward Stillingfleet in 1680, Alsop was probably the closest to Howe, notably in the degree of individualism both demonstrated. Both were nominally Presbyterians in London and were known to one another. With their congregations, both appear to have come under considerable pressure in 1681-5.[7] Yet, despite the apparent nearness of their theological positions and their similar experiences, Howe and Alsop made quite different responses to James II.

---

2 William Penn the Quaker and Stephen Lobb, a Congregationalist, were James' agents on the first of these occasions (May 23) see Lacey, *Dissent*, 211-2, 220; Thomas, 'Comprehension', 238.

3 The undertaking by the Churchmen was vague and noncommittal. It included a reference to Convocation and was given little credence by Dissenters. Lacey, *Dissent*, 187, 210-211; Spurr, *Restoration Church*, 94.

4 According to Roger Morrice, both Howe and Bates were involved. Morrice records some caution on the part of nonconformists about their prospects if both William and Mary were to come to the throne - see Lacey, *Dissent*, 186-187, 343 n 41.

5 Lacey (*Dissent*, 221-2) cites Morrice's frustration that Dissenters 'did not more openly and publicly rise for, and serve the Prince of Orange'. Baptists and Quakers, many of whom had collaborated with James II, 'were most notably absent' from William's support.

6 See Goldie, 'John Locke's Circle and James II'.

7 See Beddard, 'Vincent Alsop', 166-173. Alsop, like Howe, maintained a close relationship with Lord Wharton.

Alsop had gone underground during the worst of the persecution but appears not to have left the country. As much as he was able, he continued his ministry among small gatherings of his flock. Unlike Howe, he was in London when James issued his first Indulgence. In an act of collaboration which was much criticised by the staunchly resistant bulk of the nonconformist leaders, Alsop led the small group of Presbyterian and Congregational ministers which addressed thanks to James.[8]

Howe returned to England after James' Declaration, but joined the majority of his colleagues in refusing to accept its validity. He thus stood apart from Alsop on this important question. Prosaic reasons for their different responses are not hard to find. Alsop's son had been in the rebel army in 1685 and was facing execution. A father's need to curry favour with the King has been suggested as Alsop's motivation for addressing James.[9] Howe by contrast had become closely associated with the Prince of Orange. Calamy records that William had warned Howe not to address thanks to the King.[10] Called to a private audience with James to explain his stance, Howe 'told his Majesty that he was a Minister of the Gospel, and it was his Province to preach, and endeavour to do good to the Souls of men; but as for meddling with State Affairs; he was as little inclin'd as he was call'd to it.'[11] This explanation was disingenuous. Howe discussed politics with the likes of Hampden and Swynfen.[12] He was an active supporter of William; possibly meeting with his envoy during 1687.[13] In a later address to the then William III he claimed a clear-headed view that, under James II, 'a design hath been industriously

8 Beddard, 'Vincent Alsop', 175-180; Keeble, *Literary Culture*, 62-3.

9 Stoughton IV, 119-120. A pardon was granted to the son soon after the delivery of the Address by Alsop. On this explanation for Alsop's actions see Beddard, 'Vincent Alsop', 180-1.

10 Calamy 130-1.

11 Calamy 136.

12 See Howe's letter to John Swynfen Sept. 26, 1687 and Swynfen's draft reply, BL Add MSS 29910 ff 226-7.

13 Lacey, *Dissent*, 199-200; Ashcraft, *Revolutionary Politics*, 555. Ashcraft's assertions about Howe's actions following his return to London must be treated with caution. In places he fails to distinguish between John Howe, nonconformist divine, and 'Jack' Howe, Parliamentarian (and sometimes even with the latter's brother, Emmanuel Scrope Howe), despite the accuracy of his secondary sources - see 516-7, 558 n. 152, 595. For 'Jack' Howe's family see Henning (ed.), *The Commons 1660-1690*, 606-612.

driven, that we might be made papists, to make us slaves; and for the enslaving us, to debauch us.'[14]

After William's accession to the throne, but before the settlement of the religious question, Howe penned *The Case of the Protestant dissenters Represented and Argued*.[15] This was a political tract, containing very little theology. Howe represented the concerns of the dissenters, through all the problems of the Restoration, as being for 'the civil interests of the nation'.[16] On the reluctance of himself and others to endorse the Indulgence, he acknowledged the impact of Gaspar Fagel's letter which had circulated in late 1687 and which purported to outline William's policy on toleration.[17] Howe's opposition to James was, it appears, sustained by hope of better things, 'if ever that happy change should be brought about, which none have now beheld with greater joy than we.'[18]

How much of William's plans had been revealed to Howe cannot be determined. Nevertheless it may have been, as Goldie suggests for Locke, that Howe 'knew something his friends did not, and it made the world of difference to the contingencies of their respective political lives.'[19]

For both Alsop and Howe, then, political and personal factors came into play. Theology, after all, is not everything. Nevertheless, there was more to their actions than paternal concern or political expediency. Beddard argues that Alsop's action was consistent with the principles he espoused in 1680. In his contribution to the Stillingfleet controversy of that year, Alsop gave a high priority to independency and individual conscience. Prepared to let high politics take its course, he naturally welcomed any move which allowed the free exercise of those principles. Seen in this light, there is little surprise that Alsop joined with Anabaptists and Quakers in accepting the Indulgence. Though not as extreme as they, Alsop had in common with these groups an ecclesiology radically committed to the invisible church. The only policy they sought was toleration. They had no reason to seek the alternative of comprehension. More-

14 J. Howe, *Dedication* (prefixed to the third volume of Dr Manton's Works) [1690], *Works* III, 593-596, 594.

15 J. Howe, *The Case of the Protestant Dissenters Represented and Argued*, [London, 1689], *Works* III, 560-567.

16 Howe, *Case*, 564.

17 For the circumstances and response to Fagel's *Letter* see Ashcraft, *Revolutionary Politics*, 485-89.

18 Howe, *Case*, 564.

19 Goldie, 'John Locke's Circle', 586.

over, formal constitutional niceties, whether ecclesiastical or civil, were to them of small consequence. As Beddard points out,

> Unlike his more fastidious and discriminating brethren [Alsop] did not bother whether toleration came by way of an exercise of the prerogative or by the promulgation of statute; for him the means were subordinate to the end.[20]

By contrast, Howe's political sensibilities, apparently latent in 1680, had been awakened by 1687. Had he moved away from the ecclesiological position he and Alsop had then occupied? Had his invisiblist principles, worked out with care in the early 1680s, been overwhelmed by a political preference for William III during the stay in Utrecht and through his contact with such as Locke? Certainly *The Case of the Protestant dissenters* contained few of the themes of the earlier works. There was even a section which could have been lifted directly from Locke's political theory. Commenting on the validity of the laws requiring uniformity, Howe denied there could be 'so much as a pretence of authority derived for such purposes from the people, whom every one now acknowledges the first receptacle of derived governing power.'[21]

Yet, although by 1689 Howe was more politically involved, he had not travelled far from the ecclesiological territory he had occupied with Alsop at the beginning of the decade. In the *Case of the Protestant Dissenters* he defended the nonconformists who accepted Charles II's Indulgence in terms of which Alsop would have approved. Howe maintained that authority to govern true religion lay with God alone.

> We are therefore injuriously reflected on, when it is imputed to us that we have...acknowledged an illegal dispensing power. We have done no other thing herein, than we did when no dispensation was given or pretended, in conscience of duty to Him that gave us breath: nor did, therefore, practise otherwise, because we thought these laws dispensed with, but because we thought them not laws.[22]

In failing to respond to James II, Howe was clearly not rejecting toleration *per se*. He wanted it as much as did Alsop, but judged it advisable to wait for what William could deliver. Where he did differ significantly from Alsop was in continuing to seek comprehension (still a live, if fading, possibility when *The Case of the Protestant Dissenters* was published). His concern for charity made it natural to keep alive the possibility of a *rapprochement* with conformists. This end he judged to be best served by opposing James'

---

20 Beddard, 'Vincent Alsop', 179.
21 Howe, *Case*, 562.
22 Howe, *Case*, 563.

transparent attack on the established Church. Hopes for comprehension were to founder once more on differences in ecclesiology. Ironically it was now conformists who felt visible unity would exact too high a price. Spurr has identified in Restoration Churchmen the fear that comprehension would 'import schism into the Church'.[23] This notion was dismissed by Howe, as 'the favouring of us...will as much ruin the church as its enlargement and additional strength will signify its ruin.'[24]

Alsop and Howe both clearly emphasised the invisible church. Both stressed the transcendent relation of God to humans. Yet, their ecclesiologies were not identical in all respects. Christian love did not assume the dynamic role in Alsop's thinking that it took in Howe's. For Alsop, the dominant concepts were centrifugal: independency and individuality. By contrast, Howe spoke little of independency and, in his scheme, the centrifugal force of individual conscience was balanced by the centripetal energy of charity.

Whatever the differences in their reasoning and actions the two men remained close colleagues. Alsop was an important subscriber to the 1690 Common Fund and a signatory to the 1691 *Heads of Agreement* which established the ill-fated 'Happy Union'. Despite his unpopular line in 1687, he was soon a prominent figure again. Whatever they thought of his co-operation with James II, it is clear that his associates did not regard Alsop as beyond the pale theologically. He and Howe would be further associated in setting up the Salters' Hall lectures in 1694. The ecclesiologies of the two, albeit differently configured, remained compatible. This is important, as the vision of the church which they shared, and especially Howe's version of it, would come to dominate later Stuart nonconformity, with unexpected results.

6.2 The 'Happy Union'

Howe returned to familiar themes in a second short publication of 1689. *Humble Requests Both to Conformists and Dissenters* appeared after the passing of the Act of Toleration.[25] By now, comprehension was a dead letter. Howe's fear was that the new environment would encourage criticism and legitimate disharmony. Many of the argu-

23 J. Spurr, 'Schism and the Restoration Church,' *JEH*, Vol. 41, No. 3, July 1990, 408-424, 420.

24 Howe, *Case*, 565.

25 J. Howe, *Humble Requests Both to Conformists and Dissenters, Touching Their Temper and Behaviour Toward One Another Upon the Lately Passed Indulgence*, [London, 1689], *Works* III, 567-572.

ments of *Union Among Protestants* appeared in shortened form in *Humble Requests*. All were employed to minimise the importance of differences in 'externals'. If the 'internal principles of [Christianity] may live and flourish in our own souls...there may at length cease to be any divided parties at all.'[26]

With the failure of comprehension and the achievement of a modicum of toleration, Howe's efforts shifted to unifying dissent. Moves towards what would be called the 'Happy Union' between 'Presbyterians' and 'Congregationalists' began in 1690. The Common Fund for the support of the ministry was formally set up in London on 1 June of that year. Howe was a founding subscriber.[27] His personal commitment to the project cannot be questioned. He promised the substantial sum of one hundred and sixty pounds annually, considerably more than any other individual.[28]

The Common Fund was the precursor to a far more ambitious project. Howe was most likely the drafter of the *Heads of Agreement*, signed in 1691 and representing an attempt to provide for co-operation and support between the main nonconformist groups.[29] On 6 April, 1691 'above fourscore' Presbyterian and Congregational ministers agreed on a 'Happy Union' of those groups. It was a moment of triumph for Howe and his closest collaborators, Matthew Mead and Increase Mather, both prominent nonconformist activists for most of their careers. Howe appears to have been the senior figure in this venture.[30]

The *Heads of Agreement*, though inevitably a compromise document, is revealing. The opening clause was overtly biased towards

---

26 Howe, *Humble Requests*, 570.

27 Apparently, 'Presbyterians' took the initiative in this venture. Of the four original subscribers on 9 April 1690, three (including Howe) were 'Presbyterians'. The wording of the minutes suggests the 'Presbyterian' managers were selected first – Gordon, *Freedom*, 158-9, 164. See also W. Walker, *The Creeds and Platforms of Congregationalism*, (1893) (Boston: Pilgrim Press, 1960), 445-6; R.T. Jones, *Congregationalism in England 1662-1962* (London: Independent Press, 1962) 111; White, 'The Twilight of Puritanism', 325-6.

28 No other individual came near to Howe. Vincent Alsop subscribed a total of 110 pounds, Samuel Annesley 108. See Gordon, *Freedom*, 164-7.

29 On Howe's role see Calamy 181; Gordon, *Freedom*, 155-6, 189-90.

30 Walker, *Creeds*, (445) suggests that 'the strongest influence...in the accomplishment of the Union' was Mather. Mather certainly played a role but his recent biographer concedes that Howe was the 'main spirit behind the reconciliation' and that Mather was recruited as a 'go-between' - Hall, *Last American Puritan*, 238-9. See also Calamy 181; Gordon, *Freedom*, 155-7; Mather, 'Autobiography', 338.

the invisible church. Here, formally and explicitly stated, was the ecclesiology implicit in earlier works.

> We acknowledge our *Lord Jesus Christ* to have One *Catholick Church*, or *Kingdom*, comprehending all that are united to Him, whether in *Heaven* or *Earth*. And do conceive the whole multitude of *visible Believers*, and their Infant-Seed (commonly called the *Catholick Visible Church*) to belong to *Christ's Spiritual Kingdom* in this world: But for the notion of a *Catholick Visible Church* here, as it signifies its having been collected into any formed Society, under a Visible human Head on Earth, whether *one* person singly, or *many* collectively, We, with the rest of Protestants, unanimously disclaim it.[31]

This clause encapsulated the classic features of invisiblist ideas of the church. The true church contained all Saints, in heaven and on earth. Visibility was conceived in individualistic terms and even then served merely to demonstrate the believer's membership of the spiritual body. Ecclesiastical form and authority, so important to Stillingfleet, were specifically rejected.

The provisions of the *Heads of Agreement* seem to express Congregational principles.[32] Commentators with Congregational sympathies have explained this by downplaying Howe's 'Presbyterianism'. Their interpretation depends upon the view that Howe was Congregational from his youth, only becoming a Presbyterian nominally and late in his career. The issue of Howe's allegiance is an important one and may now be usefully addressed.

The Congregational case appears strong. Howe's associations with Congregationalists at university have been noted. The *Episcopal Return* of 1665 listed him among Congregationalists at Torrington.[33] Later, hagiographical Congregationalists Stoughton, Horton, Dale, and Scott certainly wanted to make him one of their own, at least in spirit.[34] A biographer of John Owen nominated Howe as a virtual secret agent for Owen, whilst at Whitehall.[35] Williston Walker is forthright in his account.

> So it came about that, under his desire for an honourable union with the Church of England, Howe drifted from association with the Congregationalists, and, without apparently any radical change of view

---

31 *Heads of Agreement* Clause I, 1 (Walker, *Creeds* 457).

32 On the compromise between the two positions see Watts, *Dissenters*, 290-291.

33 Turner, *Original Records* vol. II, 1174.

34 Stoughton, *Religion*, II, 210-11; Horton, *John Howe*, 55; R.W. Dale, *History of English Congregationalism* (London: 1907), 377; Scott, *Life*, 9. See also Bremer, 'Increase Mather's Friends', 71.

35 A. Thomson, 'Life of Dr Owen' in W.H. Goold (ed), *The Works of John Owen D.D.*, (16 vols, 1850-53), London, 1965, Vol. I, XXI-CXXI, XLIV.

on the subject of church polity, was numbered among the Presbyterians.[36]

Counting against the hopeful claims of Congregationalist historians are several telling features of Howe's career. He received a Presbyterian ordination. His relations by marriage were Presbyterian and it was to a Presbyterian (Baxter), rather than to Owen, that he turned for counsel when at Whitehall. His London church was Presbyterian. He was never listed among Congregationalists whilst in active ministry.

Assessments of Howe's own mind are more difficult. As he was in Antrim at the time, he never took up a licence under the Indulgence of 1672. Moreover, other than in the unique case of the *Heads of Agreement*, nowhere in his works does he align himself with any particular view on church polity. Indeed, in a concession which would later fuel the fears of the Scottish nationalist James Webster, he declared himself willing to accept and work within even an Episcopal system. '[T]he generality of the dissenters differ from the church of England in no substantials of doctrine and worship, no, nor of government, provided it be so managed, as to attain its true, acknowledged end.'[37]

Against the hopes of partisan biographers, the only acceptable view of Howe is that he preferred no one polity above any other. Walker is, in part, correct - Howe chose those allegiances which would best promote unity - but nominal 'Presbyterianism' does not imply a reluctant departure from heartfelt 'Congregationalism'. To Howe, polity was a matter of theological indifference, compromised by historical uncertainty and individual idiosyncrasy. Compared to the task he pursued, it was a distraction.

> You greatly prevaricate, if you are more zealously intent to promote independency than Christianity, presbytery than Christianity, prelacy than Christianity, as any of these are the interest of a party, and not considered in subserviency to the Christian interest, nor designed for promoting the edification and salvation of your own soul.[38]

There are ramifications which extend beyond Howe himself. The 'Happy Union' sought to secure co-operation between nascent denominational entities. Many divines gave conscious and public allegiance to one group or other. To this degree, traditional party labels retain some validity. Genuine differences of emphasis existed and would lead to division during the 1690s. Yet denominational historians have taken the subtle watercolour of later Stuart dissent

36 Walker, *Creeds*, 445. See also Dale, *History*, 475.
37 Howe, *Case*, 565.
38 Howe, *Humble Requests*, 572.

and reissued it as a heavy line drawing. The standard terms mislead, by focusing attention on narrow questions of polity. Individual allegiance was as likely determined by the form of ordination received as by views on church government. In signing the *Heads of Agreement*, 'Presbyterians' could agree to a form which amounted to 'Congregationalism'. A leading figure like Howe could transcend rigid divisions. The diverse views revealed in the controversies of 1680 found a parallel in 1691. Simple nomenclatures based on formal church polity fail to capture the complexities and shadings of the ecclesiology of dissent.

6.3 The Collapse of Unity

Because of illness, Richard Baxter had been out of the negotiations which led to the *Heads of Agreement* in 1691. Long experienced in struggles for unity, he rejoiced at the 'very attempt' but warned 'you must look that it should be assaulted by Cavil and Reproach.'[39] His caution was well-founded. The 'Happy Union' was not as happy as it appeared. Across the spectrum of nonconformist theology there were misgivings.[40] Forces which contributed to its alienation from the established Church would in turn foster the fragmentation of dissent. The *Heads of Agreement* could not hold the parties together. The irenic drive and goodwill of such as Howe and Mead had advanced the front of institutional unity well beyond the supply lines of doctrinal agreement. The Union was to crack along these lines and ultimately collapse in the following years.

Serious tactical errors by Howe would contribute to this failure. The first can be traced back to 1689. Samuel Crisp, son of the deceased antinomian Tobias Crisp (1600-1643), issued posthumously some of his father's sermons.[41] In a seemingly innocuous act, Howe and a number of other prominent ministers certified that the sermons were in fact those of the elder Crisp. However, in his preface to the published version, Samuel Crisp maligned the views of Richard Baxter. Baxter was appalled at the attack, the publication itself, and the association with it of such as Howe. He responded publicly

39 Baxter to 'The United Protestant Nonconformists in London', 23 April, 1691 - *Church Concord* (1691) (see Keeble, *Calendar*, no. 1234).

40 Nathaniel Mather (brother of Increase), though a nominated manager of the Common Fund, refused to sign the agreement. Some Independents were reluctant to be so closely tied to those (like Baxter and Howe) who favoured 'Sacramental Communion with the Church of England' – Gordon, *Freedom*, 156. See also Walker, *Creeds*, 447-8.

41 T. Crisp, *Christ Alone Exalted* (London: 1689).

with a series at the popular nonconformist forum, the Merchants' Hall lectures, and in *The Scripture Gospel Defended* (1690). Howe sought to calm the gathering storm but was able to divert Baxter from public criticism of himself only by endorsing, along with several others, two refutations of antinomianism, written respectively by John Flavel and, most damagingly, by Dr Daniel Williams.[42] This action merely complicated matters further. The controversy which resulted demonstrates the inter-relation of a variety of theological factors and their impact on church disputes. It also signalled a fundamental shift in the self-understanding of dissent.

Daniel Williams (1643?-1716) had enjoyed a long ministry in Dublin, noted for its irenic quality.[43] From 1687, when he came to London, he quickly became the heir apparent to Richard Baxter, in theology and disputation. He was a close associate of Baxter in his final years and succeeded him as a Presbyterian Merchants' Hall lecturer.[44] Calamy noted that he held to the 'divine right of presbytery'. Roger Thomas correctly interprets this phrase to mean that Williams, as had Baxter, stressed the authority of the pastor in matters of discipline.[45] Williams also carried forward Baxter's almost obsessive polemic against antinomianism. This was a point at which the theological fault lines in dissent crossed. Many who identified themselves as Independents favoured a strongly Calvinist soteriology. Extreme versions of this system were open to the very charges of antinomianism attached to Tobias Crisp.[46] It was to refute antinomianism that Williams wrote *Gospel Truth Stated and Vindicated* in 1692. Howe and the other signatories to Williams' pamphlet were all Presbyterians. Some Independents objected to what they interpreted as an oblique attack on their more orthodox views.

Williams was already involved in a parallel dispute concerning the extreme Independent, Richard Davis (1658-1714). Davis was a remarkably successful evangelist in Northamptonshire. Unfortunately his very success had seen the depletion of a number of neighbouring dissenting congregations. The London ministers

42 See J. Flavel, *Planelogia: A Succinct and seasonable discourse...with an epistle...relative to Dr Crisp's works*, (London: 1691); D. Williams, *Gospel Truth Stated and Vindicated* (London: 1692).

43 See Kilroy, *Protestant Dissent* 41, 74-5.

44 R. Thomas, *Daniel Williams 'Presbyterian Bishop'* (London: Dr Williams' Trust, 1964), 5-6.

45 Thomas, *Daniel Williams*, 7.

46 It was his concern that some versions of Calvinism encouraged antinomianism which prompted Richard Baxter to develop his 'middle way' from 1649. This modified Calvinism made Baxter suspect in the eyes of many Independents - See Lamont, *Richard Baxter*, 124-155.

sought to call him to account in May, 1692. Davis rejected this attempt to exert what he regarded as presbyteral authority. Williams added to the tension by accusing Davis of antinomianism.[47]

The Crisp and Davis controversies combined to polarise the parties to a now very unhappy union. Howe had done nothing to help. He undoubtedly blundered in putting his name to the Crisp publication. Why had he done so? He most certainly did not share Tobias Crisp's views. His ideas on grace were similar to those of Baxter. Rogers suggests that Howe and the others were tricked by the younger Crisp, who sought to garner credibility for his own attack on Baxter.[48] This may be true; Howe does not appear to have known about Crisp's preface until publication. However, a less Machiavellian explanation for Howe's action is likely. Howe may have agreed to sign the certificate as a gesture intended to promote nonconformist unity. This was of particular concern to him in 1689. His publications of that year had called for real unity among Christians, or at least a united front. The certificate to Crisp senior's *Christ Alone Exalted* was a symbol of the latter. The signatories comprise six Congregationalists (including Nathaniel and Increase Mather and Isaac Chauncey), four Presbyterians (including Howe and Vincent Alsop) and two Baptists.[49] The publication of fifty-year-old sermons must have seemed an innocuous enough vehicle for a display of unanimity. His misguided attempt to limit the subsequent damage by signing the testimonial to Williams' book, just as Williams was becoming the *bette noire* of Congregationalists, made matters worse. That these seemingly well-intended gestures contributed to such disastrous results was a major blow.

Howe took part in negotiations for a settlement of the Davis affair. Some agreement was reached but irreparable damage had already been done.[50] By 1693, Congregationalists were withdrawing in large numbers. The 'Happy Union' was clearly falling apart. In response, Howe published two sermons on *The Carnality of Religious Contention* to which he added a long 'Preface to the Reader'.[51] On its face this

47 R. Thomas, 'Presbyterians in Transition' in Bolam *et al* ed, *The English Presbyterians: From Elizabethan Puritanism to Modern Unitarianism* (London: Allen & Unwin, 1968), 113-174, 115-119; Watts, *Dissenters*, 291-297.

48 Rogers, *Life*, 272-3.

49 The Baptists were John Gammon and Hanserd 'Knowles' (Knollys).

50 This short-lived settlement was recorded in *The agreement in doctrine among the Dissenting Ministers in London* (London: 1693). See also Calamy 183-3; Gordon, *Freedom*, 156.

51 J. Howe, *The Carnality of Religious Contention: In Two Sermons, Preached at the Merchants' Lecture, in Broad Street*, (London: 1693) in *Works* III, 111-155.

work appears to add little to Howe's earlier calls to put aside differences. In sentiments which echoed those expressed as early as 1668, in *The Blessedness of the Righteous,* Howe censured all parties. Yet, *Carnality* signalled the beginning of a realignment of Howe's hopes and priorities, which became more definite as the decade progressed. It was a shift born out of disappointment.

The new mood which underlay *Carnality* is highlighted when it is compared to Howe's most important work of the 1680s: *Union Among Protestants.* In *Union,* Howe set out a positive case for unity, based upon the dynamic power of Christian love. *Carnality* gave the obverse of that case. In a detailed examination of the reasons for strife and dissension, Howe set out specific stages and facets of contention among Christians. As his chosen title suggests, he held these to spring from 'Carnality'; that is, the 'lust of the flesh', in the broad sense of the concerns and methods of the worldly. Here was the suspicion of human nature which underlay much nonconformist thought. Human products and traits, from philosophical constructs to natural passions - though acceptable, even valuable in their place - became 'strange unhallowed fire' when they usurped the prerogatives of the Gospel.[52] Even the interpretation of scripture became destructive when 'there is more of the man in it than of the Christian'.[53] Most dangerous of all,

> the contentious, disputative genius...hath grown strong and vigorous, and acquired the power to transform the church from a spiritual society, enlivened, acted and governed by the Spirit of Christ, into a mere carnal thing, like the rest of the world.[54]

The result was a fascination and passion for things not essential to the faith. 'In sum; not only are things most alien from real Christianity added to it, but substituted in the room of it, and preferred before it.'[55]

Not until these distractions were shed, would the unity which was already a fact in the spiritual realm (i.e. the invisible church) translate into a 'more entire, visible oneness'.[56] This vision was one of love and acceptance. Even earthly unity was not portrayed as a matter of structure and uniformity. Howe had no need to resort to the visiblist ecclesiology of Stillingfleet. Accordingly, he did not argue that visible disunity *in itself* constituted the destruction of the church. Rather, its effect was to cramp and weaken the Christian in-

---

52 Howe, *Carnality*, 142-147.
53 Howe, *Carnality*, 137, 142.
54 Howe, *Carnality*, 112.
55 Howe, *Carnality*, 115.
56 Howe, *Carnality*, 116.

terest. Infidels were repelled at it and the Spirit was induced to withdraw, testifying to divine displeasure. 'And hence is the growth of the church obstructed, not only naturally, but penally too.'[57]

There was nothing substantially new in Howe's argument. His relegation of the natural and his view of the church as primarily a 'spiritual society' were in line with the stress on transcendence and the invisible church which has already been noted. The logic of *Carnality* depended upon the same basic theological orientation that has been observed in his works of the 1680s. Yet, two features of *Carnality* disclosed the first stirrings of a new emphasis.

The first was a note of pessimism not found so explicitly in Howe's thought since the fall of the Protectorate. The very focus of *Carnality* was negative: the anatomy of failure. This was more than a device. Howe appeared now to doubt the possibility of achieving the oneness he sought. As noted above, he located the immediate cause of disunity in 'the addition of unnecessary things'. Until such time as these were removed, progress was impossible. 'But this amputation is, according to the present posture of men's minds all the Christian world over, a thing equally to be desired and despaired of; as a general union therefore is, in the meantime.'[58]

Howe had not given up - not yet - but *Carnality* was a decidedly more gloomy work than such as *Union Among Protestants*. 'That only which the present state of things admits of, is, that we keep ourselves united in mind and spirit with all serious Christians, in the plain and necessary things wherein they all agree.'[59]

The second feature related to doctrine, rather than mood. Parallel to the negative spur of discouragement was a positive factor which would assume great importance in Howe's thought. A decade before, in *Union Among Protestants*, Howe had briefly outlined the essentials of the faith. Then, the concentration was on Christological and soteriological doctrines.[60] In 1693, Howe repeated the exercise. Early in his preface to *Carnality*, he anticipated a crucial question. 'It will here then be inquired,...what Christianity is?...what is its essence...or wherein doth it consist?' The answer is instructive. The themes of 1683 remain, but an eschatological framework is added.

> [I]t will be readily acknowledged, that Christianity ...must be estimated more principally by its end [i.e. goal], and that its final

57 Howe, *Carnality*, 116-7.
58 Howe, *Carnality*, 117.
59 Howe, *Carnality*, 117.
60 See Howe, *Union*, 186-7.

> reference is not to this world, but to the world to come, and to a happy state there.[61]

Further on, concluding the preface, Howe made a plea which echoed the central themes of his sermons of 1677-8:

> let us supplicate more earnestly for the effusions of that Holy Spirit, which alone can give remedy to our distempers, and overcome the lusts of the flesh, of whatever kind, and restore Christian religion to itself, and make the Christian name great in the world.[62]

In the later 1690s, a growing pessimism about present prospects for unity led Howe to rely increasingly upon future hope. This would be less a new direction than the reactivation of the pneumatological eschatology of 1678.

In the meantime, efforts to preserve unity in at least 'mind and spirit' continued. A committee of five Congregationalists (Mead, Annesley, Veale, James and Lobb) and five Presbyterians (Howe, Hammond, Alsop, Mayo and Slater) met inconclusively until as late as December 1694.[63] Even this faint flicker was eventually extinguished. Once again Dr Williams was at the centre of the problem. In an April 1694 lecture at Pinners' Hall, Nathaniel Mather accused Williams of 'semi-Socinianism'. This led directly to the departure of the bulk of Presbyterians to set up their own, competing lectureship at Salters' Hall. Howe was one of those who departed but, as with his caution about joining Goodwin's group at Oxford forty years before and his decision not to conform in 1662, it was a concern *for* catholicity and latitude, rather than his own lack of these qualities, which determined his course. To Spilsbury, a year later, he declared

> God knows how I strove against that division...I have urged, both publicly and privately, that the same lecturers might alternate in both places, which would take away all appearance of disunion...Upon these terms I had preached with them [those who remained at Pinners' Hall] still; but I will not be tied to them, nor any party, so as to abandon all others.[64]

Charges of Socinianism were particularly provocative in the 1690s. The Trinitarian controversy was engaging the best minds of the established Church. Howe too played a substantial role in the

---

61 Howe, *Carnality*, 113.

62 Howe, *Carnality*, 120.

63 Walker, *Creeds*, 452.

64 Howe to John Spilsbury, April 20, [16]95, Calamy 195-198 (Rogers, *Life*, 279-281). On the Pinners' Hall - Salters' Hall split generally see O.M. Griffiths, *Religion and Learning: A Study of Presbyterian Thought from the Bartholemew Ejections (1662) to the Foundations of the Unitarian Movement* (Cambridge: CUP, 1935), 95-105; Thomas, 'Presbyterians in Transition', 117-120.

debate. Over several years he conducted a correspondence, eventually in public, with some of the principal protagonists. His approach exemplified his ideal of tolerant Christian discourse. In *A Calm and Sober Enquiry Concerning the Possibility of a Trinity in the Godhead* (1694) Howe made no attempt to resolve the paradox in the Christian declaration that God is both 'three' and 'one'. Instead he examined the narrower point as to whether it was legitimate to hold to both statements about the Godhead. True to his mitigated scepticism, he called for a looser adherence to the scholastic idea of the 'simplicity' of God, arguing that, whilst this quality excluded any 'composition' within Godhead, it did not necessarily disallow 'variety'.[65]

On this point Howe was challenged, to the extent of being charged with tritheistic heresy by one respondent. In 1695, stung by what he regarded as deliberate misrepresentation of his views, Howe made a plea for open and free debate.

> I think much service might be done to the common interest of religion, by such a free mutual communication of even more doubtful thoughts, if such disquisitions were pursued with more candour, and with less confidence and prepossession of mind, or addictedness to the interest of any party whatsoever....it being too manifest, that the same insulting genius, which makes a man think himself competent to be a standard to mankind, would also make him impatient of dissent, and tempt him to do worse than reproach one who differs from him, if it were in his power; and the club or fagot arguments must be expected to take place, where what he thinks rational ones did not do the business.[66]

In the deliberate choice of a narrow point, which considered merely whether a position was valid, rather than attempting to solve the principal issues, Howe was following the approach he had adopted in the 1677 *Reconcilableness of God's Prescience*. There were other similarities. As he had in the work on prescience, Howe faced in two directions in his writings on the Trinity. There was a presenting apologetic need (the defence of trinitarian orthodoxy) but there was also a difficult polemical context. This time the struggle was not between dissent and the Church, but within dissent itself. In his contribution to the Trinitarian debate Howe was seeking to model an alternative to the 'club or fagot arguments' he had condemned in *Carnality*. By 1695 these were reaching a fatal intensity.

---

65 J. Howe, *A Calm and Sober Enquiry Concerning the Possibility of a Trinity in the Godhead* (London: 1694), *Works* II, 527-576, 530-532

66 J. Howe, *A View of that Part of the Late Considerations Addressed to H.H. about the Trinity* (London: 1695) *Works* II, 596-628, 598-599.

If not 'tied to a party', Howe was dedicated to a cause. He made one more fruitless, but highly revealing, bid for peace. In 1695, the charge of Socinianism was again levelled at Dr Williams, this time by Stephen Lobb (1647?-1699). Since the rift between Presbyterians and Independents had flared in 1692, Howe had sought ways to lower the temperature of the debate. He had failed. The question had settled to a mutual demonisation of opposing positions. Calamy summarised the later debate in this way.

> One Party suspected (or at least pretended to suspect) the other of verging too much towards *Arminianism*, and even *Socinianism*; and they on the other side charg'd them with encouraging *Antinomianism*. Several Papers were hereupon drawn up and subscrib'd, in order to an Accommodation; there was a first, a second, and a third Paper, of this sort: and these very Papers created new Altercations and Debates, that were carry'd on with no small heat and pettishness....[67]

This terse account omits details which cast Howe in an unflattering light. Lobb's case against Williams was weak. It hinged on an allegation regarding Williams' views on the process of salvation. To the Calvinists it was crucial to deny any human agency in bringing about satisfaction for sin. Christ must in all senses be understood to have taken the place of the human individual. Anything less than such a thorough exchange would have lessened the role of Christ, potentially opening the way for Socinian views. Lobb contended that Williams denied this essential 'change of persons' between Christ and the believer. (In fact Williams had merely excluded some senses of this exchange. His formula, stated in *Gospel Truth*, had been maintained as strongly by Baxter.) Disturbed at this further tension, Howe sought to pull together a compromise statement (his was the 'first paper' in Calamy's account). To this he obtained the signatures of six other leading Presbyterians and submitted it to the Congregationalists with a covering letter dated 25 March, 1696.[68] Crucially this statement specifically distanced the subscribers from Williams, effectively conceding Lobb's point. It seems Howe negotiated this attempted settlement without consulting Williams, who was conveniently out of London, at Bath. Roger Thomas, who has examined this incident in an admiring treatment of Williams, decries this as an 'underhand' procedure. Williams himself was aggrieved at the manoeuvre and at what he held were misrepresentations of his position and 'expected better treatment at least from such whose cause I

---

67 Calamy 183.

68 The text of the paper and letter is to be found in [Anon.] *A History of the Union of between the Presbyterian and Congregational Ministers...and the causes of the Breach of it* (London: 1698), 29-34.

pleaded'.[69] He issued his own *Remarks* in protest. Howe had not submitted his paper to the Presbyterian remnant which still maintained the fiction of being the 'United Ministers'. In September 1696 both papers were before the Board of Ministers, which appointed a committee to draft a third paper, reconciling the two. Howe was nominally on this committee but took no part in framing the new document.[70] No such reconciliation could satisfy the now highly offended Independents. Howe's attempt to win back their support for the Union failed. Indeed, his action merely escalated the dispute. Williams referred the question to Stillingfleet (to whose writings Howe had appealed in his paper) who cleared Williams of the charge of Socinianism, effectively ending the controversy, though not healing the wounds.[71]

This was a humiliating defeat for Howe. If there was deceit on his part it was strangely uncharacteristic. That Howe was willing to deal in this way emphasises his personal investment in the now shattered Union. The affair was also symbolic of a deeper issue. In his willingness to isolate, even sacrifice, Williams, Howe was signalling more than the importance of compromise. Williams preserved the approach of Richard Baxter, in which pastoral discipline was crucial. Howe's concerns however were different: unity taking priority over ethical, or even doctrinal, rectitude. Though he lost out badly in 1696, a new emphasis within dissent had been signalled. The tension between Howe's irenicism and Baxterian discipline was now a clear fault line. It would open disastrously in 1719.

6.4 'A Spiritual Sort of Blessing'

The final Williams affair appears to have exhausted Howe's faith in earthly struggles for unity. Increasingly he sought a change of cosmic proportions. Yet this disillusionment with human effort reflected an intensification, rather than a radical change, of his view of the church. His commitment to an invisiblist ecclesiology remained constant. In 1695 he had published a sermon marking the death and funeral of Queen Mary. He took his text from Hebrews 12:23, which suggested the informal title of the discourse: *Heaven a State of Perfection*.[72] The principal theme was the nature of the 'per-

69 D. Williams, *The Answer to the Report Which the United Ministers Appointed the Committee to draw up…* (London: 1898), 75.

70 Compare the lists in Williams, *Answer*, 'Preface' [1] & 91-92.

71 See Thomas, *Daniel Williams*, 16-21.

72 J. Howe, *A Discourse Relating to the Much Lamented death, and Solemn Funeral of Queen Mary* (London, 1695), *Works*, III, 315-341.

fection' to which the saints aspire. However, the treatise depended upon understanding the true church to be that invisible, spiritual society which finds its proper home in heaven. This body consisted of the truly saved of all generations and, intriguingly, included the angels.

> 'And to the spirits of just men made perfect.' This shows they all make but one church, even such spirits as have dwelt in flesh, being received into the communion of those whose dwelling never was flesh. And, in the mean time, those that yet continue in these low, earthly stations, as soon as the principles of the divine life have place in them, belong, and are related to that glorious community; for they are said to be already come thereto, and all together comprise but one family. For there is but one *paterfamilias*, of whom the whole family in heaven and earth is said to be named.[73]

This passage is probably Howe's most unequivocal statement of those concepts which constitute the doctrine of the invisible church. A little further on in his sermon, he argued the absurdity of expecting entry to 'perfection' based on formal attachment rather than inward conversion.

> Let a soul be supposed actually adjoined to that glorious assembly and church above, that is yet unacquainted with God...such a soul will only seem to have mistaken its way, place, state and company...the outrage of its own lusts and passions would create to it a hell in the midst of heaven....[74]

When John Howe thought of the church, it was the invisible body that came to mind. This is most explicit in this sermon of 1695 but the same understanding underlay all of his contributions to the ecclesiological issues of the later Stuart period. It was the natural product of a theological orientation towards the spiritual, the transcendent, and Howe never departed from it.

In December 1697, Howe preached *A Sermon on Thanksgiving Day* or *Peace Considered as God's Blessing*,[75] marking the peace of Rijswick, negotiated by William III. This short discourse gives further evidence of his evolving outlook, propelled by the frustrations of his activist period of 1681 to 1695. The fundamental theology had changed little, but the focus had shifted considerably.

As clear as ever was Howe's commitment to immediate, spiritual experience. The thesis of the sermon was that, though civil and military peace was to be welcomed, it counted for little unless it was

---

73 Howe, *Funeral of Queen Mary*, 322.

74 Howe, *Funeral of Queen Mary*, 324-5.

75 J. Howe, *A Sermon Preached on Thanksgiving Day, December 2, 1697 [Peace Considered as a Blessing]* [London: 1697], *Works* III, 240-261.

accompanied by a renewal of 'substantial godliness'. Without this revival of religion, peace was merely 'external' and could not be rated a 'real and peculiar blessing'. Howe cited the example of Jabez (1 Chronicles 4:9-10) who asked for a 'blessing indeed'. In other words,

> let me have a blessing within a blessing; let me have that blessing whereof the other is but a cortex, the outside; let me have that blessing that is wrapt up and inclosed in the external blessing....There is a spiritual sort of blessing that may be enclosed in the external blessing, and particularly in this peace....[76]

This principle, applied initially to a specific situation, was rapidly made general. True value was in spiritual, rather than material, benefit. What Christians were to desire above all from God was an 'immediate, spiritual blessing'.

> Let us, I pray you, learn to distinguish between a self-desirable good, that in its own nature is such, so immutably that it can never degenerate, or cease to be such; and what is only such by accident, and in some circumstances may be much otherwise. Spiritual good, that of the mind and spirit, and which makes that better, especially that which accompanies salvation (Heb. vi. 9) that runs into eternity, and goes on with us into the other world, is of the former sort. External good is but *res media*, capable of being to us sometimes good, and sometimes evil, as the case may alter...the kindest and most benign part of the divine government lies in immediate influences on the minds of men.[77]

In such passages, Howe displayed, yet again, his attraction to the transcendent work of God. If anything, failure had strengthened, rather than weakened, this fundamental bias. Other things, however, *had* changed. Most notable was Howe's diminished confidence in institutional shows of unity.

> Men may, notwithstanding mere external peace, be as miserable in this and in the other world, as if they had never known it....Mere external peace, without [spiritual blessings] can never be a complete blessing.[78]

---

76 Howe, *Peace*, 251. The use of 'cortex' here provides another link with Henry More, Glanvill and the Platonism they shared with Howe. The *OED* identifies the first uses of 'cortex', in the sense of an 'outer shell or husk', in two works by More (1660 & 1681) and in Glanvill's *Scepsis Scientifica* (1665). This last is the same work which introduced 'idiosyncrasy' in the sense employed by Howe in *Union Among Protestants*.

77 Howe, *Peace*, 254.

78 Howe, *Peace*, 252.

In the final part of *Peace Considered as God's Blessing*, Howe directly addressed the failure of unity within the church. Not only did structural unity fail to deliver on its apparent promises, any unity short of total communion was a failure. Howe renounced half measures, which, in the past, he had accepted as the best available course.

> I also reckon it too low and narrow a design to aim at a oneness of communion among Christians of this or that single party and persuasion: which would but make so much the larger *ulcus* and *tumor*, a greater unnatural *apostem*, or secession, in the sacred body of our blessed Lord.[79]

This was an important critique. It reflected the evolution of Howe's own views. His own nearest formal success (the 'Happy Union') was limited to two groupings within dissent. It had met with failure. Further, Howe's statement of such views at this time (December, 1697) may be no coincidence. Horwitz' research suggests that 1696-7, in particular the autumn of 1697, saw yet another round of efforts towards a reconciliation with the Church of England among Presbyterians. It appears likely that John Humphrey and even Vincent Alsop reopened discussions with leading Anglican figures.[80] Congregationalists, on the other hand appear to have excluded themselves.[81] Given his espousal of unity and previous involvements in the cause, Howe might have been expected to feature alongside Humfrey and Alsop. Yet there is no evidence to connect him with these late manoeuvres. He seems to have moved away from piecemeal solutions. A unity both deeper and broader was necessary. 'Any serious living Christian of whatsoever party or denomination I ought to communicate with as such, and only as such [i.e., as a Christian].'[82]

But how was such a comprehensive unity to be achieved? Not by external measures certainly. Nor was it enough to rely upon reason and apparent goodwill.

> I cannot forget, that sometime discoursing with some very noted persons, about the business of union among Christians, it hath been freely granted me that there was not so much as a principle left...upon which to disagree; and yet the same fixed aversion to un-

79 Howe, *Peace*, 260.

80 H. Horwitz, 'Comprehension in the Later Seventeenth Century: A Postscript', *CH*, vol. 34, Sept, 1965, 342-349. Alsop's alleged involvement is intriguing, given his highly independent style of 'Presbyterianism'.

81 Horwitz, 'Comprehension', 345.

82 Howe, *Peace*, 260.

ion continued as before, as a plain proof they were not principles but ends we were still to differ for.[83]

Recent painful experience had shown that mere human efforts would amount to little. The achievement of full communion among Christians would require a dramatic alteration of the present state. This in turn could only result from an equally dramatic, 'internal blessing' of God. There were two principal elements in this blessing. The first was 'vital religion',

> wherein stands [Christians'] being at peace with God; when there is a mutual amplexus between him and them, mind touching mind, and spirit spirit; when he does, by his Spirit embrace the spirits of men, and infuse light and life into them, and adapt and suit them for his communion.[84]

The second flowed from, and into, the first: 'mutual love among Christians...to reconcile them to one another: which indeed, is also but to Christianize them, to make vital religion take place with them.'[85]

These were themes already noted in Howe's 1680s writings. The intense, unmediated, interpenetrative relationship with the divine and the dynamic power of charity were particularly evident in the most important work from that period, *Union Among Protestants*. In 1697, Howe was more explicit about the means of bringing this happy state about.

> To this purpose, we have great cause to beg and supplicate earnestly for a greater pouring forth of his Spirit....
>
> The matter speaks itself; that opposite spirit unto truly Christian peace and love, which appears amongst us, nothing but the Spirit of Christ can overcome; we are not to expect a cure of our distempers in this kind, but by the pouring forth of this blessed Spirit.[86]

In this way, in the final decade of Howe's life, cosmic eschatology reappeared as a major theme. Significant as this was in itself, it also supplies an important link. Eschatology serves as an enlightening point of comparison between Howe and Richard Baxter.

---

83 Howe, *Peace*, 258.

84 Howe, *Peace*, 256.

85 Howe, *Peace*, 257.

86 Howe, *Peace*, 256, 257.

CHAPTER 7

John Howe and Richard Baxter

When Dr William Bates died in 1699, the ageing John Howe, by then sixty-nine, was invited to preach the all-important funeral sermon. These were set piece occasions - opportunities to make trenchant religious points by appealing to the potent legacy of the deceased. The passing of his friend prompted Howe to bring together the themes of a disappointing decade. He concluded the sermon with a vision which combined sustained hope in God with pessimism about immediate success. 'Be it far from us to say, 'Let us die with him [Bates],' as despairing of our cause; if our cause be not that of any self-distinguished party, but truly that common Christian cause, of which you have heard.' The failures of the 1690s had chastened the optimistic architect of the 'Happy Union'. Now, though the dream of inclusive unity continued undimmed, it was overtly eschatological.

> When our confidences and vain boasts cease....then (and I am afraid, not till then) is to be expected a glorious resurrection, not of this or that party, for living, powerful religion, when it recovers, will disdain the limits of a party....Then will all the scandalous marks and means of division among Christians vanish….Then...will that Almighty Spirit so animate and form this body, as to make it every where amiable, self-recommending and capable of spreading and propagating itself, and to increase with the increase of God. Then shall the Lord be one, and his name one, in all the earth.[1]

Repeated and increasing reference to the sovereign work of the Holy Spirit as the means by which unity might be achieved was a feature of Howe's statements in the later 1690s. This attention to the place of the Spirit is in itself unremarkable. Geoffrey Nuttall has traced a logical continuity of views of the work of the Holy Spirit across the puritan spectrum. Likewise, Richard Greaves has asserted for the same groups that 'virtually every aspect of the Christian life was linked to the work

---

1 J. Howe *A Funeral Sermon for that Most Excellent Minister of Christ, the Truly Rev. William Bates, D.D., Works* III, 428-457, 456-7.

of the Spirit'.[2] But by the late 1690s Howe was giving particular attention to the role of the Spirit in the consummation of the purposes of God. From out of disillusionment with the schemes of himself and others, pneumatic Christian hope emerged as a major theme. Importantly, this was neither an escape to apocalypticism nor a retreat to quietism. On the one hand, Howe disliked fantastic schemes and, on the other, he never dismissed the value of active effort. In his 1698 sermon on *The Duty of Civil Magistrates*, he had insisted on strenuous involvement in society by Christians. Neither was the stress on hope a new theme for Howe. Early in the decade he had preached at length on the role of hope in personal faith. Specifically eschatological hope had appeared in his preaching much earlier. That no new treatise on eschatology appeared in the 1690s is no surprise. Howe's increasing dependence on the cosmic work of the Spirit of God was less a traumatic lurch than a fresh appreciation of an established and integral part of his theological framework.

In a series of sermons on *Ezekiel* preached in 1667-8, Howe had set out a detailed pneumatic eschatology. In the 1680s his focus had shifted. In those difficult years of pressure on dissent he had expounded on the principal qualities of life in his vision of the end: unity and charity. In the early 1690s he and others had their opportunity to build at least an attenuated spiritual Jerusalem on earth. They had failed. Howe was forced back on first principles. In the second half of the decade the focus of his hopes returned to the outpouring of the Holy Spirit. He did not have to reinvent his eschatology; he merely dusted it off. This change of focus, born out of disillusionment, nevertheless confirms the importance of key themes, already identified in Howe's theology. It provides a useful context for a detailed comparison of Howe and his most quoted older contemporary.

7.1 Richard Baxter and 'Baxterisation'

For three hundred years, the scholarly study of Restoration nonconformity has suffered from the occluding effects of 'Baxterisation'. No other individual has received the attention accorded Richard Baxter. The leading exponents are currently William Lamont and N.H. Keeble.[3] However, studies devoted to Baxter are but the tip of an

---

2 See Nuttall, *Holy Spirit, passim*; R.L. Greaves, *John Bunyan and English Nonconformity* (London: Hambledon Press, 1992), 1-35, 28. Greaves cites Howe's 1677-8 sermons as a prime example of how this was worked out in nonconformist divinity.

3 In addition to several articles, Lamont has published two books employing Baxter as a means of interpreting the Interregnum (*Godly Rule: Protestant Im-*

historiographical iceberg. Works which touch on the period are replete with entries for him, far eclipsing his important Interregnum rival, John Owen.[4] Other notable nonconformist figures, such as Milton and Bunyan, are studied more for their literary legacies than for their immediate influence on the history of English dissent.

Baxter's prominence is not without basis. He was a crucial, though ultimately destabilising, figure in negotiations towards the Church settlement in 1660-1. His desire for a broad comprehension led him to maintain numerous contacts within the established Church. He was unquestionably the pivotal figure in relations between Church and dissent in the 1660s and 1670s. His influence extended to the Presbyterians in Ireland, where it lingered long after his death.[5] However, his later significance in the English scene has been exaggerated. The signal fact that all of Baxter's Restoration schemes failed has been quietly ignored. From the late 1670s, comprehension was eclipsed by toleration as the central concern of nonconformists. Baxter's star faded with it. A powerful voice in the turbulent middle decades of the century, his theological concerns became dated and increasingly marginalised. As he died in 1691, he had no direct role in the affairs of dissent in the crucial decade of the 1690s.

Despite this unmistakable decline in influence, Baxter's shadow has been stretched to the end of the seventeenth century and beyond. This feature of the historiography may be prosaically explained: Baxter wrote a lot. His polemical fecundity and extensive correspondence have produced an incomparable record. The autobiographical *Reliquiae Baxterianae* has been trawled for pungent comment since its first publication in 1696. Indeed, the lack of a modern edition of the full available text of this hugely important work is one of the major documentary lacunae in early modern historiography. Yet it is doubtful whether Baxter ever embodied in his person the aims and aspirations of wider dissent. In many ways an

---

perialism and the English Revolution (London: Macmillan, 1969) and the later Stuart period (*Richard Baxter and the Millennium,* 1979). He has more recently edited Baxter's *A Holy Commonwealth* (Cambridge: CUP, 1994). Keeble is author of a literary biography (*Richard Baxter: Puritan Man of Letters,* 1982) and, with another 'Baxterian', G.F. Nuttall, has calendared Baxter's letters (*Calendar of the Correspondence of Richard Baxter,* 2 vols., 1991).

4 An example of this is Watts' respected work *The Dissenters*. Watts' index devotes seventeen lines to Baxter. John Howe is not mentioned at all.

5 In 1667 Baxter and others were consulted on occasional communion by Presbyterians in Dublin. Typically, Baxter made his own reply, stressing his unique combination of pastoral discipline and catholicity. He remained a respected figure into the 1690s. See Greaves, *God's Other Children,* 201-2; Kilroy, *Protestant Dissenters,* 44.

eccentric figure, he was never universally accepted as leader or prime representative by English nonconformists. Others played roles just as decisive at crucial moments. It will be argued in the next chapter that, as dissent stumbled into the eighteenth century, the irenic voice of John Howe was to be heard as often as the remembered polemical tones of Baxter. Howe met with his own failures but, as a younger man coming to prominence in the 1680s and 1690s when Baxter was imprisoned or in failing health, he was in a position to forge elements of a new post-Toleration movement which Baxter would hardly have recognised.

In *Richard Baxter and the Millennium,* William Lamont has attempted to reconstruct the development of Baxter's theology. As the title of his study suggests, Lamont argues that a hitherto unrecognised eschatological framework provides the key to understanding the sometimes baffling and apparently contradictory positions taken by Baxter at various points in his long career. Though neither Baxter nor Howe was associated with the more dramatic millennial movements such as the Fifth Monarchists, each had a sophisticated understanding of God's cosmic purpose. A comparison of their views on this and related issues sheds important light on their ideas of the church.

Lamont identifies three stages in Baxter's career. These are delineated by changes in Baxter's attitude to the idea of a 'national church'. The first and longest period ran from 1649 (the year of Baxter's first publication, the *Aphorismes of Justification,* a work admired by Howe[6]) until about 1676-7. In this period, Baxter favoured a national church supported by a strong civil magistracy. From 1677 to about 1683, he moved away from that ideal, only to return to it with even greater enthusiasm from the middle 1680s until his death.

Several features of Baxter's early national church vision are notable. The dominant concern was for Christian 'discipline'. This was the task of the pastor: to train and direct in godliness. For the effort to be effective, the role of the magistrate was crucial. He would protect the church, perhaps regulate its national affairs. All-importantly, civil authority would support, through enforcement where necessary, the local pastor. Support, but not usurp. Lamont points out that Baxter was no Erastian, in the sense in which the church is fully subject to civil authority. Pastors should avoid politics but in turn should be free to carry out their own allotted responsibility. As Lamont puts it, 'Baxter did not see the authority of the civil magistracy as a *rival* to clerical discipline, but as its *prerequisite*.'[7] A pastoral sphere of influence was thus

---

6 See Howe's first recorded letter to Baxter, March 12, 1657.

7 Lamont, *Richard Baxter,* 174.

created and preserved. In his 1659 *Holy Commonwealth* Baxter described the relationship thus:

> Magistrates and Pastors having different kinds of Power, must exercise their several Powers on one another: So that the Magistrate is the Pastors Ruler by the sword, and the Pastor is the Magistrates Pastor and Ruler by the Word.[8]

At the 1661 Savoy Conference he would seek, but fail to secure, the retention of the pastor's disciplinary control over admission to 'the Lord's table', confirmation and baptism.[9]

This feature of Baxter's ecclesiology remained constant through his career. Ironically it was this very consistency which limited the usefulness of his ideas in the rapidly changing environment facing English nonconformity. It was a vision little different from that contained in *The Form of Church Government to be used in the Church of England and Ireland*, passed by the Long Parliament in 1647. Baxter's sustained importance in Ireland reflected the very different context of the English and Scottish Presbyterians there, among whom discipline was able to be exercised and remained a strong theme.[10]

The roots of Baxter's authoritarian ecclesiology lay deep in the 1640s. His experience during the civil wars and his contact with radical sectaries engendered in him a dread of anarchy and its spiritual parallel, antinomianism.[11] His concern for discipline was one result. Indeed, he came to regard the question of discipline as a key issue underlying the conflict. His respect for magistracy was another. From this, in turn, flowed a third: a hatred of 'popery'. Significantly, to Baxter, the principal threat of Catholicism was the opposite to that of Erastianism. Instead of a secular authority ruling the church, the danger was that Roman ecclesiastics would come to rule the English nation-state. He decried as 'the way to bring in popery' suggestions that 'the Magistrate

---

8 Baxter, *A Holy Commonwealth,* Thesis 249, 167. In a 1656 letter to Edward Harley M.P. (1624-1700) Baxter had suggested how this parallel relationship between magistrate and pastor might be achieved under the Protectorate - Baxter to Harley, 15 September 1656, *Baxter Corr.* i, 226 (Keeble, *Calendar,* no. 324).

9 See Wood, *Church Unity,* 214-7; also E.C. Ratcliff, 'The Savoy Conference' in G.F. Nuttall and O. Chadwick (eds.), *From Uniformity to Unity 1662-1962* (London: Epworth, 1962), 89-148 *passim.*

10 See Greaves, *God's Other Children,* 233-241; Kilroy, *Protestant Dissenters passim.*

11 The significance of the fight against antinomianism in Baxter's career has been traced by Tim Cooper in his thesis 'Richard Baxter and Antinomianism'(University of Canterbury, New Zealand, 1997), recently published as *Fear and Polemic in Seventeenth Century England* (Aldershot: Ashgate, 2001).

should have no power in all matters of Gods Worship, Faith and Conscience'.[12]

A fourth, eschatological dimension entered in the protectorate of Richard Cromwell, when Baxter glimpsed the possibility of a 'Holy Commonwealth' in England. Lamont makes much of this, arguing that the vision 'owed most of all to the sense in which Baxter shared in the millenarian excitement of the age.' This is stating the case too strongly. In the same paragraph Lamont concedes that Baxter had little to say on the apocalypse at this time.[13] The key lies elsewhere.

Though the expectations of 1659 were dashed with the fall of the Protectorate and the subsequent Restoration, the other elements of Baxter's national church ecclesiology survived well into Charles II's reign. He continued to seek comprehension of nonconformists within the established Church. Properly modified (perhaps along lines proposed by Archbishop Ussher), even an episcopal system could promote discipline.[14] However, as the clouds of Restoration crisis gathered and doubts about the succession grew, Baxter's confidence waned. The established Church seemed to him to be drifting towards Rome. Discipline could not thrive in such conditions. His fear of popery turned cannibalistic; he now questioned the value of the magistrate. Indeed, in a series of works from this 'crisis' period Baxter argued *against* the national church (at least, in the form of the 'new prelacy' promoted in the Church of England) and flirted with the 'sect type' model of church structure.[15] We have seen that this was certainly his position in 1680.

This apparent *volte face* did not last long. Baxter soon returned to a form of his earlier model. Lamont wants to link this recovery to investigations into the book of *Revelation,* whilst in prison in 1686. Nevertheless, he concedes that the swing back had begun by 1684. Baxter began to see that the sect model was an even greater threat to discipline than the flawed Church of England. The 'nightmare of fragmentation' forced him to reconsider.[16]

---

12 Baxter, *Holy Commonwealth* 22, 30-34, 41-47. See also *Baxter Treatises* vii, f. 300v.

13 Lamont, *Richard Baxter*, 202.

14 See e.g. the letter to Harley, 15 September, 1656. Baxter's willingness to contemplate a form of Episcopacy is a central thesis in Wood's study - see Wood, *Church Unity, passim*; also Keeble *Richard Baxter*, 26-7; Lamont, *Richard Baxter*, 212-3.

15 See R. Baxter, *Church History of the Government of Bishops and their Councils Abbreviated* (1680) *A treatise of Episcopacy* (1681); *A Second True Defence of Meer Nonconformists* (1681); *The True History of Councils Enlarged* (1682). See also Keeble, *Richard Baxter*, 117-121; Lamont, *Richard Baxter*, 248-9.

16 Lamont, *Richard Baxter*, 259-261.

Baxter's millennial investigations did, however, provide a crucial plank. His description of the dispensations of history are telling

> As Moses was above Aaron & Solomon was above Abiathar, so is the King above the Archbishop....Christ's Kingdome was but in its infancy until he visibly ruled by the sword and by Christian Princes....So did he, by propheticall Apostles and inspired Teachers, keep up the Church until he had ripened it for a Christian Empire.[17]

The 'empire' was Constantine's, 'for it was at that historic point in time that Christ came to 'visibly reigne by Christian Rulers''.[18]

Lamont makes much of this development in Baxter's thought but overstates the case when he makes Baxter's prison eschatology the key to the resurgence of his 'protestant imperialism' or national church ecclesiology. The real issue for Baxter was always discipline. At no stage did he resile from this ideal. If the national church model and the magistracy as they operated in the late 1670s failed to promote that goal, both could be questioned. In the 1680s, it was his perception that the sect approach was even worse which drove him back to his earlier position. His reading of *Revelation* may have rehabilitated a crucial element of his national church model but it was the need for discipline which drove his ecclesiology.[19]

7.2 Varieties of Eschatology

Although Lamont overstates the importance of millennialism, the framework he suggests for Baxter's ecclesiology is very helpful. The categories he identifies make Baxter's ideas a potent foil to those of John Howe. The principal elements of Baxter's national church ecclesiology were four: discipline, magistracy, anti-popery and eschatology. In the final decade of his life, Howe touched directly on the last three. I will argue that the considerable differences which may be observed on these fronts signal a radical divergence on the first. More importantly, the contrast between the visions of Richard Baxter and John Howe points to a fundamental difference in theological approach. I shall consider the four categories in reverse order, beginning with eschatology.

Christian formulations of how God will consummate his relationship with creation have been notoriously complex and varied. Lamont identifies four major strands in seventeenth-century England: radical

---

17 *Baxter Treatises*, vii, f 300v.

18 Lamont, *Richard Baxter*, 263. The reference is to Constantine's conversion in 312.

19 For Baxter, it was the pastor/congregation relationship which constituted the church - See Baxter's *Answer* to Stillingfleet 43-4 and *Baxter Treatises* vi, ff 317-319.

millennialism, preterism, historicism and futurism.[20] The first depended heavily on a terrestrial rule by Christ for 1000 years. Common in extreme groups like the Fifth Monarchists and the Diggers, it typically declared an imminent commencement of Christ's reign and the creation of a holy and just society. This view depended upon association of the imagery of biblical passages from Daniel and Revelation with events and people of the present and immediate past. It was the strand which most properly deserved the description 'millennialist'.[21] By contrast, the 'preterist' interpretation, favoured by Roman scholars, located the fulfilment of the prophecies in the early years of the church. Apocalyptic images were effectively separated from the *eschaton* altogether, allowing a concentration on the Catholic church's continuing role in representing Christ on earth. The third, 'historicist' schema located the commencement of a 'flourishing time' (rather than a 'millennium') in the past. A precise, 1000 year duration was not essential. Christ's sovereignty was held to be extended by a gradual process rather than a crisis. In England, classic expression was given to this view by John Foxe (1516-1587).[22] The fourth version, 'futurism', postponed fulfilment of prophecies to the very end of time. Richard Baxter held a modified historicist view; John Howe propounded a type of the futurist interpretation.

In 1659 Baxter confessed to being confused over the details of eschatology.[23] Nevertheless, in the 1680s, influenced by Foxe, he developed a variation of the historicist view quite different from those of his friends. In most protestant versions, the Antichrist was identified with the papacy. Baxter was ambivalent on this issue; his hatred of popery was grounded elsewhere. More important was Baxter's dating scheme. Protestants had generally looked back to the first two centuries of the church as a golden period which declined rapidly under the Constantinian Catholic church. In Baxter's version, the forces of Christ were identified in the ideal of the Christian emperor. The flourishing age *began* with Constantine. It was here that Baxter's prison research was decisive. He recognised that, in the age of Constantine, 'the Church had ripened into a Christian Empire'. In this, as will be seen, Baxter

20 Lamont, *Richard Baxter*, 11-13.

21 See Cohn's list of the characteristics of millennialist movements - N. Cohn, *The Pursuit of the Millennium: revolutionary millenarians and mystical anarchists of the Middle Ages* (London: Maurice Temple Smith, 1970), 13.

22 For the details of Foxe's schema and a critique of Lamont's interpretation see J. Olsen, 'Was John Foxe a Millenarian?', *JEH*, Vol. 45, No. 4, October 1994, 600-624.

23 Baxter, *Holy Commonwealth*, 133.

was closer to the arch-conformist Samuel Parker than to the main body of dissent.

Lamont lacks precision in his analysis of Baxter's eschatology. He frequently describes Baxter's formulation as 'amillennialist', yet in other places finds him merely locating the millennium in the past. The causes of this imprecision are not hard to identify. Lamont's broad expansion of the term 'millennium' to include any vision of 'Godly rule' is unhelpful and has been criticised.[24] As important in this case is his neglect of other aspects of the end. The 'millennium' does not exhaust Christian concepts of the *eschaton*. Such aspects as the defeat of the forces of Antichrist and the final judgement are also to be incorporated. Baxter was prepared to regard the millennium as past, whilst holding that the conflict with evil was not complete and that there was judgement still to come. This caused some consternation to his historicist friends, who expected the defeat of Antichrist to be complete by the end of the reign and judgement to coincide with the close of the millennium.[25] Baxter did not deny a millennium, and is thus poorly described as 'amillennial'. Nevertheless, his 'millennium' was wrapped up. He neither accepted its currency nor looked for it in the future. It thus played a minor formal role in his eschatology. However, as will be shown, his association of the millennium with Constantine had enormous implications for his ecclesiology.

When John Howe renewed his interest in the consummate activity of God, he did not propound a detailed, new schema. Instead, he alluded in various phrases to 'the effusion of the Spirit'. These were shorthand references to the type of pneumatic eschatology he had espoused in 1677-8. When those sermons are examined, marked differences from Baxter's understanding are readily apparent.

Howe eschewed the first three models mentioned above. He rejected the preterist approach, which claimed early fulfilment of the prophecies. The suggestion, for instance, that the figures of Gog and Magog may be identified with such as Antiochus Epiphanes was specifically dismissed.[26] Neither was the radical millennialist view endorsed. It has already been noted that, in his 1681 *Thoughtfulness for the Morrow*, Howe lamented the distracted reading of signs and portents which characterised such schemes. The same position is found in the 1677-8 sermons. Millennialist speculations signalled a greater interest in the 'circumstances of such an expected state, than [in] the substantials that

24 See Bernard Capp, 'GODLY RULE and English millenarianism', *P&P*, lii, (1971), 106-17 and 'The millennium and eschatology in England', *P&P*, lvii, (1972), 152-162; Olsen, 'Was John Foxe a Millenarian?', 619-624.

25 See Lamont, *Richard Baxter*, 55, 61-64, 305-6 and *passim*.

26 *Whole Works* V, 231-2.

do belong to the state itself'.[27] In an important passage, he listed those components of eschatological views which he found untenable.

> For my own part, I will not assert any of these following things. Either, *first,* That that thousand years doth precisely and punctually mean such a limited interval of time; however more probable it may seem that it doth so, and though it be confessed to do so by them that would have these things to be in the past. Nor, *secondly,* That Christ shall personally appear...at the battle of Armageddon; and that he shall personally reign afterwards upon the earth for a thousand years. Nor, *thirdly,* That there will be any resurrection before that time do commence...nor *fourthly,* That the happiness of that time shall consist in sensual enjoyments....And least of all, *fifthly,* That in this state of things the saints as such, shall have any power or right given them in the properties of other men; or that there shall be a disturbing and overturning of ranks and orders in civil societies.[28]

There could be no acceptance of the claims of the radical millenaries. The fourth and fifth propositions, in particular 'carry no other face, than of things to be abhorred and detested.'

If Howe was clear on his distaste for preterist and radical millennialist views, he was just as adamant in rejecting the historicist interpretations which Lamont suggests were favoured most by orthodox protestants. He linked the second proposition above to 'them that would have these things to be past'. Here he came directly against Baxter's views. Baxter looked at history and held it to be obvious that Constantine's conversion ushered in a golden era, no less than the 'reign of Christ'. Howe rejected such a view. His reasons are revealing. He argued that the 'millennium' would be recognised by Christians in 'first, the destruction of their external enemies; secondly, a very peaceful, composed united state of things among themselves; and thirdly, a very lively, vigorous state of religion.'[29]

Never in the history of Israel or the church had these conditions coincided. Specifically, 'there was in Constantine's time, and after, much of tranquillity, by the cessation of persecution from without; but there was less of the life and vigour and power of religion.'[30]

This points to a crucial difference between Baxter and Howe. Richard Baxter held the 'visible rule' by the Christian magistrate to be essential for the operation of discipline and, therefore, a prerequisite for holy living. Howe was not as confident.

---

27 *Whole Works* V, 224.

28 *Whole Works* V, 234.

29 *Whole Works* V, 232.

30 *Whole Works* V, 233.

> Experience hath done very much...to refute the folly of any such hope, that any external good state of things can make the church happy....There can be no good time in the church of God, without the giving of...his own Spirit. That, or nothing, must make the church happy.[31]

This was exactly the distinction Howe would later delineate in his preference for 'internal' above 'external' blessings. Baxter believed that the right civil conditions would help create the 'holy commonwealth'. For Howe the process was quite different. The 'happy time', the millennium, would be the direct result of the effusion of the Spirit.

> I conceive that thousand years to intend a very long…time, wherein the state and condition of the Church shall be peaceful and serene and happy; but especially…by a large communication of the Holy Ghost, that shall make men have very little mind to this world, and very little seek such a things as serving secular interests, and pleasing and gratifying their senses and sensual inclination….And that this state of things is not yet past.[32]

The last statement is crucial. The key point for Howe was that the 'happy time' had not yet occurred. He thus rejected historicist, along with preterist and radical millennialist eschatologies. Instead, he unequivocally propounded a 'futurist' schema. Lamont suggests this interpretation was favoured by some seventeenth-century Catholics because, by it, the Antichrist would not appear until the very end of time. The current papacy was thus let off the hook. For that very reason, Lamont suggests, it was not 'attractive to protestants'.[33] Yet, Howe (unquestionably not a papist) espoused an overtly futurist view as he concluded the argument of the first two sermons in the 1677-8 series.

> And therefore we have the thing first proposed I conceive in good measure cleared, that there is a state yet to come of very great tranquillity and prosperity to the church of God for some considerable tract of time.[34]

If Howe was unusual in propounding a futurist view, he was doubly so when the most obvious feature of his schema is recognised. Howe's eschatology was almost exclusively pneumatological. The bodily return of Christ did not feature. Neither did the associated events of tribulation and judgement play a significant role. The 'effusion of the Spirit' effectively replaced the 'second coming'. This was a notable departure from popular views. Its direct roots may be found in Howe's textual base. Whereas Baxter and most theologians of the *eschaton* seem

---

31 *Whole Works* V, 225.

32 *Whole Works* V, 234.

33 Lamont, *Richard Baxter*, 12.

34 *Whole Works* V, 236.

to have found the bulk of their source material in *Daniel* and *Revelation*, Howe based his description of the end upon *Ezekiel*, specifically 34:29: 'Neither will I hide my face any more from them; for I have poured out my Spirit upon the house of Israel, saith the Lord.' Although he occasionally cited both *Daniel* and *Revelation*, Howe kept coming back to this verse and its context for the framework of his eschatology.

Why did Howe take this path? Nuttall has argued that a 'spiritualised' eschatology is to be found among erstwhile Fifth Monarchists, whose expectation of material change faded with the passage of time.[35] This cannot have been Howe's history. There is no suggestion that he ever held such radical millennialist hopes. Nevertheless, the repristination of his eschatology was clearly linked to his personal disillusionment in the later 1690s. Futurist views may not have appealed to protestants in general but, as Christopher Hill has suggested, a postponement of the 'millennium' into the distant future seems to have been part of the response of Interregnum activists to defeat.[36] For similar reasons, a futurist eschatology may have had renewed attraction for Howe in the aftermath of his 1690s disappointments.

Whatever the external causes, the theological roots of Howe's pneumatological eschatology lay in his fundamental orientation towards transcendent divine activity. The member of the Trinity from whom such activity would naturally be expected is the Holy Spirit. When, in the later 1690's, John Howe returned to the eschatology of 1678 he was merely following a career-long path. The underlying feature of his theology, which has been identified numerous times, may be stated again. Howe's primary interest was in the internal, direct work of God. It was this bias which lay at the heart of the contrast between Howe and Baxter.

7.3 The Pope and the Magistrate

From their disparate eschatologies there flowed other differences. One, though not immediately apparent, was in their attitudes to the papacy. On the face of it, Baxter and Howe held quite similar views on Rome. Although both regarded Catholicism as anathema to the Christian cause, neither was keen to identify the papacy with the Antichrist in his eschatology. For Baxter, this was because he found the evidence for such an association unconvincing. To Howe, taking his prophetic cues from *Ezekiel*, the figure of Antichrist was not even a major symbol. His preferred personifications were Gog and Magog (Ezekiel 38:2). Even

---

35 Nuttall, *Holy Spirit*, 110-2.

36 C. Hill, *The Experience of Defeat*, 164, 318.

these apocalyptic figures he declined to identify with historical persons.[37]

What, then, lay behind the implacable opposition of both nonconformists to Catholicism? Baxter found the crime of the Papists to be their usurpation of the role of the magistrate. They dared to elevate the visible church in the form of ecclesiastical hierarchy above civil authority. This was an error wherever it manifested itself.

> And hereby the Glory of Christ's Kingdome as set up in Power, by Christian Emperors and Kings is clouded, and the sense of the Revelation perverted, by Papists and too many Protestants, who call for the exercise of Christ's Kingly office by a vile mistake as if it were only in the hands of pope, prelates, presbyters or popular congregations.[38]

The danger of popery (and some protestantism!) was thus visible. It threatened to check the flow of the power of God, immanent in the civil magistrate.

In contrast to Baxter's concerns, Howe was worried about the invisible effects of Catholicism. On Guy Fawkes' day, 1703, he preached *Deliverance from the Power of Darkness*. In this sermon he celebrated past deliverances from popery in the uncovering of the gunpowder plot and in the glorious revolution. The devil, he asserted, exerts power at two levels, 'first, spiritual and internal: secondly, secular and external'. Of these, the first was to be feared above the second and, consequently, 'it is manifestly a far greater deliverance to be freed from his spiritual power, and the horrid effects thereof, than from that which he may use in reference to our outward concernments.'[39] England, in being rescued from Catholicism, was delivered from the power of darkness at both levels. Explaining this, Howe passed very quickly over the external threat but dealt in some detail with the internal dangers. These consisted of certain doctrinal 'infatuations' (e.g. transubstantiation, apostolic succession) and, most damning of all, 'the monstrous degeneracy, not from Christianity only, but even from humanity too, that is to be found in the temper of their spirits'.[40]

Where Baxter feared for the magistrate, Howe was concerned with the direct effect of popery on the individual soul. 'Infatuation' with 'absurd' doctrines created, in turn, a need aggressively to defend those positions, turning 'reasonable creatures…into ravenous, wild beasts'.[41]

---

37 *Whole Works* V, 231-233.

38 *Baxter Treatises*, vii, f. 300v.

39 J. Howe, *Deliverance from the Power of Darkness*, (1703), *Works* III, 189-206, 193-4.

40 Howe, *Deliverance*, 198.

41 Howe, *Deliverance*, 199.

The greatest effect of this 'degeneracy' was to be seen in its impact on unity. Weaving in his favourite theme, Howe identified the ultimate threat of popery as the destruction of Christian communion. Full communion may be had only

> wheresoever the essentials of Christianity do not appear to be subverted by the addition of other things, that are inconsistent with any of those essentials: as is the case with them, whose black character hath been given in this discourse.[42]

The papacy was to be feared, not for its apocalyptic significance, but as an insidious threat to Christian unity. Thus, though at first glance Baxter and Howe seemed to be of one mind regarding Rome, it is clear they came to this shared abhorrence from different places. In Howe's terms, Baxter was above all concerned with the 'secular and external' power of this darkness. Howe himself declined to be frightened by such 'outward concernments'. The real battlefield, as always for him, was within.

Similar differences are found when a third element in Lamont's picture of Baxter's ecclesiology, the role of magistracy, is considered. Baxter's position has already been outlined sufficiently to require only brief restatement. By godly rulers, Christ ruled visibly. These magistrates supplied security and (when required) enforcement, to enable pastors to promote holy discipline.

As with the question of the papacy, an initial reading of Howe's view of magistrates suggests that he and Baxter were very close. As Nuttall points out, 'in Puritanism, what...springs from concentration on the doctrine of the Holy Spirit may be seen...as a concern with immediacy, as an insistence on the non-necessity of a *vehiculum* or medium.'[43] However, 'non-necessity' does not mean impossibility. In the 1678 sermons, Howe acknowledged two means by which the Spirit would operate in the 'happy time'.

> There is nothing that is so genuine and natural a product of the effusion of the Spirit, as the *life of religion* in the world. And it may be shewn, how the Spirit may have an influence to this purpose both *mediately* and *immediately*.[44]

The immediate operation of the Spirit was conceived in terms of its effects.

> When I say immediate, I do not mean, as if it did work without means; but that by the means it doth itself immediately reach its subject; and therefore, that all the operations of the Spirit, whether in

42 Howe, *Deliverance*, 203.

43 Nuttall, 'Holy Spirit', 102-103.

44 *Whole Works* V, 256.

> converting or in building up of souls, lie not in the instruments, but strike through all, so as to reach their subject.[45]

Ultimately, it was direct encounter with God through the Spirit, which brought about change. Nevertheless 'mediate' influences were acknowledged. Of these there were four principal cases:

1. 'kings and potentates',
2. 'ministers of the gospel',
3. 'family order' and
4. the example of 'serious and exemplary religion in the professors of it.'[46]

Never did Howe come closer to the heart of Richard Baxter. Magistrates, pastors, family life, exemplary living - all were crucial elements in Baxter's practical theology. Howe seemed to confirm the parallel when, in his 1698 *Sermon for the Reformation of Manners*, he described magistrates as 'gods among men'.[47] In this work, the theme of mediation (even amounting to general revelation) was again present.

> The magistrate is God's minister to men for their good. Next to the sweet airs and breathings of the gospel itself, where have we a kinder or more significant discovery of God's will to men?...This is, we find, another medium by which God testifies, or leaves not himself without witness, besides what we have elsewhere; that he gives men rain from heaven, and fruitful seasons.[48]

As magistrates were God's agents for good, Christians were to do more than submit to civil authority - they were actively to cooperate with it.

Reformation of Manners provides a useful reminder that, for all his predilection for immediate encounter, Howe was not abandoned to the concept. There was no room for Quaker-like civil disobedience.[49] Nevertheless, too much should not be made of his apparent closeness to Baxter on this point. Howe's entreaty to co-operate with the authorities was a response to Romans 13:4. Active compliance was to be less for dread than 'for conscience sake'. Indeed, *Reformation of Manners* was as much a treatise on the civil ramifications of following individual conscience as it was a defence of magistracy *per se*. It was precisely because of the individual's reverence for God that he would be eager to obey those who exercised a divine commission.

---

45 *Whole Works* V, 265-6.

46 *Whole Works* V, 254-262.

47 J. Howe, *A Sermon for the Reformation of Manners* (1698), *Works* III, 262-280, 269.

48 Howe, *Reformation of Manners*, 268.

49 For instance, as Keeble points out, Howe and other 'Presbyterians' generally eschewed unauthorised publication - Keeble, *Literary Culture*, 112-3.

> It is the authority of God that he is invested with....What an awe this should lay upon our spirits! It is, therefore, to be served for conscience' sake, which hath principal reference to God. We need not here dispute whether human laws bind conscience; no doubt they do, when they have an antecedent reason or goodness.[50]

Howe deliberately avoided considering the opposite case, where human laws have no 'antecedent reason or goodness'. Baxter by contrast was prepared to accept even tyranny in preference to anarchy.[51] Moreover, the bulk of Howe's case was directed to 'the grand precept first laid down' - in other words, the *ideal* of magistracy. This was no accident. An important distinction between Baxter and Howe on the magistracy is evident when their eschatologies are added to the picture. Baxter's case had to deal with the realities of history. As has been shown, his 'millennium' was already in the past. Howe, when he acknowledged the mediating role of the magistrate in 1678, was relating a vision for the future. Magistrates, pastors, families and exemplary Christians would be effective only with the benefit of the 'effusion of the Spirit'. That 'effusion' was still awaited in 1698. Overt eschatology was absent from *Reformation of Manners*, but the thrust of the argument remained limited to the as yet unrealised ideal.

7.4 Discipline and Peace

A further difference related to the pastoral role itself. For Baxter, ministers were figures crucial to the development of the 'holy commonwealth' for 'making them indeed Divine, is the first thing in the making a Common wealth divine.'[52] If released to get on with the role of discipline, pastors were truly effective. In 1656, Baxter had sought for himself merely to be freed for 'Church guidance and that little part of Discipline which I exercise'.[53] Two decades later, in 1678, Howe had little such faith in the efforts of ministers.

> It is plain, too sadly plain, there is a great retraction of the Spirit of God even from us: we know not how to speak living sense unto souls, how to get within you: our words die in our mouths, or drop and die between you and us. We even faint, when we speak; long experienced unsuccessfulness makes us despond: we speak not as

50 Howe, *Reformation of Manners*, 276.

51 R. Baxter, *A Christian Directory* (1673) in *Richard Baxter's Practical Works* (London, 1990), vol. 1, esp. 722-745. See also Lamont, *Richard Baxter*, 235.

52 Baxter, *Holy Commonwealth*, 145.

53 Baxter to Harley, 15 September, 1656.

> persons that hope to prevail, that expect to make you serious, heavenly, mindful of God, and to walk more like christians.[54]

The difference in mood was, of course, partly due to the reverses of the years which had passed since Baxter's *Holy Commonwealth*. By 1678, Baxter too had grown disillusioned with some parts of his national church vision. The efficacy of pastoral discipline was, however, the notable exception. It was precisely because effective discipline was impossible in the prevailing climate that Baxter toyed with Independency. This could never have been more than a short-lived flirtation. In Baxter's scheme, pastoral discipline depended upon the exercise of the parallel authorities of magistrate and pastor. He expected civil back-up to pastoral discipline. In contrast, even in his age of the Spirit, Howe never extended the function of the magistrate into spiritual affairs beyond encouragement and example. Further, Baxter accorded considerable authority to the pastor himself. As Lamont puts it, 'the neglect of ministerial *rule* was as grave as the neglect of preaching.'[55] Although following ejection he would speak of discipline to John Wilkins and as late as 1680 would cite parochial reformation as a necessary prerequisite for comprehension, Howe made nothing of discipline and control in his published works. The only 'authority' which the pastor might gain with the Spirit was the limited power to persuade.[56] Indeed, the anticipation of the Spirit's effusion should temper the aggression of pastors towards their flocks.

> Our experience shews us, alas! It is not this or that external frame of things, that can mend our case…And to have a disposition to be continually making attempts, wherein we are sure to be disappointed, and can bring about nothing, so that we shall but traffic for the wind; it is but to add mockery, to the torment of our disease….We shall deliver ourselves and the world about us from a great deal of inconvenience, if once this be but understood…that we only expect the Spirit of the blessed God to change the state of things in the world, and to make it better and more favourable unto the religion of serious christians.[57]

Considerable differences can, then, be observed between the ecclesiologies of Richard Baxter and John Howe. These in turn signal

54 *Whole Works* V, 257.

55 Lamont, *Richard Baxter*, 167. See esp. the 'Preface' to 'Richard Baxter's Confession of his Faith' (London: 1655)

56 *Whole Works*, V, 257-8. Howe questioned the likelihood of success even in this venture. In the 1683 *Union Among Protestants* he was very cautious about attempts at persuasion. In his 1699 sermon on Bates' death he confessed 'our very sermons are lost upon most' - *Works* III, 442.

57 *Whole Works* V, 258.

differences in the ultimate concerns and fundamental theological biases of these men. As argued above, Richard Baxter's ecclesiology was consistently driven by the importance he placed on discipline. The goal of this discipline was holiness, which Baxter prized above all. This was recognised by a critic of Baxter's national church model, the Dean of Durham, Thomas Comber (1645-1699), who in 1691 wrote: 'it is *Peace* I perceive you would have, but *Holiness* more'.[58] Comber hit the nail on the head. As Lamont concedes, 'if a 'National Church' meant no more than *peace* Baxter would not have been interested. The argument for Baxter was not over whether a 'National Church' secured *peace*, but over whether it secured *holiness*.'[59]

Howe too was concerned with holiness, though he regarded peace in a different light. Holiness would arise naturally, not from mere discipline, but from the action of the Holy Spirit. The key product of this action would be love and its concomitant, peace. From out of these basic Christian characteristics, holiness would automatically flow. For both Baxter and Howe 'peace' was a prerequisite for holiness. Yet, whereas Baxter conceived of a peace enforced in the civil realm, for Howe it was the fruit of the internal, regenerative power of the Spirit.

Peace almost defined holiness, indeed Christianity itself, for Howe. In the 1678 sermons, it was the principal sign of the effusion of the Spirit. Conversely, in 1693, he linked its absence with 'carnality' - 'as the Christian church hath grown more carnal, it hath grown more contentious; and as more contentious, still more and more carnal'.[60] Although many did not address the topic directly, all Howe's works from the 1690s turned at some point to the question of unity. The message was clear: 'The more truly catholic the communion of Christians is, it is the more truly Christian.'[61]'To reconcile [Christians] to one another...is also but to Christianize them.'[62] Always this unity was conceived in invisible, spiritual terms, 'mere external peace…can never be a complete blessing.'[63] Outward uniformity was certainly not Howe's goal: 'I must avow it to all the world, it is not this or that external form I so much consider in the matter of Christian union and communion, as what spirit reigns in them with whom I would associate myself.'[64]

---

58 Thomas Comber, *Union Pursued* (1691), 12-13 - cited in Lamont, *Richard Baxter*, 274.

59 Lamont, *Richard Baxter*, 274.

60 Howe, *Carnality*, 112.

61 Howe, *Deliverance*, 203.

62 Howe, *Peace*, 257.

63 Howe, *Peace*, 252.

64 Howe, *Union Among Protestants*, 183.

Howe's theology depended upon his bias to the invisible, the transcendent, the spiritual arena. Baxter allowed a greater role for the mediated power of God. In chapter four it was shown that among the nonconformists who responded to Stillingfleet in 1680 Baxter and Howe were a considerable distance apart. Baxter's vision for the church depended less on the concept of the invisible church than did those of Howe and Vincent Alsop. If this was true for 1680 when (if Lamont is right in his argument) Baxter was in the middle of a brief period in which he was more sympathetic to the 'sect-type' model generally favoured by invisiblists, it was doubly so for Baxter's main line of thought. As Lamont's analysis implies, and the evidence in this chapter demonstrates, for the bulk of his career Baxter was even further away from Howe in his fundamental ecclesiology than the 1680 controversy suggests.

7.5 Baxter and Radical Dissent

Two further pieces of evidence may be cited to support this view of Baxter. The first is his concern to establish some visibility for the 'true' church. In 1660 he published *The Successive Visibility of the Church,* a defence of protestant claims to visible continuity.[65] In 1684 he was making a similar point when, returning to his national church model, he criticised the sect approach.

> This opinion must needs make men seekers, who say, that the church was in the wilderness, and lost all true Ministry...after the first...century...And consequently we have no wiser answer to the Papist [challenge (where was your church before Luther?)] than to say that it was *Invisible;* that is, that we cannot prove that there was any such thing on earth.[66]

Such passages do not imply that Baxter rejected the basic protestant view that the 'true' church was the invisible communion of the saints. What they do show is the importance he consistently placed on corporate, institutional visibility. In John Howe, such a concern was much less evident.

Further support for a more visiblist interpretation of Baxter comes from the intriguing parallels between his ideas and those of the virulent anti-dissenter, Samuel Parker. The association initially seems bizarre, but Baxter was closer to Parker than has hitherto been acknowledged. Lamont recognises, but hurriedly discounts, any real similarity. 'Baxter was not a Samuel Parker or a Roger L'Estrange. His

65 R. Baxter, *The Successive Visibility of the Church* (London: 1660).

66 R. Baxter, *Whether Parish Congregations be True Christian Churches* (London: 1684), 27.

support for the magistrate on the throne stemmed from his principles, not from his lack of them.'[67] This is both to slight and to misunderstand Parker and to miss the significance of evidence Lamont himself cites. Interesting parallels between Baxter and Parker are not lacking. On two occasions Baxter may be found rejecting arguments originally directed against Parker.[68] As in Parker, much in Baxter's case for the 'unfettered authority of the magistrate' sounded like an argument from Thomas Hobbes. Both were, indeed, accused of 'Hobbism'.[69]

There are, moreover, more direct, intellectual parallels. The emphasis on immanence they shared produced at least two similar positions on seemingly unrelated issues. Both distinguished themselves from Hobbes precisely because he discounted providential, immanent divine activity in favour of a godless, mechanical determinism.[70] Further, in a particularly interesting parallel, both criticised excessive use of florid language and metaphor. Although this may seem an inconsequential, even eccentric, attitude, it was one they shared with Hobbes. Baxter and Parker, however, were merely being true to their immanentalist theology. One result of a stress on divine immanence was to place greater value on the apparently ordinary. As God is present in the most commonplace of objects and situations, immanentalism led naturally to an elevation of the mundane. The obverse of this could be a suspicion of the florid and overwrought. This negative reaction is what explains the objection of both Parker and Baxter to complicated imagery and analogy. Parker called for metaphor to be outlawed.[71] Baxter asserted that

> the plainest words are the profitablest oratory in the weightiest matters. Fineness is for ornament, and delicacy for delight; but they answer not necessity though sometimes they may modestly attend that which answers it.[72]

---

67 Lamont, *Richard Baxter*, 93.

68 Baxter counselled John Humfrey against publishing *A Case for Conscience* (1669) which was largely addressed against Parker's *Ecclesiastical Polity* - see Baxter to Humfrey (undated), *Baxter Corr.* iii, 11-12 & ii, 108 (Keeble, *Calendar*, no 766). He also rejected the quite different arguments of Henry Dodwell as set out in the latter's *Two Letters of Advice* (Dublin: 1672). - see R. Baxter, *An Answer to Mr Dodwell and Dr Sherlocke* (1682) esp. 70-89. Importantly, in the Dodwell case the key issue was discipline. Lamont cites both these instances - *Richard Baxter*, 223, 230.

69 Lamont, *Richard Baxter*, 103-4.

70 On Parker in this regard, see G.J. Schochet, 'Between Lambeth and Leviathan', 201. On Baxter see Lamont, *Richard Baxter*, 140-142.

71 Parker, *Discourse of Ecclesiastical Politie*, 75-6.

72 R. Baxter, *A Treatise of Conversion* (1657) in *Richard Baxter's Practical Works* (London: 1990), vol. 2, 397-500, 399. On this aspect of Baxter's style see Kee-

Baxter was not merely a nonconformist Parker. Parker had virtually no place for immediate contact with the divine. He was totally committed to the immanent operation of God's authority through the magistrate. It is his radical consistency in this regard which makes him difficult for modern interpreters to fathom. Baxter departed from this in two ways. Firstly he was not as exclusively dedicated to immanence. His concern for individual holiness signalled a deep interest in personal religion which went beyond Parker's definition of religion as virtue.[73] The greatest reservation Baxter had about the national church idea was his fear of admitting to communion those who lacked this personal commitment. Secondly, unlike Parker who seated authority solely in the magistrate, Baxter preserved an oasis of ecclesiastical immanence in the discrete function he reserved for the pastor. Nonetheless, despite these important differences, the similarities between the two men are striking.

Howe and Baxter, on the other hand, represented two fundamentally different theological styles within mainstream dissent. The significance and extent of this diversity has not fully been recognised. Studies of Restoration theology have tended to describe nonconformist theology as an undifferentiated whole. Yet, in fact there was a dynamic development on crucial fronts as the later Stuart age progressed. The result was an increasingly complicated ecclesiological map.

Anglican High-Churchmen such as Thorndike and Henry Dodwell (1641-1711) found divine activity to be immanent in the institutions and hierarchies of the visible church. Individual conscience was not trustworthy, magisterial authority must not impinge upon the proper functions of the church. Only to this approach, with its radical dependence on ecclesiastical structures may be properly attached the label 'visiblist'. By contrast, the 'Constantinian' view, of which Samuel Parker was the prime example, did not locate God's immanent activity in ecclesiastical structures. Instead it found God working primarily through the magistrate. Within conformist thought there were variations on these themes. As has been shown, Edward Stillingfleet and John Tillotson employed moderate versions of the visiblist and Constantinian views respectively.

In mainstream dissent there was a similar degree of variation. In general, nonconformist ecclesiology tended to stress the invisible church. Richard Baxter was an important exception. Though he had a lively sense of personal religion he called for a national church, ac-

---

ble, *Richard Baxter*, 48-54; Lamont, *Richard Baxter*, 140-1.

73 'And all true Religion can consist in nothing else but either the Practice of Vertue it self, or the use of those Means and Instruments that contribute to it.' Parker, *Ecclesiastical Politie*, 69.

corded an authoritarian role to the pastor and was prepared to accept a modified episcopacy. Most intriguingly, Baxter placed great value on the magistrate as the means by which Christ 'visibly reigns'. That he thus located immanence primarily in civil authority is of enormous importance. His close friendship with Tillotson and the conceptual links with Parker become explicable. If a pivotal figure is to be found in the confusion of ecclesiological ideas which followed the Restoration, Richard Baxter is surely a candidate. This made him a key individual in the first decades, when comprehension might have been possible. But his incorporation of Constantinian immanentalism, ecclesiastical visiblism and intense puritan piety was uncommon, probably unique. It is this very singularity which casts doubt on his legitimacy as a representative of dissent in general.

Baxter represents the opposite case to that of John Locke. Locke was a radical innovator whose heterodoxy reduced his immediate impact of dissent. By contrast, there was no doubting Baxter's doctrinal orthodoxy, but he was no innovator. His ecclesiology was forged in the Interregnum. By the 1680s, new challenges, requiring different solutions, were pressing upon dissent. In the next chapter I will question the conventional reliance on Baxter as a guide to nonconformist ideas. I will argue that we must go beyond Baxter, to include divines like John Howe, if we are fully to understand the dynamics of later Stuart dissent. Howe called for peace, toleration and unity, but his personal vision was fractured from within, compromised by its own inadequacies. The relegation by Howe and others of 'mere external peace' would be an important factor in the decay of dissent.

CHAPTER 8

'Moderate Nonconformity'

If John Howe was a key figure in the 1690s, his influence over the theology of dissent in the ensuing decades would also be profound. His irenic ecclesiology enabled nonconformity to enjoy a degree of comfort within the legal, political and religious framework of England following the Act of Toleration. It was, however, an evanescent solution, eventually overwhelmed by unresolved tensions. The dissenting interest was decaying from within.

8.1 Occasional Conformity

The Act of Toleration was little more than an Indulgence, and freedoms under it were always tenuous. Earlier restrictive legislation continued. Particular problems were caused by the sacramental requirements of the Test and Corporations Acts. Dissenters who sought some official offices were required to establish a level of conformity. The high churchman Henry Sacheverell denounced such aspirants as 'double-dealing practical atheists'.[1] Attacks from outside were one thing; ultimately more corrosive were divisions within dissent. The issue highlighted internal tensions which within two decades would bring schism.

Objections to occasional conformity drew from Howe a final entry into controversy. Sir Thomas Abney, Lord Mayor of London in 1700, was a regular at Howe's congregation and an occasional conformist. Daniel Defoe, in the middle of a polemical binge which would end with his imprisonment on charges of sedition, challenged Howe to account for his acceptance of Abney's practice. Implicit in Defoe's criticism was an assault on Howe's own integrity. Howe replied in *Some Consideration of a Preface to an Inquiry Concerning The Occasional Conformity of Dissenters*, in which he summarised the attitude he had

1 Cited by G.S. Holmes, *The Trial of Doctor Sacheverell* (London: Eyre Methuen, 1973), 54.

taken to such matters throughout his career.[2] This work depended in large part on the recollections of an old man seeking to justify himself. It was, by Howe's standards at least, an unusually polemical work. The pamphlet nevertheless displayed the crucial components of Howe's mature ecclesiology.

The first was Christian love. In the 1680s Howe had developed a dynamic theology of charity, which formed the centrepiece of his case for unity. This was also evident in his 1702 recollection.

> [W]hen the love of God comes to govern the Christian Church, and reign in the hearts of men; then will the kingdom of God come in power. For I am sure the spirit of love is the spirit of power, and of a sound mind.[3]

Charity, the source of 'a sound mind', was more important than precision in small matters. It was what should determine attitudes to those who conform, even if conformist practices were held to be wrong.

> Wheresoever such a spirit appears of zeal against such and such external forms…of pride and self-esteem, for so contemptibly little things; of malice and cruelty, that they could persecute even to the death…or into strange countries, such as differ from them in things of no greater moment: I would sooner be of a fellowship with drunkards, or other sensualists…than with them; as much as I count a devil somewhat worse than a brute.[4]

In similar vein, Howe concluded his defence of occasional conformists with a parting shot at Defoe. 'Mr Prefacer, if your judgment on the case itself be true; I conceive that truth, accompanied with your temper and spirit, is much worse than their error.'[5]

Next was Howe's mitigated scepticism. In his reply to Stillingfleet in 1680 and, more directly, in *Union Among Protestants* in 1683, Howe called for tolerance of different views. In his reply to Defoe, he quoted a passage from the preface to his 1674 collection of Torrington sermons, *Delighting in God*, in which he signalled his epistemological caution.

> I have little reason to be conceited of any advantage I have of [those who differ from me] in point of knowledge...and can with the less confidence differ from them, or contend with them: being thereby,

2 J. Howe, *Some Consideration of a Preface to an Inquiry Concerning The Occasional Conformity of dissenters etc*, (1702), *Works* III, 536-552. On this clash with Defoe see Calamy, *Historical Account*, I, 464. See also P.R. Backscheider, *Daniel Defoe: His Life* (Baltimore: Johns Hopkins University Press, 1989), 84-105.

3 Howe, *Some Consideration of a Preface*, 547.

4 Howe, *Some Consideration of a Preface*, 546.

5 Howe, *Some Consideration of a Preface*, 552.

> though I cannot find that I err in these matters, constrained to have suspicion lest I do.[6]

Howe claimed, flowing from this caution, a deep respect for the decisions of others. 'Where is the man that can say I ever persuaded him to conform, or not to conform?'[7] Philosophical constraint in turn informed Howe's respect for sincerity. 'A sincere conscience is invulnerable'[8] to criticism and is, by nature, not open to scrutiny or judgement.

> If God have authorized you, and revealed to you, not only what was right or wrong, in the case itself, but the secrets of his heart whom you judge; and that he practised what he thought to be wrong....then hath he indeed set you over him...dignified you with an authority superior to what he ever conferred upon any apostle, or on the whole Christian church, or on any, beside his own Son.[9]

In 1680 Howe had accorded a central place to conscience. Again in 1702, the individual alone before God was the scene of divine encounter and, hence, true religion. The transcendent activity of God was the sole power to which Christians could respond.

> The matter were indeed easy, if (for instance) in a select gathered church...one conscience, or a few men's would serve the whole body; or, by parity of cases, of a whole parish or nation. But when we consider, that every one must give an account of himself to God; and that in matters which concern our own duty God-ward, we are no more capable of having it done by another for us, than...of being represented by another in the day of judgment; this will bring the matter with weight upon our own spirits, lest we should be found transgressors in Bethel, and to have offered strange fire, instead of a sacrifice, on the one hand; or needlessly, on the other, set on fire the temple itself.[10]

Here, in essence, was Howe's radically invisiblist ecclesiology. There was no mediation, no escape from direct contact with and responsibility to, the Spirit. It was a beguiling vision, though one with ramifications which Howe did not imagine. Intended as pleasing sacrifice it would contribute instead to events which would 'set on fire the temple itself'. This unanticipated outcome was not yet evident. Howe would not live to see it; on 2 April, 1705 he passed away

---

6 Howe, *Delighting in God*, 475-6, cited in Howe, *Some Consideration of a Preface*, 537.

7 Howe, *Some Consideration of a Preface*, 538.

8 Howe, *Some Consideration of a Preface*, 548.

9 Howe, *Some Consideration of a Preface*, 542.

10 Howe, *Some Consideration of a Preface*, 538.

at his home in London.[11] The influence of his approach to Christian unity, however, did not die with him. Indeed, Howe's ecclesiology already had a persuasive new champion.

8.2 Edmund Calamy and 'Moderate Nonconformity'

Roger Thomas has credited Edmund Calamy Jnr (1671-1732) with inaugurating 'an epoch in the evolution of dissent' in a series of works in 1703-5 which articulated a version of *Moderate Nonconformity*. Calamy's prescription placed emphasis firmly on individual conscience and congregational autonomy. The effect was twofold. First, the 'presbyterian' drive for a national structure was removed. Secondly, the Church of England could be portrayed as merely another Christian body with which nonconformist groups could happily coexist. Calamy thus at once dissipated the threat of sedition, perceived in nonconformity by the establishment, and liberated dissent to irenic engagement.[12]

Though Calamy was an important figure, his role was more pivotal than original. Crucially, his categories and concerns stood in the same line as Howe's. The connection has hitherto been missed. Both Roger Thomas and William Lamont have instead identified Richard Baxter's ecclesiology as the principal influence on Calamy's thought. This view may be challenged as a prime example of the effects of 'Baxterisation'. Both Thomas and Lamont manifest the presumption towards Baxter which has dominated the historiography of Stuart dissent. Their analyses, however, are quite different. According to Thomas, Baxter provided the essential positive foundation for Calamy's ecclesiology. By contrast, Lamont suggests that Calamy's concern was not to promote but rather to sanitize Baxter's ideas. Recognizing the significance of Baxter, Calamy was compelled to revise him in a manner which would support his own, rather different, ecclesiology. Nevertheless, for both Thomas and Lamont, Baxter is central. This is no small matter. I have argued that Baxter's importance in the history of dissent has been exaggerated. Moreover, Baxter propounded an ecclesiology which was fundamentally different from that of Howe. Where Baxter's ecclesiology was discipline-centred, Howe's was charity-centred. The visible church played a surprisingly important role for Baxter, placing him closer to Tillotson and others in the established Church than to many nonconformists, especially the younger group which included Howe and

11 See the account in Calamy 225-227.

12 Thomas, 'Presbyterians in Transition', 128 and 127-138 *passim*. See also Lamont, *Richard Baxter*, 210-212, 273-276.

Alsop. Howe, on the other hand, displayed a radical bias to the invisible church. Given these differences, some assessment of their relative influences over subsequent developments must be attempted.

Baxter's importance in the 1660s and 1670s cannot be doubted. However, in the 1680s, the picture changed. Howe was minister to an important London congregation. Baxter, ill and with no appointment, sought to maintain his influence through his publications and his extensive correspondence. Calamy himself directly questioned Baxter's pre-eminence in this period. 'That Mr Baxter was a man of interest and influence among them, I freely own; but that he was any thing of a proper head, I know not.'[13] As we have seen, on at least one occasion (1681) Howe was preferred by Churchmen as a negotiating partner. While Baxter was in prison in the mid-1680s, Howe was in the Netherlands, consorting with dissident leaders and establishing a relationship with William of Orange. It was in this period that he was 'esteemed as one of the greatest preachers in England'.[14] It was Howe who led the welcoming nonconformist ministers in 1689, and who drew up the *Case of the Protestant Dissenters* before the Act of Toleration. It was Howe who headed the subscribers to the Common Fund and who helped to compose the *Heads of Agreement* in 1691. Baxter died in that year; Howe's role continued through the 1690s.

There is of course no denying Baxter's significance. His 'middle way' on predestination was sophisticated and influential long into the eighteenth century. But the half-life of his discipline-centred ecclesiology is less clear. Certainly it survived his death, featuring in the 1690s polemics of Daniel Williams. Williams argued against Baxter's *bête noire*, antinomianism, in his controversy with Crisp. The Pinners' Hall/Salters' Hall split was precipitated by Williams' Baxterian, modified Calvinism. When he was accused of socinianism in 1695, Williams' ideas were again linked to Baxter.[15] But this was a means of accusation, rather than approbation. Even Thomas concedes that identification with Baxter's legacy was hardly likely to add to Williams' prestige.[16] Moreover, it has recently been shown that the protagonists in the 1690s antinomian debates rarely invoked Baxter's arguments or referred to his works. A likely reason for this

13 Calamy, *Historical Account*, I, 213.

14 J. Erskine, *Journal of the Hon. John Erskine of Carnock, 1683-1687*, Edinburgh, 1893, 174.

15 See Thomas, *Daniel Williams*, 117-123. Thomas describes Williams as 'a devout disciple of Baxter'.

16 Thomas, *Daniel Williams*, 6.

avoidance of Baxter lay in the new circumstances of toleration. Baxter's ecclesiology had always pointed to comprehension as the desired outcome. With this option (and Baxter himself) now dead, alternative frameworks were more attractive. Even Williams, who clearly did hold to a version of Baxter's 'rectoral theory of the ministry,' felt only occasional need to refer to his mentor's arguments for support.[17]

When one turns to the specific case of Edmund Calamy Jnr, the argument for Baxter's influence initially appears strong. The principal evidence lies in the fact that Calamy issued a revision of the *Reliquiae Baxterianae*, in 1702.[18] This included the first version of his own account of ejected ministers and was edited by Calamy 'with freedom'.[19] Edited with considerable 'freedom', in fact. Calamy seized on the inadequacy of Sylvester's edition of *Reliquiae* as providing an opportunity to construct his own apology for nonconformity. Calamy suggested that Sylvester's 'esteem for Mr Baxter...ran as high, as it was fit it should towards any Mortal Man: Perhaps he exceeded.'[20] But if Sylvester's edition of Baxter's memoirs was an act of homage, Calamy's most certainly was not. Rather, the text was appropriated to what Calamy regarded as a far greater end: defining a new nonconformity in an increasingly hostile environment. David Wykes has shown that the history he presented, both in tone and in detail, was very different from Baxter's account.[21] The controversy which followed its publication had more to do with Calamy's presentation of the issues than the contents of the manuscript with which he began. The addition of the famous ninth chapter, which gave biographical details of ejected ministers and which would later be greatly expanded, was felt to be particularly offensive, leading to the riposte that Calamy sought to 'Canonize... those very men...whose misguided Zeal had filled the former Age with Blood and Confusion.'[22]

---

17 Cooper, 'Richard Baxter and Antinomianism', 282-293.

18 See Thomas, 'Presbyterians in Transition', 127; Lamont, *Richard Baxter*, 79-81.

19 See Calamy, *Historical Account*, I, 442-459.

20 E. Calamy, *A funeral sermon occasion'd by the sudden death of the Reverend Mr Matthew Sylvester* (London: 1708), 37.

21 See D.L. Wykes, 'To let the memory of these men dye is injurious to posterity': Edmund Calamy's *Account* of the Ejected Ministers' in N. Swanson (ed), *The Church Retrospective, Studies in Church History* 33 (Woodbridge: Ecclesiastical History Society, 1997), 379-392, 382-390 & *passim* and *To Revive the Memory of Some Excellent Men: Edmund Calamy and the Early Historians of Nonconformity* (London: Dr Williams Trust, 1997), 19-20.

22 Anon. *Seditious Preachers, Ungodly Teachers* (London: 1709), Preface, sig. A2. - cited Wykes, 'To let the memory of these men dye', 389.

Calamy's three-volume *Defence of Moderate Nonconformity* (1703-5) was his response to criticisms of his gloss on nonconformist history. The key principles for this 'moderate nonconformity' were spelled out in a long 'Introduction' attached to volume two of the *Defence* but which Calamy stated really served as an opening to the entire work. One of his principal antagonists was Benjamin Hoadly (1676-1761), who would later provoke the Bangorian controversy. Picking up departures from Baxter, Hoadly questioned the faithfulness of Calamy's vision to that of earlier nonconformists. 'I think there is reason to judge that the best of them would sooner have chosen the continuance of the present Establishment than the alteration of it into such an one as is here contrived.'[23]

Thomas suggests that Hoadly missed the mark, asserting instead that Calamy

> was in many ways a typical Baxterian but, although he stuck to the theological pattern inherited from Baxter more faithfully than some of his younger contemporaries, he did so with a magnanimity that was perhaps more faithful to Baxter's genius than Baxter might have been himself.[24]

The 'genius' to which Thomas refers is Baxter's supposed 'catholicity'. In his new system, Calamy held that 'each worshipping society must determine for itself all necessary circumstances and each private Christian has his own judgement and discretion left untouched.'[25] This provision for 'each worshipping society' signalled a shift away from strictly Presbyterian polity. Calamy sanguinely acknowledged that his could be represented as a 'meer Independent scheme.' However, it is the protection of the individual conscience in this passage which most impresses Thomas. He asserts that Calamy came to this position by 'remodelling' Baxter. At this point Thomas introduces a second key figure, arguing that the 'remodelling' was achieved by incorporating John Locke's views on toleration.[26] This dual association is important in the light of the analysis of both Baxter and Locke in this study. It does not stand up to scrutiny.

---

23 B. Hoadly, *The Reasonableness of Conformity*, 4th ed, (London: 1720), 528.

24 Thomas, 'Presbyterians in Transition', 127.

25 E. Calamy, 'Introduction' to *A Defence of Moderate Nonconformity - Second Part* (London: 1704), 87.

26 Thomas, 'Presbyterians in Transition', 130. This is not surprising as Locke is an important factor in Thomas's view of later dissent. Thomas also contends for Locke's influence on Doddridge - see R. Thomas, 'Philip Doddridge and Liberalism in Religion' in G. Nuttall (ed.) *Phillip Doddridge 1702-51: His Contribution to English Religion* (London: Independent Press, 1951), 122-153.

William Lamont is another who identifies Calamy's 1704 'Introduction' as a crucial turning point in the 'emancipation' of dissent. He too argues for the seminal importance of Baxter.

> To emancipate Restoration dissent...Calamy would have to revise Baxter. But Calamy did not need to invent new concepts. He transformed Protestant Nonconformity, not by ignoring Baxter or by misunderstanding him, but by developing arguments that had already been advanced by Baxter, *particularly in his writings of the late 1670s and the early 1680s*. Indeed, in that period of his writings, there is evidence to suggest that the development of his views might have led logically to the philosophy that Calamy expressed in 1704. *Baxter might have been the man to emancipate Restoration dissent.* (original emphasis)[27]

According to Lamont, that Baxter was not himself the agent of emancipation was due to his recovery of an apocalyptic vision and subsequent return to the national church dream. He insists that Thomas's account 'misses the final *distance* between Baxter's answers in the [later] 1680s and Calamy's in 1704'.[28] Lamont identifies Calamy's key revision to have been his removal of the eschatological structure from Baxter's ecclesiology. With the stakes thus lowered, both separatist and established churches could be viewed in a more sober manner.[29]

The distance correctly identified by Lamont between the mature Baxter and Calamy is highlighted by the reaction to Calamy's 'Introduction' by the undoubted 'Baxterian' Daniel Williams. In his account of his own life, Calamy records that Williams, alone of his colleagues, objected to the scheme, advancing that 'when a proper season came...he could overthrow the whole fabric, with ease'. Calamy's confident response to Williams is instructive.

> I told him, frankly, that the principles there advanced were spreading so wide, and prevailing so generally among us, that if he neglected the present opportunity, he might afterwards find it very difficult to make way for other notions.[30]

Far from being a disciple, Calamy rejected the national church structure which was crucial to Baxter's vision for most of his career. Even more significant was his relegation of discipline. Calamy specifically distanced himself from Baxter's alleged practice of imposing his own requirements on communicants.[31] He stated as a founda-

---

27 Lamont, *Richard Baxter*, 211-2.
28 Lamont, *Richard Baxter*, 275.
29 Lamont, *Richard Baxter*, 278-9.
30 Calamy, *Historical Account*, II, 30.
31 Calamy, 'Introduction', 63-4.

tional principle that 'conscience is the great engine by which God hath maintained religion in the world ever since he has had a Church in it.'[32] Thomas concedes that 'Baxter's adherence to "discipline" naturally conflicted with his catholicity.'[33] Yet, discipline (not 'peace', and certainly not catholicity) was the very key to Baxter's ecclesiology. Lamont suggests that Calamy repristinated ideas which Baxter flirted with in 1677-82. Yet Lamont's own analysis demonstrates that this was the period when Baxter departed from his main line of thought. This would merely have been honouring Baxter in the breach. Moreover, as has been shown, even in his aberrant period Baxter was not prepared to give individual conscience the high place Calamy accorded it. Calamy was right in claiming to represent the mainstream of nonconformist thought, the new consensus did not spring from Baxter's legacy.

Was Calamy's emphasis on individual conscience, then, the result of the growing influence of John Locke? Certainly Calamy cites Locke's first *Letter Concerning Toleration*, in his 'Introduction', but only in so far as Locke argues for the 'Civil Interests of Mankind'.[34] Thomas notes that Calamy went 'even further than Locke himself'. Locke may have called for civil freedom of association with churches, 'Calamy, however, clearly envisages a measure of toleration within the worshipping community itself...he acted on the principle of a good deal of internal latitude and toleration within the Church.'[35]

This is a vital point of difference, signaling the influence of a third stream of thought. Calamy did not have to extend Locke's position to reach such an irenic view. There was already a model for intra-church toleration of which Calamy was well aware.

The assumption that the combined influences of Baxter and Locke provided the theological context for Calamy's restatement of nonconformist principles is open to serious challenge. The likely role of John Howe in particular must be recognised. It was Howe who had advised the young Calamy to seek education in Utrecht. In 1692, Howe endorsed Calamy for a position in a large congregation in Bristol and subsequently advised him. During the 1690s Calamy attended a weekly meeting for 'amicable discussion', at the home of Howe's relation, Dr Francis Upton. Calamy's closest friend in the 1690s was Howe's assistant, Thomas Reynolds, with whom he also

32 Calamy, 'Introduction', 3.

33 Thomas, 'Presbyterians in Transition', 127 n.1. This concession is based on R. Schlatter, *Richard Baxter and Puritan Politics*, New Brunswick, 1957, 33-37.

34 Calamy, 'Introduction', 29.

35 Thomas, 'Presbyterians in Transition', 130.

shared a lodging. It was to Howe that both younger men first applied for ordination.[36] Neither should it be missed that, though Calamy edited Baxter's autobiography and gathered material on a whole generation of ejected ministers, his only full-scale biography was a study of John Howe. The significance of that project will become evident.

Such circumstantial links on their own are not conclusive. The dissenting clerical world was small. Calamy was assistant at various times to the true 'Baxterians', Sylvester and Williams. There were, moreover, other important senior figures. R.A. Beddard argues for the pivotal role of Vincent Alsop.[37] Alsop was an acute thinker who, despite the fact that he broke ranks over James II's Indulgence, remained a leading nonconformist until his death. Beddard contends that Alsop recognised the inevitability and desirability of independence from the established Church. This insight makes Alsop a candidate as a principal figure in the evolution of dissent. Yet Beddard ignores Horwitz's suggestion that Alsop was among those who, in the 1690s, made belated overtures towards comprehension.[38] Calamy and the bulk of nonconformists showed no interest in such a prospect.

Positive points of agreement between Calamy and Howe are more telling. On the key issue of toleration, Lamont, recounting Thomas's interpretation of Calamy, inadvertently identifies a crucial category. 'Charity' he notes, 'weighs more with Calamy than the "plausible Pleas of Uniformity and Decency".'[39] As we have seen, it was John Howe, rather than Richard Baxter, who built his ecclesiology around charity. Similarly Calamy's supposed extension of Locke may be better understood as mirroring Howe's concerns. As has been shown, a key difference between Locke's *Letter Concerning Toleration* and Howe's *Union Among Protestants* was that Locke's work addressed a merely civil context, whereas Howe's called for tolerance within and between the congregations.

Calamy himself testified to the harmony of his ideas with those of Howe. That Howe endorsed Calamy's moderate nonconformity scheme is mentioned only in passing by Thomas and Lamont.[40] Yet Calamy's account of the approbation is important, suggesting the ecclesiologies of the two men were very close indeed.

---

36 Howe ultimately declined. This seems not to have damaged their relationship - Calamy, *Historical Account*, I, 139, 311-7, 324, 339.

37 Beddard, 'Vincent Alsop' *passim.*

38 Horwitz, 'Comprehension', 345.

39 Lamont, *Richard Baxter*, 276.

40 Thomas, 'Presbyterians in Transition', 130; Lamont, *Richard Baxter*, 274.

> In the last visit I made to Mr Howe, a very few days before he died, speaking of this Introduction, and signifying his hearty approbation of it, he made it his request to me, that, at a proper juncture, I would take it off the stocks, (as he was pleased to express it,) make it more general, without a reference to any particular persons or writings, and publish it as an Essay towards an Ecclesiastical Settlement. It was his opinion it might be of considerable service.[41]

Though Calamy does not mention Howe in the 'Introduction', the significance of this omission is mitigated by the fact that those writers Calamy cites approvingly tend to be limited to those who carried the added authority of being already dead. When Calamy's ideas are considered in detail, his argument is revealed to draw heavily on the invisiblist categories which also drove Howe's ecclesiology. The futurist, pneumatological eschatology revived by Howe in the 1690s removed the spotlight from current institutions, either separatist or established. More fundamentally, Howe's key category of charity was, as Lamont notes, of paramount importance also to Calamy. 'The aim and drift of our Holy Institution…is to diffuse among us a Noble spirit of Love.'[42] On the thorny issue of occasional conformity Calamy matches Howe's 1702 argumentation in *Consideration of a Preface*.

> But why may not I shew my peacable Disposition in communicating occasionally, with those, a Total compliance with whose Impositions I judge Unlawful, without being charged with Hypocrisie? My Aim is visible; I don't seek to conceal it; nor is there any need I should: I would shew my Charity to them, tho' I dare not own their Autority (sic), or encourage their encroachments.[43]

The novelty of Calamy's 'Introduction' has been overstated. He was merely synthesizing for a new generation the type of ecclesiology which had already found sophisticated expression in Howe's work.

8.3 The Division at Salters' Hall, 1719

The evidence for Howe's influence over later dissent goes beyond Calamy's *Defence of Moderate Nonconformity*. Subsequent developments sadly, but powerfully, validated his 1690s pessimism. Despite considerable, even ardent, good will from individual nonconformists and various attempts (some remarkably sustained) to create structures for cooperation, the ideals of the 'Happy Union' would never

41 Calamy, *Historical Account* II, 31.

42 Calamy, 'Introduction', 12; cf. Howe, *Union Among Protestants*, 160.

43 Calamy, 'Introduction' 82. cf. Howe, *Some Consideration of a Preface*, 544-5.

be achieved. This inability to forge effective connections may have reflected a broader, even more disconcerting drift. By the fourth decade of the new century, some were warning of the 'decay' of dissent. Precise indicators of the nature and extent of any retreat are difficult to specify. J.C.D. Clark estimates that the combined population of dissenters and Roman Catholics had declined to half by the 1740s.[44] Richard Brown is reluctant to quantify numerical decline but nevertheless describes dissent as 'an increasingly demoralized, introverted movement'.[45] Many, including some of the brightest, of the second generation after toleration elected to conform. More worrying to contemporary leaders was a perceived decline in spirit and enthusiasm.[46] Hard evidence is patchy and ambiguous. If it ever was, it is now impossible to quantify these alleged trends. It is clear, however, that Howe's fears were justified. The most obvious characteristic of early eighteenth-century dissent was its failure to unite.

A series of controversies in the early decades of the century absorbed huge energy and left a deposit of hostility in later dissent. The evidence is complex. Formal schism is a particularly ambiguous sign. Michael Watts has pointed out that some denominations fared better than others. The Congregationalists and the Particular Baptists appear to have maintained unity more successfully than the Presbyterians, General Baptists and Quakers. That appearance may, however, be misleading. The three latter groups were those which strove for some central organisation and national cohesion. This simply meant that occasion was given for division to be stated and formalized. Neither the Congregationalists nor the Particular Baptists attempted any national structure in this period. Their unity cannot therefore be asserted with confidence, as it was never tested.[47] In any case the outstanding symbol of disunity was the failure to again bridge the differences *between* denominations, as Howe and others thought they had in 1691. This did not mean that efforts were not made to that end. In the first decade of the eighteenth century the 'General Body of Protestant Dissenting Ministers in and about London' was formed. This was a looser body than the 'Happy Union' and, in any case, was limited to the capital and to largely political ends.[48] In 1718 Edmund Calamy considered that 'closer union'

44 Clark, *English Society 1688-1832*, 137.

45 Brown, *Church and State in Modern Britain 1700-1850*, 110-111.

46 See Watts, *Dissenters*, 384-386.

47 Watts, *Dissenters*, 297-303.

48 Thomas, 'Presbyterians in Transition', 125-6. This 'Committee of the Three Denominations' supposedly included both Baptists groups in the one membership. General Baptists, however, felt excluded from the arrangement, as the Baptist

was again a possibility and that 'the thoughts of several were working that way...and some previous steps had been taken in order to it.'[49] These steps would, however, stumble into the breach at Salters' Hall in 1719.

The Salters' Hall controversy had roots deep in the 1690s. Debates over the Trinity had rumbled among both conformists and nonconformists since Stephen Nye's 1687 *A Brief History of the Unitarians, called also Socinians*. As we saw, Howe took part in this debate, drawing criticism for not being positive enough on the unity of the Godhead. The issue surfaced periodically thereafter. Thomas Emlyn was deposed from his Presbyterian congregation in Dublin for Socinian views in 1702. Among the conformists, William Whiston was expelled from his professorship at Cambridge in 1710, whilst Samuel Clarke's 1712 *Scripture Doctrine of the Trinity* was denounced as Arian and he was threatened with prosecution for heresy.

The immediate causes of the controversy which led to the Salters' Hall division have been detailed elsewhere.[50] The crisis was forced on dissent when heterodox views on the Trinity were avowed by Hubert Stogdon, a Presbyterian candidate for ordination in Exeter. Suspicion was also cast on a number of his senior colleagues. The matter was referred for advice to the London ministers who gathered at Salters' Hall on 19 February, 1719. However, it is important to note that the famous 'upstairs/downstairs' division at this meeting was not taken over a doctrinal affirmation about the Trinity. Rather the issue turned on whether such doctrinal affirmations should be demanded of ministers at all. Thus, the division was not over a particular doctrine but over the broader question as to whether confessional agreement was an essential element in unity. By 57 votes to 53 it was decided not to recommend a doctrinal 'subscription' in the advice to Exeter. The voting fell broadly along denominational lines: Congregationalists and Particular Baptists generally favoured subscription; General Baptists and (though less overwhelmingly) Presbyterians opted for non-subscription. The controversy was far-reaching in its consequences. It provoked bitter polemic and made formal unity between the disputing groups well-nigh impossible.

Acknowledged by students of the crisis as a key figure, Calamy continued to plead the case for a unified 'moderate nonconformity'.

---

representatives were all Particular Baptists. See R. Brown, *The English Baptists of the 18th Century* (London: Baptist Historical Society, 1986), 25-27.

49 Calamy, *Historical Account*, II, 401. See UHST, xiii (1966) 168-71.

50 In most detail in R. Thomas, 'The Non-Subscription Controversy amongst dissenters in 1719: the Salters' Hall Debate', *JEH*, 4, 1953, pp 162-186.

His 1724 biography of Howe must be interpreted in the light of this polemical context. Salters' Hall signalled the end of his dream. The impact of the split can be observed in the policies of the two denominational funds. The Congregational Fund appears to have increasingly insisted on doctrinal standards before making grants to ministers. In the Presbyterian Fund, by contrast, Calamy was able to propose and have adopted a policy that the issue of subscription be left out of deliberations. In this continuing crusade he employed Howe as an exemplar. Calamy summed up Howe's approach in pertinent terms. 'He was for having nothing remain as a Test or Boundary of Christian Communion, but what has its Foundation as such, in plain Reason or express Revelation.'[51]

Wykes' studies of Calamy's 1702 *Abridgement* and the 1727 *Continuations* have highlighted his apologetic interest in demonstrating the qualities of ejected ministers. It has not been recognised that Calamy's 1724 *Memoirs* of Howe served a similar purpose. The *Memoirs* appeared in the contentious period following the Salters' Hall split. Calamy reissued Howe's published works in the same year. Howe was presented as the ideal representative of the 'generous liberty' Calamy favoured. Calamy acknowledged that this position has been defended only by 'some among the dissenters' and lamented that 'unaccountable Heats' had weakened the nonconformist cause. If the wider movement had only kept to that 'large and noble' foundation its success would have been much greater.[52] The *Memoirs* must be interpreted as both *apologetic* (addressed to conformists, in keeping with Calamy's other historical works) and *polemic* (aimed at those less 'generous' within dissent). Howe thus served as a potent symbol for Calamy's brand of ecclesiology. As Calamy's account remains the principal source for the details of Howe's life, this likely motivation raises inevitable questions about the accuracy of the representation. Calamy undoubtedly presents an idealized account of his subject in the *Memoirs*. Yet on the key issues examined here there does not appear to have been any significant distortion of Howe's views. Indeed, an examination of Howe's own writings indicates that the 'reason and revelation' position endorsed by Calamy is implicit throughout Howe's works and is clearly enunciated as early as 1693.

In the 'Preface to the Reader' which accompanied the two sermons on *The Carnality of Religious Contention* Howe expressed his pessimism that 'a general union' would be possible. He abandoned hopes for institutional, visible unity and shifted his focus to the invisible

---

51 Calamy 239.
52 Calamy 129-130.

realm, proffering terms by which Christians might keep themselves 'united in mind and spirit'. The scheme depended on the attitude to creeds, reason and scripture which Calamy would later champion. First, Christians must join 'for actual and local communion' with others of like mind, who share in 'some such scheme of doctrinals' which they all respect. Howe placed value on these creeds, which were like 'gold formed into a vessel whereas truth as it lies in the holy Scriptures is as gold in the mass.' However, this value was principally as a means of informing outsiders of what the group believed. Whereas, in the 'Heads of Agreement' in 1691, creeds were accorded a secure role as interpreters of scripture, Howe makes it clear in *Carnality* that they are to be looked upon as '*mensura mensurata*, reserving unto the Scriptures the honour of being the only *mensura mensurans*; and so that we only own them as agreeable to the Scriptures.'

If Scripture was to prevail over doctrines, so also was reason. The creeds, 'human compositions', were not to be regarded as sacred, nor indeed were 'words used in the translation of the Bible itself'. Moreover 'we believe them with a degree of assent proportionable to their greater or less evidence.' Creeds, then, were for information and convenience only, not imposition. Thus

> while we look upon an agreement therein as a sufficient character of one sound in the faith, we... do never intend our communion shall be limited by other bounds than only agreement in those things for doctrinals, which we take to be of such importance and necessity as without the belief whereof a man cannot be a sincere Christian.[53]

Howe declined to specify these 'necessary doctrines'. However, he affirmed that their number would be small and, most importantly, determined by Scripture, as understood using common sense methods. Such key beliefs 'cannot but be a very few, less disputed things, among them that profess to believe the divine authority of the Scriptures, and that will allow them to be interpreted according to the ordinary ways of interpreting other writings.'[54]

Thus 'plain reason or express Revelation' were for Howe the determinants of communion as early as 1693. He was not alone. Locke and some moderate conformists called for similar standards and methods of exegesis. Yet Howe differed from latitudinarians and especially from Locke in his employment of both reason and revelation to the end of 'heart religion'. His vision, after all, was for a unity of 'mind and spirit'. His definition of the 'essence' of Christianity was just as short as Locke's but was of a fundamentally different or-

53 Howe, *Carnality*, 117-8.
54 Howe, *Carnality*, 118.

der. Where Locke demanded only acceptance that Jesus was the Messiah, Howe called for covenanted submission to the lordship of this Christ.[55]

8.4 Rational Toleration and Heart Religion

The combination of heart and head is important. In an early essay Thomas pointed out that the Salters' Hall controversy had more than one context. Not only did it stand at the end of three decades of Socinian debate within dissent, but it also existed within the wider setting of the Bangorian controversy which for two years had been exercising both conformists and nonconformists.[56] In March, 1717 Benjamin Hoadly, Bishop of Bangor, preached an inflammatory sermon on *The Nature of the Kingdom, or Church, of Christ*. Hoadly reduced the church to a purely human institution, with no claim to existence independent of the State. Hoadly's call for toleration on this basis was received with cautious approval by dissenters, at that time actively seeking to broaden their legal rights. Among conformists, however, the sermon provoked a storm of protest.

The logic of Hoadly's argument has recently been examined.[57] Drawing deeply on Locke's toleration theory, Hoadly added an argument based on incremental changes in the meanings of words across time. The only remedy was 'recourse to the Originals of Things: to the Law of Reason...and to the Declarations of Jesus Christ and his immediate Followers.'[58] In particular, 'Kingdom' had come to mean an earthly reality, rather than one, as Christ declared it, 'not of this world.' This original sense should be recovered. Hoadly went on to deny the authority of any humans to 'either to make *New Laws* for *Christ's* Subjects; or to impose a sense on the *Old* Ones...or to *Judge*, Censure or Punish the Servants of *Another Master*, in matters relating purely to *Conscience* or *Salvation*.'[59]

Thomas suggested that Hoadly's sermon 'gave active encouragement' to an emerging rational toleration within dissent, and Presbyterianism in particular. By this interpretation, Salters' Hall was a turning point in the development of rational dissent, from which there emerged a 'movement to leave the mind free and unfet-

55 Howe, *Carnality*, 113.

56 Thomas, 'The Non-Subscription controversy' 180-182.

57 M.A. Stewart, 'Rational dissent in early eighteenth-century Ireland' in L. Haakonssen (ed.) *Enlightenment and Religion: Rational dissent in eighteenth-century Britain* (Cambridge: CUP, 1996), 42-63, 51-55.

58 B. Hoadly, *The Nature of the Kingdom, or Church, of Christ* (London: 1717), 4.

59 Hoadly, *Nature of the Kingdom*, 16.

tered in its search for truth.'[60] Thus, echoing Calamy, 'plain reason or express Revelation' are named by Thomas as the determinant categories for the non-subscription party at Salters' Hall. David Wykes, following Thomas, has argued that the fault-line which widened in the decade up to 1720 grew out of a combination of divergent responses to Baxter's 'Middle Way' on doctrines of grace and to Locke's philosophy and biblical exegesis. Michael Watts, less enthusiastically, identifies a growing breach between a rationalistic approach, tolerant of diversity and tending to Arminianism, and one based on evangelical 'heart religion' and tied more closely to Calvinistic theology.[61]

Once again the historiography has missed the contribution of Howe's ideas. That the legacy of Baxter and the new thinking of Locke played significant roles in these developments is undoubted. Yet it is a mistake to locate the cause of the stresses within dissent simply in the confluence of these two streams. A third stream – Howe's invisiblist stream – must be recognised.

Isabel Rivers has explored this set of questions fruitfully in her study of developments in dissent. There is clear merit in the various analyses which identify a tension between rational toleration and evangelical religion. They have the significant advantage of employing categories suggested by contemporary nonconformists themselves. In 1630 Strickland Gough called for a renewed emphasis on toleration of different views within dissent. Too many ministers, he felt, were departing because they were being asked to subscribe to creeds they found too narrow. Such 'impositions' were the underlying cause of 'the Decay of the Dissenting Interest'. Salters' Hall was the symbol of the failure of dissent to live up to its heritage of liberty. Polite conversation would be the mark of authentic and attractive religion. It would moreover, be shorn of the unnecessary and divisive accretions of the past as 'what was fashionable to our forefathers is now as disagreeable to us as their dress'.[62]

Nevertheless, although the issues take a prominent place in contemporary discourse, it is not so clear that a divergence between head and heart religion, broadly coinciding with denominational loyalties, was widespread or even common. Key leaders like Isaac

60 Thomas, 'Presbyterians in Transition', 169. See also the note in Bogue and Bennett, *History of the Dissenters* III, 226.

61 Watts, *The Dissenters*, 371-393.

62 [S. Gough], *An Enquiry into the Causes of the Decay of the dissenting Interest*, London, 1730. Cited in I. Rivers, *Reason, Grace and Sentiment: A Study of the Language of Religion and Ethics in England, 1660-1780*, Vol. I, Cambridge: CUP, 1991), 168-9.

Watts and Phillip Doddridge sought a sound balance of mind and heart in 'affectionate religion'. Both were Congregationalists who, despite their criticism of Gough, maintained a clear emphasis on reasonable faith. Watts argued that 'Man is obliged to religion because he is a reasonable creature.'[63] Doddridge, as R.K. Webb has shown, 'had no doubt that rationality and piety could be, had to be, combined'.[64] Both responded to Gough's attempt to define dissent in rationalistic terms. It was, in their view, a too simplistic recipe. The problem lay not in the abandonment of rationalism but in the decay of its necessary associate: piety.[65] Doddridge would later sum up the case.

> I am heartily concerned for the interest of virtue, if by that be meant the advancement of practical religion; but I never expected to see it promoted by the most philosophical speculations concerning its nature, or the finest harangues of its innate beauties, when the name and peculiar doctrines of Christ are thrown off, as unfashionable incumbrances of a discourse.[66]

Isaac Watts and Phillip Doddridge were crucial to the development of eighteenth-century nonconformity. They had roots deep in the puritan authors whist at the same time they were key transitional figures in the relationship between dissent and evangelicalism. Attempts to establish the key influences on these two leaders have named the usual suspects: John Locke and Richard Baxter. Doddridge, for instance, placed importance in the curriculum of his Academy on the philosophy of Locke and has been cited as the outstanding heir to Richard Baxter in later dissent.[67] However, it was to John Howe that Doddridge and Watts looked for an archetype of the style of faith they sought to promote. Doddridge's student and biographer, Andrew Kippis, listed Howe with Baxter and Tillotson as Doddridge's principal models in practical divinity.[68] Watts, even more than Doddridge, described the relative roles of

---

63 I. Watts, *The Rational Foundation of a Christian Church*, cited Rivers, *Reason*, 186.

64 R.K. Webb, 'The emergence of Rational dissent', in K. Haakonssen (ed.) *Enlightenment and Religion: Rational dissent in eighteenth-century Britain* (Cambridge: CUP, 1996), 12-41, 29-36.

65 [P. Doddridge], *Free Thoughts on the Most Probable Means of Reviving the dissenting Interest*, 1730; I. Watts, *An Humble Attempt towards the Revival of Practical Religion among Christians*, 1731.

66 Doddridge, 'Sermons to Young Persons', Works II, 116-7.

67 Notably in G.F. Nuttall, *Richard Baxter and Philip Doddridge: A Study in a Tradition* (London: Dr Williams Library, 1951).

68 See the entry for Doddridge in A. Kippis, *Biographica Britannica*, 1791, (Vol. 5).

reason and revelation in terms very similar to Howe's.[69] Nuttall has shown how Howe's account of two experiences, years apart, of profound spiritual intensity had a lasting effect on Doddridge.[70] Citing the same intense experiences, Isaac Watts praised Howe for his exemplary openness to 'extraordinary witness'.[71] The originals of these accounts are recorded in Howe's Bible, one of the few items which survived his instructions to his son.

> Dec. 26. 89 After that I had long, seriously, and repeatedly thought with my self, that besides a full and undoubted Assent to the Objects of Faith, a vivifying savory Taste and Relish of them was also necessary, that with stronger Force and more powerful Energy they might penetrate into the most inward Center of my Heart, and there being most deeply fix'd and rooted, govern my life; and that there could be no other sure Ground whereon to conclude and pass a sound Judgment on my good Estate Godward....This very morning I awoke out of a most ravishing and delightful Dream, that a wonderful and copious Stream of Celestial Rays...did seem to dart into my open and expanded Breast...But what of the same kind I sensibly felt...on Oct 22. 1704 far surpass'd the most expressive words my thoughts can suggest...Tears gushing out of mine eyes for Joy that God should shed abroad his Love abundantly though the Hearts of men, and that for this very purpose mine own should be so signally possess'd of and by his blessed Spirit.[72]

It would be difficult to find an account closer to Richard Greaves' description of the essence of 'puritanism' as an emotional, pneumatic, immediate communion with God.[73] This impulse was a central feature in Howe's spirituality. Indeed, so important was it to his understanding of religion, that it provided the only 'sure ground' on which to judge his 'good Estate Godward'.

Howe's piety was not the only point at which he touched Doddridge. As important were his theological formulations. Doddridge

---

69 Compare Watts in the Preface to *Ruin and Recovery* (cited Rivers, *Reason*, 186) to Howe in *The Living Temple* 19-20.

70 G. Nuttall, 'Phillip Doddridge – A Personal Appreciation' in Nuttall (ed) *Philip Doddridge 1702-51: His Contribution to English Religion* (London: Independent Press, 1951), 154-163, 159-162.

71 See Rivers, *Reason*, 197-8.

72 Calamy 229-231. The original was written in Latin. Calamy adopts the translation made by Spademan and published with the funeral sermon for Howe. Doddridge recounts a similar experience, 'which indeed put me in mind of Mr Howe's 'full-stream of rays'' – Letter to Mercy Doddridge, 8 March 1742/3, in Doddridge, *Correspondence and Diary* (ed) J. Humphreys, 1829-31, IV, 211.

73 Greaves, 'The Nature of the Puritan Tradition', 258.

wrote of Howe to John Wesley, 'I cannot but say that he seems to me to have understood the gospel as well as any uninspired writer I have ever read...[his] two posthumous volumes on the Spirit...you must read.'[74]

In those sermons on the Holy Spirit which Doddridge praised, Howe insisted that Christians must depend upon the 'immediate influence' of the Spirit. 'I am very much persuaded, that [the lack of this dependence] is the great worm at the root of religion this day.'[75]

The significance of this connection between Howe and the later leaders of dissent emerges more fully when their cases for toleration are examined. In his writings on later nonconformity Thomas cites Baxter and Locke as the two great pillars of tolerationist thought. This is too simple a picture. Both Isaac Watts and Doddridge were readers and respecters of Locke's philosophy but each expressed important reservations. Thomas puts this down to their need to be cautious about endorsing publicly a figure not yet fully accepted within dissent.[76] The analysis in this study suggests more fundamental reasons. As shown in chapter four, Locke's case for toleration was different in type from the charity-based argument of Howe's *Union Among Protestants*. In particular Locke's view of conscience lacked Howe's 'inward, vital owning' – sentiments typical of the type of piety Howe represented and which Doddridge and Watts sought to preserve. The absence of key elements of orthodoxy and faith further distanced Locke from dissent. Watts complained that Locke's *Reasonableness of Christianity* 'has sunk some of the divine themes and glories of that dispensation too much below the original design.' Doddridge, before he could adjudge it valid, had to read crucial nonconformist themes into Locke's single fundamental of Christianity (that Christ is the Messiah).[77]

In the case of Baxter the converse applies. Whereas they were disquieted at Locke's heterodoxy, Isaac Watts and Doddridge were less insistent on doctrinal purity than Baxter. Baxter could comprehend 'godly men' from across the spectrum, whilst simultaneously denouncing their views. However, Watts and Doddridge were generally unwilling to condemn the doctrines themselves.[78] This

74 Doddridge, *Correspondence and Diary*, II, 230.

75 Howe, *Whole Works* V, 155-6.

76 Thomas, 'Philip Doddridge', 128-129.

77 Thomas, 'Philip Doddridge', 127-8.

78 On Doddridge, see A. Saunders, 'The State as highwayman: from candour to rights', in K. Haakonssen (ed.), *Enlightenment and Religion: rational dissent in eighteenth-century Britain* (Cambridge: CUP, 1996), 241-271. Watts was open

trend came to be suspected of weakening dissent. Reviewing the eighteenth century, the evangelical historians, David Bogue (1750-1825) and James Bennett (1774-1862) condemned applications of such 'candour'.

> The influence of this idea was exceedingly pernicious; for it led to an indifference with respect to truth and error, which depraved both their sentiments and dispositions, which relaxed the springs of Christian integrity and conduct, and gradually brought them to call good evil and evil good, to put light for darkness and darkness for light.[79]

Bogue and Bennett had the generation of Priestley in mind when they wrote this, but more orthodox dissenters like Watts and Doddridge had also exhibited Calamy's 'generous Liberty'. As with Calamy it is not a sufficient explanation to cite, as Thomas does, the rationalism of Locke and the toleration of Baxter as the obvious influences. Each, in different ways, was fundamentally discontinuous with the later men. Locke lacked connection with heart piety; Baxter eschewed scepticism on matters of doctrine. Neither modelled the mix of ideas which motivated Doddridge and Watts. They had access to a third approach, with its own integrated logic, in the irenic vision of John Howe. Calamy's 'moderate nonconformity' and, later, the pious rationalism of Doddridge and Watts were versions of this radically invisiblist ecclesiology. Each in their own way promoted Howe's fusion of love and forbearance, heart and head.

Yet even this was not enough. Howe imagined that religion lived in these terms would restore the life and spirit of the church, that once again it would be energized and winsome. Guided by such precepts, Christianity might even repeat its extraordinary primitive spread. It was a bold, but cruelly misguided, hope. His ecclesiology would not prevent the break up of old dissent. Indeed, it would contribute to the process. Revival would come, but the rise of eighteenth-century evangelicalism would depend on additional elements, lacking in Howe's vision.

The genius of the new elements lay in their inherent optimism. David Bebbington has shown the importance of Enlightenment empiricism in the development of evangelicalism.[80] Both Watts and Doddridge were influenced by this trend. Here the role of Locke is unquestionably key. From the 1630s Locke's influence increased markedly, heralding a fundamental change in philosophical fashion.

---

even to Socinian views – see A.P. Davis, *Isaac Watts: His Life and Works* (London: Independent Press, 1943), 109 & 103-126 *passim*.

79 Bogue and Bennett, *History of the Dissenters* III 384.

80 See D.W. Bebbington, *Evangelicalism in Modern Britain: History from the 1730s to the 1980s* (London: Unwin Hyman, 1989) esp. 42-55.

The impact was profound. Howe had built his ecclesiology on scepticism, mitigated by his Platonic expectation of divine illumination. Empiricism, by contrast, drew primarily on observation and experiment. Evangelicals applied this method to their religious life. The result was a greater potential for assurance. If the right evidence was present one could be sure of salvation.

A further element was the rise of post-millennial eschatology, different in type from the strands of millennial thinking prevalent in the seventeenth century. Enlightened millennialism looked to gradual improvement and progress towards the arrival of Christ.[81] Howe had no such confidence. His hope lay in the eventual intervention by God. In the mean time the church would struggle. Evangelicals would translate this optimism into a confidence in using 'means' for evangelism and mission. Howe's eschatology was essentially pessimistic. Until Christ returned, the church's efforts would be compromised, its plans thwarted.

Historical factors like the influences of continental Protestantism, the advance of exploration and a growing consciousness of the potential of the first empire all added to the transformation of British Atlantic religion. As the century unfolded the decline of dissent was reversed only as it came to terms with the new movement. Howe's strand of heart and head religion contributed to the Evangelical mix. On its own, however, it did not contain the resources to sustain such an advance.

---

81 Bebbington, *Evangelicalism*, 60-63.

CONCLUSION

The Ecclesiology of Later Stuart Dissent

John Howe represented a stream of dissent which increasingly came to focus on individual conscience and irenic forbearance in all but the most central questions of faith. This was an ecclesiology biased towards the invisible church - a view which relegated institutional and credal structures. As union based on such structures became increasingly problematic, even impossible, the appeal of this alternative foundation for harmony 'in mind and spirit' grew accordingly. Invisiblist ecclesiology naturally fitted with a futurist eschatology which enabled dissent to come to terms with defeat. It had the further advantage of cohesion with important philosophical trends. The recognition of its presence allows a new theological perspective on the religious history of the period.

Definition is a perennial problem in the history of ideas. As this study of Howe's career and theology has shown, traditional party tags are unhelpful, more likely to mask real issues than reveal them. The question of Howe's own allegiance highlights the ambiguity of the familiar labels 'Presbyterian' and 'Congregational'. Each of the debates considered has cast further doubt on their usefulness. Though for convenience they must remain in use, an understanding which recognises and incorporates various spectra of emphasis is clearly more able to deal with the surprising subtleties of later Stuart religion. Interestingly, this makes possible the partial restoration of a label once thought too compromised for continued use.

Attempts to define 'puritanism' as a discrete set of commonly held doctrines have proved fruitless. However, if understood as a concern for immediate piety, puritanism can be seen to have survived the downfall of the republic and protectorates. Further, if, as Wallace suggests,[1] piety is the soil out of which theology grows, some bridge between the two should be possible. I have proposed that an underlying spectrum of emphasis on the immanence or transcendence of

1 Wallace, *Puritans and Predestination*, ix.

God provides such a link. This spectrum was manifested the range of ecclesiologies which may be observed in the later Stuart period.

As outlined in chapter one, Anthony Milton and others have convincingly propounded a similar analysis for the early Stuart church. Those issues did not disappear in the turmoil of revolution and restoration. Indeed, fundamental tensions remained unresolved in 1660. Yet, continuity with the past does not imply that theology is static. Whilst it is unhelpful to set an impermeable boundary at 1660, it is as misleading to ignore the pressures of the later political and ecclesiastical context. Moreover, as Jonathan Scott has argued, seventeenth-century England was a place of restless innovation, a restlessness in which theology shared. The later Stuart period witnessed an increasing divergence of fundamental ecclesiology. In the established Church, two competing emphases developed. Both stressed the immanent activity of God. One located this in the Church, represented by its Bishops; the other found it in the state. Within dissent, the prevailing interest came to be in the transcendent operation of God's will, with a concomitant stress on the church as an invisible society.

I have suggested three broad phases in the history of later Stuart nonconformity. The first spans the 1660s and 1670s. The failure of the Savoy Conference, the rejection of the Worcester House declaration and the Act of Uniformity, led to enormous pressure on dissent. Work continued for a comprehensive Church and limited toleration, but all efforts failed, slipping into a widening ecclesiological gap.

To the leaders in the Church of England, the requirements of the Act of Uniformity were entirely logical. The visible church concept carried with it the imperatives of obedience to authority and institutional unity. More extreme visiblists employed an assumption in favour of episcopal rulings. The Bishops, as *jure divino* symbols of the church, should be obeyed. All visiblists placed importance on uniformity. They were happy to concede that the act required uniformity on many matters of 'indifference' (i.e. those questions of form and ritual which all agreed did not in themselves determine salvation). However, even small issues assumed a kind of significance when set in the context of the Church. If matters were truly indifferent, scruples over them could validly be set aside in the interest of what was important: visible unity. The proper response of all Christians was clearly to conform.

Nonconformists saw things differently. Their leaders emphasized (though to varying degrees) the invisible church above the visible. Episcopal rule, institutional unity and shared ritual gave way to local authority and individual conscience. Questions of 'indifference' took on an aspect markedly different from that of the Churchmen. If individuals scrupled at particular practices, forced conformity would require transgression of conscientious principles - tantamount to sin. Those who were relaxed about particulars felt that acquiescing in uniformity would put undue pressure on others. As Howe put it to Bishop Wilkins, his 'latitude...was the very thing which made him a Non-conformist'.[2]

Discussions between the parties were handicapped by these different ecclesiological biases. Some nonconformists, uninterested in national church structures, sought only toleration. Nevertheless, until the end of the 1670s, comprehension seemed a possibility. The most consistent interest in comprehension was shown by Richard Baxter. In the first decades of the Restoration, Baxter was at the peak of his influence within dissent. His concerns placed him near the middle of the ecclesiological spectrum. In this period at least, he continued to favour a national church and was thus open to institutional expressions of unity. In Churchmen such as Stillingfleet and Tillotson, he had natural partners who shared many of his interests.

By the end of the 1670s, Baxter's efforts were looking increasingly futile. Genuine interest in comprehension was fading on both sides. It would briefly revive in 1680, but all proposals foundered. The shift away from comprehension has been correctly linked to the burst of relative freedom under the 1672 Indulgence.[3] Yet, neither the Indulgence, nor a simple generational shift from 'Dons' to 'Ducklings', can satisfactorily explain the change. More complicated forces were at work. The shifting sands of political allegiance in the exclusion crisis had its counterpart in theology. Indeed the crisis signalled a second phase in the history of dissent.

The controversies of 1680 revealed significant ecclesiological fault lines. These did not, however, neatly correspond with those traditionally assigned. The so-called 'latitudinarians', Stillingfleet and Tillotson, did not share the same ecclesiology. By 1680 Stillingfleet had moved to a greater reliance on the visible church; Tillotson had adopted a moderate 'Constantinian' position. That both men were less willing than previously to make concessions to dissenters reflects the fact that, in different ways, they had shifted towards immanence. The mediated action of God had become more important to their ecclesiology. Accordingly, dissenters' claims to follow conscience carried less weight.

Among the nonconformists a corresponding, though opposite, process of innovation was occurring. As Lamont has shown, in the face of increasing official hostility and the threat of Roman Catholic

2 Calamy 31-3.

3 Watts, *The Dissenters*, 248-9; Thomas, 'Comprehension', 209.

ascendancy, even Richard Baxter moved to a more sectarian ecclesiology during the exclusion crisis. For Baxter as an individual, the tilt was temporary. Eventually his discipline-based national church ecclesiology gyroscopically reasserted itself. For the larger body of dissent, the shift was more telling. The most influential ecclesiology of the 1680s would not be Baxter's catholic Presbyterianism. Yet neither did dissent simply lurch to established versions of Independency. Rather, it drifted to the more thoroughgoing invisiblism of such as John Howe.

If Howe's importance is accepted, the theological dynamics of later Stuart dissent take on a different aspect. Our understanding of the 1680s and 1690s needs to incorporate the increasing power of an ecclesiology which emphasised the invisible church and which drew its logic from a radical bias to the transcendent activity of God. The result of these developments among both Churchmen and dissenters was the removal of the common ground that Baxter had exploited in the preceding decades. The intensified pressure of the early 1680s, followed by the accession of James II, served to confirm the widening rift. Comprehension would be discussed again in 1688-9, but it was no longer a realistic possibility. Spurr has shown that committed Churchmen were opposed to a broad comprehension for fear it would compromise uniformity, thereby 'importing schism into the Church.'[4] Theological barriers to comprehension were not confined to the Anglicans. Dissenters like Howe, desirous of unity based on the principle of charity, were, nevertheless, unwilling to enter into any arrangement which threatened the exercise of individual conscience. A form of toleration would be required.

By the glorious revolution, nonconformists were speaking an ecclesiological language quite different from that of even moderate Churchmen. When it was referred to Convocation in 1689, comprehension finally died as a viable option. The pattern had, however, been set a decade before. Crucial leaders on both sides had moved closer to opposing poles on the ecclesiological spectrum. The 1680s witnessed the final alienation of dissent from the established Church. With the passing of the Act of Toleration, nonconformity entered a new era.

The 1690s began with expectations of success and reconstruction. These were to be disappointed. Assessing the ultimate demise of comprehension, Spurr concludes that 'the cost to the Church of England was incalculable'.[5] Not immediately obvious was the profound effect radical invisiblism would have on the fate of dissent. In devel-

4 Spurr, 'Comprehension', 944 and *passim*.

5 Spurr, *Restoration Church*, 103.

opments which mirrored the failure of a wider comprehension, nonconformists were unable to effect a strong institutional unity. The 1690s onward was the third phase of later Stuart nonconformity. The theological dynamics which contributed to its alienation from the Church of England, would play a major role in its fragmentation and decay.

The importance in this process of invisiblist ecclesiology may be illustrated by a comparison of the history of later nonconformity with that of the Church of England in the same period. In the Common Fund of 1690 and the 'Happy Union' of 1691, Presbyterians and Congregationalists achieved a modicum of institutional unity. It was not, however, robust enough to survive the series of disputes which centred on Daniel Williams. The Baptists, who also attempted institutional unity among themselves, likewise ended the 1690s disunited.[6] Less formal vehicles for co-operation were shattered in 1719. Although some collaboration in the training of ministers continued into the 1730s, nonconformists were unable to sustain any form of institutional unity.

The established Church too, was wracked by doctrinal disputes in the decades following the accession of William and Mary. Anglicans were embroiled even more deeply in the various outbreaks of the Socinian controversy. There were long-running disputes over Convocation and, in 1710, the trial of Dr Sacheverell exposed significant differences. The Bangorian controversy raised crucial issues of authority and the role of the church.[7] Yet, despite these considerable strains, the Church of England did not divide. Even the 1689 departure of the Non-jurors had not precipitated a significant schism. Most high churchmen remained within the established body. Torn by similar disputes, the nonconformists had broken down to their constituent parts by 1730. The Church of England remained largely intact.

A direct comparison between nonconformists and the Church of England has obvious problems. It is likely that the smaller numbers of dissenters magnified personal and doctrinal differences. Legal and constitutional factors placed a presumption of institutional unity on Anglicans. Nevertheless, the impact of fundamental ecclesiology should not be discounted. The security of the Church of England as a national Church was built on two foundations. One

6 See White, 'Twilight', 318-325.

7 E.G. Rupp, *Religion in England 1688-1791* (Oxford: Clarendon Press, 1986), 88-101. Thomas links the nonconformist controversy which culminated in the 1719 Salters' Hall split directly with the Bangorian Controversy see Thomas, 'Nonsubscription Controversy', 180-185.

was its confidence in itself as the visible church of Christ. The second was its connection with the constitution and particularly the sovereign. Both of these depended upon an acceptance of the immanent activity of God. To those who emphasised this basic position, the rending of a body so established was inconceivable. The presumption towards institutional unity thus engendered proved able to withstand the considerable centrifugal forces of doctrinal dispute.

Dissent, by contrast, lacked a secure motivation for visible unity. In Howe's ecclesiology, this function was performed by the dynamic power of Christian charity. Yet it was just this quality which most quickly disappeared in the polemical exchanges associated with early modern theological controversy. It was, in any case, an *invisible* measure of unity. It promoted the fiction that, despite institutional factionalism, spiritual unity could be maintained. Nonconformists did not have the momentum for visible unity which kept the Church of England together. The centrifugal pressure of doctrinal dispute was not balanced by an effective centripetal force.

This leads to an important conclusion about the fate of later Stuart nonconformity. It is not sufficient merely to explain the decay of dissent in terms of individual controversies and doctrinal differences. Even the different church polities associated with Presbyterians, Congregationalists and Baptists do not, in themselves, provide the key. By the time of Queen Anne these differences were small. All operated on an essentially similar model: effective congregational autonomy, tempered by association over issues such as ordination. Underlying the organisation of nonconformists was an ecclesiology which, by its emphasis on the invisible church and on individual conscience, provided little foundation for the institutional unity periodically attempted. Ultimately the fragmentation of dissent may be traced, not to the doctrines on which the parties differed, but to the ecclesiology they shared.

As dissent maintained this decline, a vigorous movement was being born which would both fill the void created and win new ground. Evangelicalism was far more than puritanism preached in the fields. Ecclesiology was a principal focus of the leaders of dissent. It had to be - the Stuart context demanded it. By the 1730s the issues had changed. The world of evangelicalism was bigger, and it created a different story altogether.

This study has explored the earlier tale. Centred on the theology of John Howe, it calls for a reinterpretation of later Stuart dissent. When the effects of the Howe myth and generations of 'Baxterisation' are stripped away, Howe's individual importance in the history of nonconformity becomes more evident. His view of the church has been distinguished from that of the Latitudinarians, John Locke and

Richard Baxter, opening up a new perspective on events. This ecclesiology ostensibly transcended party division and made space for individual conscience. Yet, Howe's and Calamy's approach would not sustain dissent. Indeed it contained the seeds of its own destruction. The division at Salters' Hall in 1719 merely demonstrated its inadequacy. Thomas misrepresents those who held out for subscription when he dismisses them as vestiges of a less enlightened era. It is perhaps more accurate to interpret their stand as an unwillingness, when the issue was forced, to persevere with the strictly invisiblist model. Their instinct was that some visible basis for unity, in this case confessional agreement, was essential.

In 1707, the Scot James Webster was suspicious of the legacy of the irenic leaders of English dissent. By 1750, even such an admirer as Philip Doddridge had concluded that the open policy of Howe and others on occasional conformity had served 'very unhappily for the dissenting interest'.[8] The paradox of this should not be lost. John Howe, for all his iconic status, bequeathed a troublesome ecclesiological legacy. He had built his career and his theology around concerns for Christian peace. His long commitment to schemes for unity was no aberration. Peace and toleration were natural to him. Indeed, the generosity of his personality and thought was the very thing which made him so attractive to later generations. Yet, lacking any seat for unity in the visible sphere, his ecclesiology was exposed to the risk of institutional fragmentation and division. In a tragic irony he had fuelled the decay of dissent.

8 Letter, Doddridge to Simon Reader, 5 November, 1750. See G.F. Nuttall (ed), *Calendar of the Correspondence of Phillip Doddridge DD (1702-1751)* (London: H.M. Stationary Office, 1979), No. 1671.

Bibliography

Abbreviations

The following abbreviations are used in the bibliography:

CH	*Church History*
EHR	*English Historical Review*
EMH	*Early Modern History*
HJ	*Historical Journal*
JEH	*Journal of Ecclesiastical History*
JBS	*Journal of British Studies*
JRH	*Journal of Religious History*
P&P	*Past and Present*
TRHS	*Transactions of the Royal Historical Society*

Primary Sources

MANUSCRIPTS

Bodleian Library:

Ms. Rawl. C. 739. 139,140 - Letters from Bishop Lamplugh (Sept & Oct 1680)

Ms. Rawl. C. 983. 102 - Letter from Dr Stanley to Compton (Aug. 1686).

Ms. Rawl. D. 1350. 329 - Memorandum of Devon ministers who took the Oxford Oath.

British Library:

Add. Ms 4166, f. 146 - Letter, Anne Thurloe to Howe (1668)

Add. Ms 4275, f. 331 - Letter, Howe to J. Spademan (1697)

Add. Ms 11,342 A - Information laid ats Howe (1660)

Add. Ms 29,910 ff 226r,227v - Letter: Howe to John Swynfen, draft reply.

Add. Ms 41,812, f. 106 - Letter B. Skelton (May 1685), ff. 208-9 - Letter B. Skelton (Oct. 1685); ff 222-225 - Report to Skelton from Utrecht (Nov. 1685)

Add. Ms 41,818 f. 238 - unsigned report from Utrecht (Feb. 1686)

Add. Ms 41819, f. 213 (Middleton Papers) - Letter Howe to B. Skelton (1686)

Dr. Williams' Library:

Ms 59, vols. i-vi - Baxter Correspondence

Ms 59, vols. vii-viii 61 vols. i-vi, xi-xvii - Baxter Treatises

William Salt Library:

SMS 454 -Letter, Lord Massarene to John Swynfen (Feb. 1675)

PRINTED PRIMARY SOURCES (published in London unless otherwise noted)

--- *Religions Lotterie*, 1642 (reprinted in L.A. Sasek, *Images of English Puritanism: A Collection of Contemporary Sources 1589-1646* (Baten Rouge: Louisiana State University Press, 1989), 329-334).

--- *Heads of Agreement Assented to by the United Ministers in and About London* ([1691]).

---- *The agreement in doctrine among the Dissenting Ministers in London* (1693).
---- *A History of the Union Between the Presbyterian and Congregational Ministers...and the Causes of the Breach of It* (1698).
--- *Seditious Preachers, Ungodly Teachers* (1709)
--- *Calendar of State Papers Domestic: Charles I, Charles II, James II*
Alsop, V., *The Mischief of Impositions or, A Soveraign Antidote Against a Late Discourse Called the Mischief of Separation* (1680).
Assheton, W., *Toleration Disapprov'd and Condemned,* (2nd ed) (Oxford: 1670).
Baxter, R., *A Holy Commonwealth,* (1659) (Cambridge: Cambridge University Press, 1994) (ed. W.M. Lamont).
- *The Successive Visibility of the Church* (1660)
- *The Judgment of Nonconformists of the Interests of Reason in Religion* (1676).
- *Richard Baxter's Answer to Dr Stillingfleet's Charge of Separation...* (1680).
- *Church History of the Government of Bishops and their Councils Abbreviated* (1680).
- *A Treatise of Episcopacy* (1681).
- *A Second True Defence of Meer Nonconformists* (1681).
- *The True History of Councils Enlarged* (1682).
- *An Answer to Mr Dodwell and Dr Sherlocke* (1682).
- *Church Concord* (1691).
- *Reliquiae Baxterianae* (1696) (ed. Sylvester).
- *An Abridgement of Mr Baxter's History of his Life and Times* (1702) (ed. Calamy).
- *Autobiography of Richard Baxter* (1931) (edited J.M. Lloyd Thomas).
- *Richard Baxter's Practical Works* (4 vols.) (1990).
Boyle, R., *The Works of the Honourable Robert Boyle* (1772) (ed. T. Birch)
Burnet, G. *Bishop Burnet's History of His Own Time: from the Restoration of Charles II to the Treaty of Peace at Utrecht in the Reign of Queen Anne,* (2 vols.), (1838).
Calamy, E., *A defence of Moderate Nonconformity* (1703-05).
--- *Memoirs of the Life of the Late Revd Mr John Howe* (1724).
--- *An Historical Account of My Own Life, with some Reflections on the Times I have Lived In (1671-1731)* (2 vols.) (1829).
Calvin, J., *Institutes of the Christian Religion* (1559), J.T. McNeill (ed), *The Library of Christian Classics,* Vol. XXI, (2 vols.) (Philadelphia: 1960).
Conway, A. and ors, *The Conway Letters: the Correspondence of Anne, Viscountess Conway, Henry More and Their Friends* (Oxford: 1992) (ed. M.H. Nicholson).
Crisp, T., *Christ Alone Exalted* (1689).
D[anson], T., *De Causa Dei; or a Vindication of the Common Doctrine of Protestant Divines concerning Predestination* (1678).
Doddridge, P., (G.F. Nuttall, ed.) *Calendar of the Correspondence of Phillip Doddridge DD (1702-1751)* (H.M. Stationary Office, 1979).
Erskine, J., *Journal of the Hon, John Erskine of Carnock, 1683-1687* (Edinburgh: 1893) (ed. W. MacLeod).
Fell, P., *Lex Talionis: or, the Author of the Naked Truth Stript Naked* (1676).
Ferguson, R., *The Interest of Reason in Religion with the Import & Use of Scripture-Metaphors; and the Nature of the Union Betwixt Christ and Believers* (1675).
Filmer, R., *Patriarcha and Other Writings,* (1680) (Cambridge: Cambridge University Press, 1991) (edited J.P. Sommerville).
Flavell, J., *Planelogia: A Succinct and seasonable discourse...with an epistle...relative to Dr Crisp's works* (1691).

Fuller, T., *The Church History of Britain* (1655) (6 vols.) (Oxford: 1845).
Gale, T., *The Court of the Gentiles* (1678)
Glanvill, J., *Scepcis Scientifica: or, Confest Ignorance the way to science in an essay of the vanity of dogmatizing, and confident opinions* (1665).
- *Catholic Charity Recommended in a Sermon, before the Right Honourable the Lord Mayor Of London...,* (1669).
- *A Seasonable Recommendation and Defence of Reason, in the Affairs of Religion; Against Infidelity, Scepticism and Fanaticisms of all sorts* (1670).
Hall, R. *The Works of Robert Hall A.M.* (5 vols.) n.d..
Hickes, J., *A True and Faithful Narrative of the Unjust and Illegal Sufferings of Many Christians...in Devon* (1671).
Hoadly, B., *The Nature of the Kingdom, or Church, of Christ* (1717)
- *The Reasonableness of Conformity*, 4th ed, (1720)
Hobbes, T., *Leviathan* (1651) (Cambridge: Cambridge University Press, 1990).
Hooker, R., *Of the Lawes of Ecclesiasticall Politie* (Cambridge, MA: Folger Library, 1977).
Howe, J., *The Works of the Rev. John Howe, M.A. as Published During His Life*, (ed. E. Calamy, 1724) (ed. J.. Hewlett, 1848) (3 vols.) (Ligonier, PA: Soli Deo Gloria, 1990).
- *The Whole Works of the Rev. John Howe, M.A. with a Memoir of the Author*, (ed. J. Hunt), 8 vols. (1827).
Humfrey, J. (1620-1719), [N.B.], *A Modest and Peacable Inquiry into the Design and Nature of Some of those Historical Mistakes that are found in Dr Stillingfleet's PREFACE to his Unreasonableness of SEPARATION* (1681).
- *Pacification touching the Doctrinal Dissent among our United Brethren in London, Being an Answer to Mr Williams and Mr Lobb* (1696).
- *The friendly Interposer between the Authors of those Papers, the one called A Report; the other, A Rebuke of that Report* (1698).
- *Animadversions: Being the Last Two books of My Reverend Brother Mr Williams...Conscientiously Examined* (1699).
Humfrey, J. and S. Lobb, *The Peaceable Design* (1675).
- *An Answer to Dr Stillingfleet's Sermon, by Some Nonconformists, Being the Peaceable Design Renewed* (1680).
Laud, W., *The Works of the Most Reverend Father in God, William Laud D.D.* (Oxford: Library of Anglo-Catholic Theology, 1854).
- *A Letter from Some Aged Nonconforming Ministers, to their Christian Friends, Touching the Reasons of their Practice, August 24, 1701* (1702).
[Locke, J.], *A Letter from a Person of Quality to His Friend in the Country* (1675).
Locke, J., *Two Treatises of Government* (1689) (Cambridge: Cambridge University Press, 1967).
- *A Letter Concerning Toleration* (1689).
- *Essay Concerning Human Understanding* (1689) (Oxford: Oxford University Press, 1975).
- *The Correspondence of John Locke,* (ed. E.S. De Beer) (8 vols.) (Oxford: Oxford University Press, 1976-89).
Mather, C., *Diary of Cotton Mather* (New York: 1911).
More, H., *A Collection of Several Philosophical Writings* (1662).

Neal, D., *The History of the Puritans or Protestant Nonconformists,* (4 vols.) (1732-9) (abridged in 2 vols. by E. Parsons, 1811).

Owen, J. O., *The Works of John Owen, D.D.* (ed W.H. Goold), 16 vols., (1850-53), (1965).

Parker, S., *An Account of the Nature of the Nature and Extent of the Divine & Goodnesse* (Oxford: 1666).

- *A Discourse of Ecclesiastical Politie* (1669).

Sheldon, G., *David's Deliverance and Thanksgiving: A Sermon Preached before the King at Whitehall Upon June 28, 1660* (1660).

Sherlock, W., *A Discourse Concerning the knowledge of Jesus Christ, and Our Union and Communion with Him* (1674).

Spademan, J., *A Sermon on the Occasion of the Justly Lamented Death of the Truly reverend Mr John Howe* (1705) (Howe, *Works,* Vol. III, 609-624).

Sterry, P., *A Discourse of the Freedom of the Will* (1675).

Stillingfleet, E., *Irenicum: A Weapon-Salve for the Church's Wounds* (1661).

- *The Mischief of Separation: A Sermon Preached at Guild-Hall Chapel, May 11 MDCLXXX...Before the Lord Mayor, &c* (1680).

- *The Grand Question, Concerning the Bishops' Right to Vote In Parliament in Cases Capital* (1680).

- *The Unreasonableness of Separation: or An Impartial Account of the History, Nature, and Pleas of the Present Separation from the Communion of the Church of England...* (1681).

- *Origines Britannicae, or the Antiquities of the British Churches* (1685).

Thorndike, H., *Works,* Library of Anglo-Catholic Theology.

Tillotson, J., (1630-94), *The Protestant Religion Vindicated from the Charge of Singularity and Novelty* (1680).

- *The Lawfulness and Obligation of Oaths* (1681).

- *A Letter Written to My Lord Russel in Newgate, the Twentieth of July, 1683* (1683).

Troughton, J., *A Letter to a Friend, touching God's Prescience about Sinful Actions* (1678).

Upton, W.H., *Upton Family Records, being Genealogical Collections for and Upton Family History* (1893).

Webster, J., *Lawful Prejudices Against an Incorporating Union with England; or, Some Modest Considerations on the Sinfulness of this Union, and the Danger Flowing from it to the Church of Scotland* (Edinburgh: 1707).

Whitelock, B., *The Diary of Bulstrode Whitelock* (ed. R. Spalding) (Oxford: Oxford University Press, 1990).

Williams, D., *Gospel Truth Stated and Vindicated* (1692).

- *The Answer to the Report &C Which the United Ministers Appointed their Committee to Draw Up* (1698).

Wolsely, C., *Liberty of Conscience the Magistrate's Interest* (1668).

Secondary Sources

Abernathy, G.R., 'Clarendon and the Declaration of Indulgence', *JEH,* Vol. XI, 1960, 55-73.

Ahlstrom, S., *Theology in America: The Major Protestant Voices from Puritanism to Neo-Orthodoxy* (New York: Bobbs-Merrill, 1967).

Ashcraft, R., *Revolutionary Politics & Locke's Two Treatises of Government* (Princeton: Princeton University Press, 1986).

- 'John Locke, Religious Dissent, and the Origins of Liberalism', in G.J. Schochet (ed), *Restoration, Ideology, and Revolution* (Washington: Folger Institute, 1990) 149-167.

- 'Latitudinarianism and toleration: historical myth versus political history' in R. Kroll, R. Ashcraft and P. Zagorin (eds), *Philosophy, science, and religion in England 1640-1700* (Cambridge: Cambridge University Press, 1992), 151-177.

Aubrey, P., *Mr Secretary Thurloe: Cromwell's Secretary of State 1652-1660* (London: Althone Press, 1990).

Avis, P., *Anglicanism and the Christian Church* (Edinburgh: T&T Clark, 1989).

Aylmer, G.E., *The State's Servants: The Civil Servants of the English Republic, 1649-1660* (London: Routledge & Kegan Paul, 1973).

Backscheider, P.R., *Daniel Defoe: His Life* (Baltimore: Johns Hopkins University Press, 1989).

Baker, J.W., 'Church, State and Toleration: John Locke and Calvin's Heirs in England' in W.F. Graham (ed), *Later Calvinism: International Perspectives,* Vol. XXII (Kirksville: Sixteenth Century Journal Publishers, 1994), 525-543.

Barry, J., 'The Politics of Religion in Restoration Bristol' in T. Harris, P. Seaward and M. Goldie (eds) *The Politics of Religion in Restoration England* (Oxford: B. Blackwell, 1990), 163-189.

Bebbington, D.W., *Evangelicalism in Modern Britain: History from the 1730s to the 1980s* (London: Unwin Hyman, 1989).

Beddard, R.A., 'Vincent Alsop and the Emancipation of Restoration Dissent', *JEH,* Vol. XXIV, No. 2, April 1973, 161-184.

- 'Sheldon and Anglican Recovery', *HJ,* Vol. 19, no. 4 (1976), 1005-1017.

- 'The Restoration Church', in J.R. Jones (ed), *The Restored Monarchy 1660-1688* (London: Macmillan, 1979), 155-175.

- 'Bishop Cartwright's Death-bed', *Bodleian Library Record,* Vol. 11, 1984, 220-230.

Bernard, G.W., 'The Church of England c1529-c1642', *History,* 75, 224 (June 1990), 183-206.

Birch, T., *Life of John Tillotson,* (1752) abridged in *Gentleman's Magazine,* December, 1752, 543-546.

Bogue, D. and J. Bennett, *History of the Dissenters from The Revolution in 1688, to the Year 1808* (London: 1808-12).

Bolam, C.G. J. Goring, Short, H.L. and Thomas, R., *The English Presbyterians: From Elizabethan Puritanism to Modern Unitarianism* (London: Allen & Unwin, 1968).

Bolam, C.G. and J. Goring, 'Presbyterians in Separation: The Cataclysm' in Bolam *et al The English Presbyterians* (London: Allen & Unwin, 1968), 73-92.

Bosher, R.S., *The Making of the Restoration Settlement: The Influence of the Laudians, 1649-1662* (Westminster: Dacre Press,1951).

Bozeman, T.D., *To Live Ancient Lives: The Primitivist Dimension in Puritanism* (Chapel Hill: University of North Carolina Press, 1988).

Bremer, F.J., 'Increase Mather's Friends: The Trans-Atlantic Congregational Network of the Seventeenth Century' *Proceedings of the American Antiquarian Society*, Vol. 94, Pt 1, 1984, 59-96.

Breward I., 'The Abolition of Puritanism', *JRH*, Vol. 7,No. 4, Dec. 1973, 20-34.

Bronner, E.B., 'Quaker Discipline and Order, 1680-1720: Philadelphia Yearly Meeting and London Yearly meeting', in R.S. & M.M. Dunn (eds), *The World of William Penn* (Philadelphia: University of Pennsylvania Press, 1986), 323-335.

Brown, R., *Church and State in Modern Britain 1700-1850* (London: Routledge, 1991).

Brown. R., *The English Baptists of the 18th Century* (London: Baptist Historical Society, 1986).

Campbell, T.A., *The Religion of the Heart: A Study of the European Religious Life in the Seventeenth and Eighteenth Centuries* (Columbia, S.C.: 1991).

Capp, B.S., 'Extreme Millenarianism' in P. Toon (ed) *Puritans, the Millenium and the Future of Israel: Puritan Eschatology 1600-1660* (Cambridge: J. Clark, 1970) 66-90.

- 'GODLY RULE and English millenarianism', *P&P*, lii, (1971), 106-17.

- 'The millennium and eschatology in England', *P&P*, lvii, (1972), 152-162.

Carrol, R.T., *The Common-Sense Philosophy of Religion of Bishop Edward Stillingfleet 1635-1699* (The Hague: Nijhoff, 1975).

Carson, J.T., 'John Howe: Chaplain to Lord Massarene at Antrim Castle, 1671-1677', *Bulletin of the Presbyterian Historical Society of Ireland*, vii, (1977), 11-16.

Carswell, J., *The Descent on England: A Study of the English Revolution of 1688 and its European Background* (London: Barrie & Rockliff, 1969).

Cassirer, E., *The Platonic Renaissance in England* ((ET) Edinburgh: Nelson, 1953).

Champion, J.A.I., *The Pillars of Priestcraft Shaken: the Church of England and its Enemies 1660-1730* (Cambridge: Cambridge University Press, 1992).

Christianson, P., *Reformers and Babylon: English apocalyptic visions from the reformation to the eve of the civil war* (Toronto: University Toronto Press, 1978).

- 'Reformers and the Church of England under Elizabeth I and the Early Stuarts', *JEH*, Vol. 31. No. 4, October 1980, 463-482.

Clark, J.C.D., *English Society 1688-1832: Ideology, social structure and political practice during the ancien regime* (Cambridge: Cambridge University Press, 1985).

- *Revolution and Rebellion: State and Society in England in the Seventeenth and Eighteenth Centuries* (Cambridge: Cambridge University Press, 1986).

- 'England's Ancien Regime as a Confessional State', *Albion*, 2, 1989, 450-474.

Clark, J.K., *Goodwin Wharton* (Oxford: Oxford University Press, 1984).

Cliffe, J.T., *The Puritan Gentry Besieged, 1650-1700* (London: Routledge, 1993).

Cohn, N., *The pursuit of the Millennium: revolutionary millenarians and mystical anarchists of the Middle Ages* (revised ed) (London: Maurice Temple Smith, 1970).

Colie, R.L., *Light and Enlightenment: A Study of the Cambridge Platonists and the Dutch Arminians* (Cambridge: Cambridge University Press, 1957).

Collinson, P., *The Elizabethan Puritan Movement* (London: Cape, 1967).

- *Archbishop Grindal, 1519-1583: the struggle for a reformed Church* (London: Cape, 1979).

- 'A Comment: Concerning the Name Puritan', *JEH*, Vol. 3, No. 4, October 1980, 483-488.
- *The Religion of Protestants: The Church in English Society, 1559-1625* (Oxford: Clarendon Press, 1982).
- 'Towards a Broader Understanding of the Early Dissenting Tradition', reprinted in P. Collinson, *Godly People: Essays on English Protestantism and Puritanism* (London: Hambledon Press, 1983) 527-562.
- 'Sects and the Evolution of Puritanism' in F.J. Bremer (ed) *Puritanism: Transatlantic Perspectives on a Seventeenth-century Anglo-American Faith* (Boston: Massachusetts Historical Society, 1993) 147-166.

Compagnac, E.T. (ed.), *The Cambridge Platonists* (Oxford: Clarendon Press, 1901).

Cope, J.I., *Joseph Glanvill, Anglican Apologist* (St Louis: Washington University Press, 1956).

Cragg, G.R., *Puritanism in the Period of the Great Persecution 1660-1688* (Cambridge: Cambridge University Press, 1957).
- (ed.) *The Cambridge Platonists* (New York: Oxford University Press, 1968).
- *Freedom and Authority: A Study of English Political Thought in the Early Seventeenth Century* (Philadelphia: Westminster Press, 1975).

Dale, R.W., *History of English Congregationalism* (London: 1907).

Davis, A.P., *Isaac Watts: His Life and Works* (London: Independent Press, 1943).

Davies, C. and J. Facey, 'A Reformation Dilemma: John Foxe and the Problem of Discipline', *JEH*, Vol. 39, No. 1, Jan. 1988, 37-65.

Davies, J., *The Caroline Captivity of the Church: Charles I and the Remoulding of Anglicanism* (Oxford: Clarendon Press, 1992).

Davis, J.C., 'Cromwell's Religion', in J. Morrill (ed),*Oliver Cromwell and the English Revolution* (London: Longman, 1990), 181-208.
- 'Religion and the Struggle for Freedom in the English Revolution', *HJ*, Vol. 35, No. 3, (1992), 507-530.
- 'Against Formality: One Aspect of the English Revolution', *TRHS*, 6th series, Vol. 3, 1993, 265-288.

De Krey, G.S., 'The London Whigs and the Exclusion Crisis reconsidered' in A.L. Beier, D. Cannadine and J.M. Rosenheim (eds), *The First Modern Society: Essays in English History in Honour of Lawrence Stone* (Cambridge: Cambridge University Press, 1989), 457-482.
- 'London Radicals and Revolutionary Politics, 1675-1683' in T. Harris, P. Seaward and M. Goldie (eds), *The Politics of Religion in Restoration England* (Oxford: B. Blackwell, 1990), 133-162.
- 'The First Restoration Crisis: Conscience and Coercion in London, 1667-73', *Albion*, 25, (Winter 1993), 565-580.
- 'Party Lines: A Reply', *Albion*, 25, (Winter 1993), 639-643.
- 'Rethinking the Restoration: Dissenting Cases for Conscience 1667-1672', *HJ* 38, 1 (1995), 53-83.

Dunn, J., 'The Claim to Freedom of Conscience: Freedom of Speech, Freedom of Thought, Freedom of Worship?', in O.. Grell, J.I. Israel and N. Tyacke (eds), *From Persecution to Toleration: The Glorious Revolution and Religion in England* (Oxford: Clarendon Press, 1991), 171-193.

Endy, M.B. Jnr, *William Penn and Early Quakerism* (Princeton: Princeton University Press, 1973).

- 'Puritanism, Spiritualism and Quakerism: An Historiographical Essay', in R.S. and M.M. Dunn (eds), *The World of William Penn* (Philadelphia: University of Pennsylvania Press, 1986), 281-301.
Every, G., *The High Church Party 1688-1718* (London: SPCK, 1956).
Fallon, S.M., *Milton Among the Philosophers: Poetry and Materialism in Seventeenth-Century England* (Ithaca, NY: Cornell University Press, 1991).
Field, D.P. '"Rigide Calvinisme in a Softer Dresse": The Moderate Presbyertiansim of John Howe (1630-1705)' unpublished PhD Thesis (University of Cambridge, 1993).
Fielding, J., 'Arminianism in the Localities: Peterborough Diocese, 1603-1642', in K. Fincham (ed), *The Early Stuart Church, 1603-1640* (Basingstoke: Macmillan, 1993), 93-113.
Fincham, K., 'Episcopal Government, 1603-1640' in K. Fincham (ed), *The Early Stuart Church, 1603-1640* (Basingstoke: Macmillan, 1993), 71-91.
Finlayson, M.G., 'Puritanism and Puritans: Labels or Libels?', *Canadian Journal of History*, Vol. VIII, No.3, Dec. 73, 201-223.
- *Historians, Puritanism and the English Revolution: The Religious Factor in English Politics before and after the Interregnum* (Toronto: University of Toronto Press, 1983).
Flaningam, J., 'The Occasional Conformity Controversy: Ideology and Party politics, 1697-1711', *JBS*, Vol XVII, No. 1, Fall 1977, 38-62.
Fletcher, A., 'The Enforcement of the Conventicle Acts 1664-1679' in W.J. Sheils (ed.) *Persecution and Toleration*, Studies in Church History, 21 (Oxford: B. Blackwell, 1984), 235-246.
Fletcher, W.G.D., 'The Parish Registers of Loughborough in the County of Leicester', *The Reliquary Quarterly Archaeological Journal and Review*, London, 1873, 194-202.
- *The Rectors of Loughborough* (Oxford: 1882).
Gabbey, A., '"A disease incurable": scepticism and the Cambridge Platonists' in R.H. Popkin and A. Vanderjagt (eds) *Scepticism and Irreligion in the Seventeenth and Eighteenth Centuries* (Leiden: Brill, 1993), 71-91.
Gascoigne, J., *Cambridge in the Age of Enlightenment: Science, religion and politics from the Restoration to the French Revolution* (Cambridge: Cambridge University Press, 1989).
George, C.H. and K., *The Protestant Mind of the English Reformation 1570-1640* (Princeton: Princeton University Press, 1961).
George, C.H., 'Puritanism as History and Historiography', *P&P*, No. 41, Dec. 1968, 77-104.
Godwin, W., *History of the Commonwealth of England* (London: 1828).
Goldie, M., 'John Locke and Anglican Royalism', *Political Studies*, XXXI, (1983), 61-85.
- 'Sir Peter Pett, Sceptical Toryism and the Science of Toleration in the 1680s' in W.J. Sheils (ed.), *Persecution and Toleration*, Studies in Church History 21 (Oxford: B. Blackwell, 1984), 247-273.
- 'Danby, the Bishops and the Whigs' in T. Harris, P. Seaward, and M. Goldie (eds), *The Politics of Religion in Restoration England* (Oxford: B. Blackwell, 1990), 75-105.

- The Political Thought of the Anglican Revolution' in R.A. Beddard (ed), *The Revolutions of 1688* (Oxford: Clarendon Press, 1991), 102-136.
- 'The Theory of Religious Intolerance in Restoration England' in O.. Grell, J.I. Israel and N. Tyacke (eds.), *from Persecution to Toleration: the Glorious Revolution and Religion in England* (Oxford: Clarendon Press, 1991), 331-368.
- 'Roger Morrice and the History of Puritanism', *Early Modern History*, Vol. 1, No. 2, Jan. 1992, 19-20.
- 'John Locke's Circle and James II', *HJ*, 35, 3 (1992), 557-586.
- 'James II and the Dissenters' Revenge: the Commission of Enquiry of 1688', *Historical Research*, Vol. 66, No. 159, Feb. 1993, 53-88.
- 'Priestcraft and the Birth of Whiggism' in N. Phillipson and Q. Skinner (eds), *Political Discourse in Early Modern Britain* (Cambridge: Cambridge University Press, 1993), 209-231.

Gordon, A. (ed.), *Freedom After Ejection: A Review (1690-1692) of Presbyterian and Congregational Nonconformity in England and Wales* (Manchester: Manchester University Press, 1917).

Goring, J., 'The Break-Up of the Old Dissent', in Bolam *et al*, *The English Presbyterians: from Elizabethan Puritanism to Modern Unitarianism* (London: Allen & Unwin, 1968), 175-218.

Greaves, R.L., 'The Nature of the Puritan Tradition' in R.B. Knox (ed), *Reformation, Conformity and Dissent: Essays in Honour of Geoffrey Nuttall* (London: Epworth, 1977), 255-273.
- *Society and Religion in Elizabethan England* (Minneapolis: University of Minnesota Press, 1981).
- *Deliver Us from Evil: The Radical Underground in Britain, 1660-1663* (New York: Oxford University Press, 1986).
- *Enemies Under His Feet: Radicals and Nonconformists in Britain, 1664-1677* (Stanford: Stanford University Press, 1990).
- *Secrets of the Kingdom: British Radicals from the Popish Plot to the Revolution of 1688-89* (Stanford, Stanford University Press, 1992).
- *John Bunyan and English Nonconformity* (London: Hambledon Press, 1992), 1-35.
- 'Great Scott! The Restoration in Turmoil, or Restoration Crisis and the Emergence of Party', *Albion*, 25, (Winter 1993), 605-618.
- 'The Rye House Plotting, Nonconformist Clergy, and Calvin's Resistance Theory' in W.F. Graham (ed), *Later Calvinism: International Perspectives*, Vol. XXII (Kirksville: Sixteenth Century Journal Publishers, 1994), 505-520.
- *God's Other Children: Protestant Nonconformists and the emergence of denominational churches in Ireland 1660-1700* (Stanford: Stanford University Press,1997).

Greaves R.L. and R. Zaller, *Biographical Dictionary of British Radicals in the Seventeenth Century*, (3 vols.) (Brighton: Harvester Press, 1982).

Grell, O.P., J.I. Israel and N. Tyacke, 'Introduction', in O.P. Grell, J.I. Israel and N. Tyacke (eds), *From Persecution to Toleration: the Glorious Revolution and Religion in England* (Oxford: Clarendon, 1991), 1-16.

Green, I.M., *The Re-establishment of the Church of England, 1660-1663* (Oxford: Oxford University Press, 1978).

Griffin, M.J., *Latitudinarianism in the Seventeenth-Century Church of England* (Leiden: Brill, 1992).

Griffiths, O.M., *Religion and Learning: A Study of Presbyterian Thought from the Bartholemew Ejections (1662) to the Foundations of the Unitarian Movement* (Cambridge: Cambridge University Press, 1935).

Gysi, L., *Platonism and Cartesianism in the Philosophy of Ralph Cudworth* (Bern: Lang, 1962).

Hall, B., 'Puritanism: the Problem of Definition', in C.J. Cuming (ed) *Studies in Church History II* (London: Nelson, 1965) 283-296.

Hall, D.D., 'Understanding the Puritans', in H.J. Bass (ed), *The State of American History* (Chicago: Quadrangle Books, 1970) 330-349.

Hall, M.G. (ed), 'The Autobiography of Increase Mather', *Proceedings of the American Antiquarian Society*, Oct. 1961, 271-360.

- *The Last American Puritan: The Life of Increase Mather 1639-1723* (Middleton, Conn.: Wesleyan University Press, 1988).

Haller, W., *The Rise of Puritanism*, (1938) (New York: Columbia University Press, 1947).

Harris, T., 'Introduction: Revising the Restoration' and 'Lives Liberties and Estates: Rhetorics of Liberty in the Reign of Charles II' in T. Harris, Paul Seaward and M. Goldie (eds), *The Politics of Religion in Restoration England* (Oxford: B. Blackwell, 1990) 1-28.

- *Politics Under the Later Stuarts: Party Conflict in a Divided Society 1660-1715* (London: Longman, 1993).
- 'Party Turns? Or, Whigs and Tories Get Off Scot Free', *Albion*, 25, (Winter 1993), 581-590.
- 'Sobering Thoughts, But the Party is Not yet Over: A Reply', *Albion*, 25, (Winter 1993), 645-647.

Harrison J.R. and P. Laslett, *The Library of John Locke* (Oxford: Oxford University Press, 1965).

Henning, B.D. (ed.), *The House of Commons 1660-1690*, (The History of Parliament) (London: Secker & Warburg, 1983).

Hewlett, J.P., 'A Brief Memoir etc', Howe's *Works*, Vol. 1, ix-xxix.

Hexter, J.H., 'The Problem of the Presbyterian Independents' in J.H. Hexter, *Reappraisals in History: New Views on History and Society in Early Modern Europe* (Chicago: University of Chicago Press, 1961), 219-240.

Hill, C., *Society and Puritanism in Pre-Revolutionary England* (London: Secker & Warburg, 1964).

- *The Experience of Defeat: Milton and Some Contemporaries* (London: Faber, 1984).
- 'History and Denominational History', reprinted in C. Hill, *The Collected Essays of Christopher Hill - Volume Two: Religion and Politics in 17th Century England* (Brighton: Harvester Press, 1986), 3-10.
- 'Occasional Conformity and the Grindalian Tradition', reprinted in C. Hill, *The Collected Essays of Christopher Hill - Volume Two: Religion and Politics in 17th Century England* (Brighton: Harvester Press, 1986), 301-320.

Holmes, G.S., *The Trial of Doctor Sacheverell* (London: Eyre Methuen, 1973).

- *Religion and Party in Late Stuart England* (London: Historical Assn, 1975).
- *The Making of a Great Power: Late Stuart and early Georgian Britain 1660-1722* (London: Longman, 1993).

Honeygoskey, S.R., *Milton's House of God: The Invisible and Visible Church* (Columbia: University of Missouri Press, 1993).

Hopfl, H., '-Isms' *British Journal of Political Science*, No. 13 (1983), 1-17.
Horne, S., *A Popular History of the Free Churches* (London: James Clarke, 1903).
Horton, J. and S. Mendus (eds.), *John Locke: A Letter Concerning Toleration in Focus*, (London: Routledge, 1991).
Horton, R.F., *John Howe* (London: Methuen, 1895).
Horwitz, H., 'Protestant Reconciliation in the Exclusion Crisis', *JEH*, Vol. 15, 1964, 201-217.
- 'Comprehension in the Later Seventeenth Century: A Postscript', *CH*, Vol. 34. Sept, 1965, 342-349.
Hoyles, J., *The Waning of the Renaissance 1640-1740: Studies in the Thought and Poetry of Henry More, John Norris and Isaac Watts* (The Hague: Nijhoff, 1971).
Hunter, M., 'Casuistry in Action: Robert Boyle's Confessional Interviews with Gilbert Burnet and Edward Stillingfleet, 1691.', *JEH*, 44 (1993), 80-98.
Hutton, R., *The Restoration: A Political and Religious History of England and Wales 1658-1667* (Oxford: Clarendon Press, 1985).
Hutton, S., 'Science, philosophy, and atheism: Edward Stillingfleet's defence of religion' in R.H. Popkin and A. Vanderjagt (eds) *Scepticism and Irreligion in the Seventeenth and Eighteenth Centuries* (Leiden: Brill, 1993), 102-120.
Israel, J.I., 'William III and Toleration' in O.P. Grell, J.I. Israel and N. Tyacke (eds.), *From Persecution to Toleration: The Glorious Revolution and Religion in England* (Oxford: Clarendon Press, 1991) 129-170.
Jacob, J.R., *Henry Stubbe, radical Protestantism and the early Enlightenment* (Cambridge: Cambridge University Press, 1983).
Jay, E.G., *The Church: Its Changing Image Through Twenty Centuries*, Vol. 1 (London: SPCK, 1977).
Jolley, N., *Leibniz and Locke: A Study of the New Essays on Human Understanding* (Oxford: Clarendon Press, 1994).
Jones, G.F.T., *Saw-Pit Wharton: The Political Career from 1640-1691 of Philip, fourth Lord Wharton* (Sydney: Sydney University Press, 1967).
Jones, J.R., 'Introduction' and 'The Revolution in Context' in J.R. Jones (ed), *The Restored Monarchy, 1660-1688* (London: Macmillan, 1979), 1-9 & 11-52.
- 'A Representative of the Alternative Society of Restoration England?' in R.S. and M.M. Dunn (eds), *The World of William Penn* (Philadelphia: University of Pennsylvania Press, 1986), 55-69.
Jones, R.T., *Congregationalism in England 1662-1962* (London: Independent Press, 1962).
Jordan, W.K., *The Development of Religious Toleration in England*, (3 vols.) (London: Allen & Unwin, 1932-8).
Kearney, H.F., 'Puritanism and Science: Problems of Definition', in C. Webster (ed) *The Intellectual Revolution of the Seventeenth Century* (London: Routledge & Kegan Paul, 1974), 254-261.
Keeble, N.H., *Richard Baxter: Puritan Man of Letters* (Oxford: Clarendon, 1982).
- *The Literary Culture of Nonconformity in Later Seventeenth-Century England* (Leicester: Leicester University Press, 1987).
- *The Restoration: England in the 1660s* (Oxford: Blackwell, 2002)
- (ed.) *The Autobiography of Richard Baxter* (London: Dent, 1974).
Keeble, N.H. and G. R. Nuttall (eds.), *Calendar of the Correspondence of Richard Baxter*, 2. vols., (Oxford: Clarendon, 1991).

Keble, J., 'Editor's Preface' in J. Keble (ed.) *The Works of Mr Richard Hooker* (Oxford: 1888) vol. 1, ix-cxvi.

Kelly, J.N.D., *Early Christian Doctrines* (London: A&C Black, 1977).

Kenny, A., 'The Conscience of Sir Thomas More' in *The Heritage of Wisdom: Essays in the History of Philosophy* (Oxford: B. Blackwell, 1987), 108-115.

Kilroy, P., *Protestant Dissent and Controversy in Ireland 1660-1714* (Cork: Cork University Press, 1994)

Kirk, L., *Richard Cumberland and Natural Law: Secularisation of Thought in Seventeenth-Century England* (Cambridge: James Clarke, 1987).

Kishlansky, M., *A Monarchy Transformed: Britain 1603-1714* (London: Allen Lane Penguin, 1996).

Kroll, R., R. Ashcraft and P. Zagorin (eds), *Philosophy, Science and Religion in England 1640-1700* (Cambridge: Cambridge University Press, 1992).

Lacey, D.R., *Dissent and Parliamentary Politics in England, 1661-1689: A Study in the Perpetuation and Tempering of Parliamentarianism* (New Brunswick: Rutgers University Press, 1969).

Lake, P., 'Calvinism and the English Church 1570-1635', *P&P*, No. 114 (Feb. 1987), 32-76.

- *Anglicans and Puritans?: Presbyterianism and English Conformist Thought from Whitgift to Hooker* (London: Unwin Hyman, 1988).

- 'Lancelot Andrewes, John Buckridge, and Avant-Garde Conformity at the Court of James I', in L.L. Peck (ed), *The Mental World of the Jacobean Court* (Cambridge: Cambridge University Press, 1991), 113-133.

- 'The Laudians and the Argument from Authority' in B.Y. Kunze and D. Brautigan (eds.), *Court, Country, and Culture: Essays on Early Modern British History in Honour of Perez Zagorin* (Rochester: University of Rochester Press, 1992), 149-175.

- 'The Laudian Style: Order, Uniformity and the Pursuit of the Beauty of Holiness in the 1630s', in K. Fincham (ed), *The Early Stuart Church, 1603-1640* (Basingstoke: Macmillan, 1993), 161-185.

- 'Defining Puritanism - again?' in F.J. Bremer (ed), *Puritanism: Transatlantic Perspectives on a Seventeenth-Century Anglo-American Faith* (Boston: Massachusetts Historical Society, 1993), 3-29.

Lamont, W.M., 'Puritanism as History and Historiography: Some Further Thoughts', *P&P*, No. 44, Aug. 1969, 133-146.

- *Godly Rule: Protestant Imperialism and the English Revolution* (London: Macmillan, 1969).

- *Richard Baxter and the Millennium: Protestant Imperialism and the English Revolution* (London: Croom Helm, 1979).

- 'The Religion of Andrew Marvell: locating the "Bloody Horse"', in C. Condren and A.D. Cousins (eds), *The Political Identity of Andrew Marvell* (Aldershot: Scolar Press, 1990), 135-156.

- 'Arminianism: the controversy that never was' in N. Phillipson and Q. Skinner (eds), *Political Discourse in Early Modern Britain* (Cambridge: Cambridge University Press, 1993), 45-66.

Laslett, P., 'Introduction' to J. Locke, *Two Treatises of Government* (Cambridge: Cambridge University Press, 1967), 3-126.

Lichtenstein, A., *Henry More: The Rational Theology of a Cambridge Platonist* (Cambridge, MA: Harvard University Press, 1962).

Little, D., *Religion, Order and Law: A Study in Pre-Revolutionary England* (Oxford: B. Blackwell, 1970).

Loeb, L.E., *From Descartes to Hume: Continental Metaphysics and the Development of Modern Philosophy* (Ithaca, NY: Cornell University Press, 1981).

Lovejoy, A.O., *The Great Chain of Being: A Study of the History of an Idea* (Cambridge, MA: Harvard University Press, 1950).

McAdoo, H.R., *The Spirit of Anglicanism* (London: SCM, 1965).

McGrath, P., *Papists and Puritans Under Elizabeth I* (London: Blandford Press, 1967).

Marshall, J., 'The Ecclesiology of the Latitude-men 1660-1689: Stillingfleet, Tillotson and "Hobbism"', *JEH,* Vol. 36, No.3. July 1985, 407-427.

- 'John Locke and Latitudinarianism' in R. Kroll, R. Ashcraft and P. Zagorin (eds), *Philosophy, science and religion in England 1640-1700* (Cambridge: Cambridge University Press, 1992), 253-282.

- *John Locke: Resistance, Religion and Responsibility* (Cambridge: Cambridge University Press, 1994).

Matthews, A.G., *Calamy Revised: Being a Revision of Edmund Calamy's Account of the Ministers and Others Ejected and Silenced, 1660-2* (Oxford: Oxford University Press, 1934).

- *The Savoy Declaration of Faith and Order 1658* (London: Independent Press, 1959).

Merchant, C., *The Death of Nature: Women, Ecology, and the Scientific Revolution* (San Francisco: Harper & Row, 1980).

Miller, J., *Popery and Politics in England, 1660-88* (Cambridge: Cambridge University Press, 1973).

- 'The Later Stuart Monarchy' in J.R. Jones (ed), *The Restored Monarchy, 1660-1688* (London: Macmillan, 1979), 30-47.

Milne, D.J., 'The Results of the Rye House Plot and Their Influence Upon the Revolution of 1688', *Proceedings of the Royal Historical Society,* Fifth Series, Vol. 1, 1951, 91-108.

Milton, A., 'The Church of England, Rome and the True Church: The Demise of the Jacobean Consensus', in K. Fincham (ed), *The Early Stuart Church, 1603-1642* (Basingstoke: Macmillan, 1993), 187-210.

- *Catholic and Reformed: the Roman and Protestant Churches in English Thought 1600-1640* (Cambridge: Cambridge University Press, 1995).

More, E., 'John Goodwin and the Origins of the New Arminianism', *JBS,* Vol. XXII, No. 1, Fall, 1982, 50-70.

Morgan, E.S., *Visible Saints: The History of a Puritan Idea* (New York: New York University Press, 1963).

Morgan, J., *Godly Learning: Puritan Attitudes towards Reason, Learning and Education* (Cambridge: Cambridge University Press, 1986), 9-22.

New J.F.H., *Anglicans and Puritans: The Basis of Their Opposition, 1558-1640* (London: 1964).

- 'Cromwell and the Paradoxes of Puritanism', *JBS,* Vol. V, No. 1, Nov. 1965, 53-59.

Nuttall, G.F., *The Holy Spirit in Puritan Faith and Experience* (Oxford: B. Blackwell, 1947).

- 'Richard Baxter's correspondence: a preliminary survey', *JEH*, Vol 1 (1950), 85-95.
- 'The Worcestershire Association: Its Membership' *JEH*, Vol. 1 (1950), 197-206.
- 'Doddridge's Life and Times' and 'Philip Doddridge – A Personal Appreciation' in G. Nuttall (ed) *Philip Doddridge 1702-51: His Contribution to English Religion* (London: Independent Press, 1951), 11-31 & 154-163.
- *Richard Baxter and Philip Doddridge: A Study in a Tradition* (London: Dr Williams Library, 1951).
- 'Presbyterians and Independents: Some Movements for Unity 300 Years Ago', *Journal of the Presbyterian Historical Society*, 10, (1952), 4-15.
- *Visible Saints: The Congregational Way 1640-1660* (Oxford: B. Blackwell, 1957).
- 'The First Nonconformists' in G.F. Nuttall and O. Chadwick (eds.), *From Uniformity to Unity 1661-1962* (London: SPCK, 1962), 149-187.
- *Richard Baxter* (London: Nelson, 1965).
- *The Puritan Spirit: Essays and Addresses* (London: Epworth, 1967).
- 'English Dissenters in the Netherlands 1640-1689' in *Nederlands Archief voor Kerkgschiedenis*, 59, 1978, 37-54.

Oakley, F., *Omnipotence, Covenant and Order: An Excursion in the History of Ideas from Abelard to Leibniz* (Ithaca, NY: Cornell University Press, 1984).

Olsen, P.J., 'Was John Foxe a Millenarian', *JEH*, Vol. 45, No. 4, October 1994, 600-624.

Packer, J.W., *The Transformation of Anglicanism 1643-1660: with Special Reference to Henry Hammond* (Manchester: Manchester University Press, 1969).

Plum, H.G., *Restoration Puritanism: A Study of the Growth of English Liberty* (Chapel Hill, NC: University of North Carolina Press, 1943).

Pocock, J.G.A., 'Thomas Hobbes: Atheist or Enthusiast? His Place in a Restoration Debate', *History of Political Thought*, Vol. XI, No. 4, Winter 1990, 737-749.

- 'Enthusiasm: The Antiself of Enlightenment' in Miles Fairburn and W.H. Oliver (eds.) *The Certainty of Doubt: Tributes to Peter Munz* (Wellington: Victoria University Press, 1996), 117-39.

Popkin, R.H., 'Introduction' to (R.H. Popkin (ed)), J. Glanvill, *Essays on Several Important Subjects in Philosophy and Religion* (New York: Johnson Reprint, 1970), v-xxxiii.

- *The Third Force in Seventeenth-Century Thought* (Leiden: Brill, 1992).

Porter, H.C. (ed.), *Puritanism in Tudor England* (London: Macmillan, 1970).

Powicke, F.J., *A Life of the Reverend Richard Baxter 1615-1691* (London: Jonathan Cape, 1924).

- *The Cambridge Platonists, a Study* (London: Dent, 1926).

Ramsbottom, J.D., 'Presbyterians and "Partial Conformity" in the Restoration Church of England', *JEH*, Vol. 43, No. 2, April 1992, 249-270.

Ratcliff, E.C., 'The Savoy Conference and the Revision of the Book of Common Prayer', in G.F. Nuttall and O. Chadwick (eds), *From Uniformity to Unity 1662-1962* (London: Epworth, 1962) 89-148.

Reay, B., *The Quakers and the English Revolution* (London: Temple Smith,1985).

Remer, G., 'Rhetoric and the Erasmian Defence of Religious Toleration', *History of Political Thought*, Vol. X, No.3, Autumn 1989, 377-403.

- 'Humanism, Liberalism, & the Skeptical Case for Religious Toleration', *Polity*, Vol. XXV, No. 1, Fall, 1992, 21-43.
- 'Hobbes, the Rhetorical Tradition, and Toleration', *Review of Politics*, 54:1, 1992, 5-33.

Rivers, I., *Reason, Grace and Sentiment: A Study of the Language of Religion and Ethics in England, 660-1780* (Cambridge: Cambridge University Press, 1991).

Rogers, G.A.J., 'Locke and the latitude-men: ignorance as a ground for toleration' in R. Kroll, R. Ashcraft and P. Zagorin (eds), *Philosophy, science and religion in England 1640-1700* (Cambridge: Cambridge University Press, 1992), 230-252.

Rogers, H., *The Life and Character of John Howe, M.A with an Analysis of His Writings* (London: Religious Tract Society, 1863).

Rupp, E.G., 'A Devotion of Rapture in English Puritanism' in R.B. Knox (ed), *Reformation, Conformity and Dissent: Essays in Honour of Geoffrey Nuttall* (London: Epworth, 1977), 115-131.
- *Religion in England 1688-1791* (Oxford: Clarendon Press, 1986).

Russell, C., 'Arguments for Religious Unity in England 1530-1650', (1967) reprinted in *Unrevolutionary England, 1603-1642* (London: Hambledon Press, 1990), 179-204.
- (ed.), *The Origins of the English Civil War* (London: Macmillan, 1973).

Sasek, L.A. (ed.), *Images of English Puritanism: A Collection of Contemporary Sources 1589-1646* (Baton Rouge: Louisiana State University Press, 1989).

Saunders, A., 'The State as highwayman: from candour to rights', in K. Haakonssen (ed.) *Enlightenment and Religion: rational dissent in eighteenth-century Britain* (Cambridge: Cambridge University Press, 1996), 241-271.

Schlatter, R., *Richard Baxter and Puritan Politics* (New Brunswick: Rutgers University Press, 1957).

Schneider, C.G., 'Roots and Branches: From Principled Nonconformity to the Emergence of Religious Parties' in F.J. Bremer (ed) *Puritanism: Transatlantic Perspectives on a Seventeenth-Century Anglo-American Faith* (Boston: Massachusetts Historical Society, 1993), 167-200.

Schochet, G.J., *Patriarchalism in Political Thought: The Authoritarian Family and Political Speculation and Attitudes Especially in Seventeenth Century England* (New York: Basic Books, 1975).
- 'Toleration, Revolution, And Judgment In the Development of Locke's Political Thought', *Political Science*, Vol. 40, No. 1, July 1988, 84-96.
- 'Radical Politics and Ashcraft's Treatise on Locke', *Journal of the History of Ideas*, 50:3, July/Sept. 1989, 491-510.
- '"The Tyranny of a Popish Successor" and the Politics of Religious Toleration', in G.J. Schochet (ed), *Restoration, Ideology and Revolution* (Washington: Folger Institute, 1990), 83-103.
- 'From Persecution to "Toleration", in J.R. Jones (ed) *Liberty Secured? Britain Before and After 1688* (Stanford: Stanford University Press, 1992), 122-157.
- 'Between Lambeth and Leviathan: Samuel Parker on the Church of England and political order' in N. Phillipson and Q. Skinner (eds), *Political Discourse in Early Modern Britain* (Cambridge: Cambridge University Press, 1993), 189-208.

- 'Samuel Parker, religious diversity, and the ideology of persecution' in R.G. Lund (ed.) *The Margins of Orthodoxy: Heterodox Writing and Cultural Response, 1660-1750* (Cambridge: Cambridge University Press, 1995) 119-148.

Scott, J., 'England's Troubles: Exhuming the Popish Plot' in T. Harris, P. Seaward and M. Goldie (eds.), *The Politics of Religion in Restoration England* (Oxford: B. Blackwell, 1990), 107-131.

- *Algernon Sidney and the Restoration Crisis, 1677-1683* (Cambridge: Cambridge University Press, 1991).

- 'Restoration Crisis. Or, If This Isn't a party, We're Not Having a Good Time.', *Albion*, 25, (Winter 1993), 619-637.

- *England's Troubles: Seventeenth Century English Political Leadership in European Context* (Cambridge: Cambridge University Press, 2000).

Scott, W.M., *The Life of John Howe* (London: Congregational Union, 1911).

Seaton, A.A., *The Theory of Toleration Under the Later Stuarts* (Cambridge: Cambridge University Press, 1911).

Seaward, P., *The Cavalier Parliament and the Reconstruction of the Old Regime 1661-1667* (Cambridge: Cambridge University Press, 1989).

- 'Gilbert Sheldon, the London Vestries and the Defence of the Church of England', in T. Harris, P. Seaward and M. Goldie (eds), *The Politics of Religion in Restoration England* (Oxford: B. Blackwell, 1990), 49-73.

Sherwood, R.F., *The Court of Oliver Cromwell* (London: Croom Helm, 1977).

Shifflett, A., *Stoicism, Politics & Literature in the Age of Milton: War and Peace Reconciled* (Cambridge: Cambridge University Press, 1998).

Simon, W.G., 'Comprehension in the Age of Charles II', *CH*, Vol. 31, 1962, 440-448.

Skeats, H.S. and C.S. Miall, *History of the Free Churches of England 1688-1691* (London: Alexander & Shepherd, 1891).

Sommerville, C.J., *The Secularization of Early Modern England: From Religious Culture to Religious Faith* (New York: Oxford University Press, 1992).

Sommerville, J., *Politics and Ideology in England 1603-1640* (London: Longman, 1986).

- 'Introduction' to R. Filmer, *Patriarcha and Other Writings*, Cambridge: Cambridge University Press, 1991, ix-xxiv.

Spalding, J.C. and M.F. Brass, 'Reduction of Episcopacy as a Means to Unity in England, 1640-1662.', *CH*, Vol. 30, 1961, 414-432.

Spalding, R., *The Improbable Puritan: A Life of Bulstrode Whitelocke 1605-1675* (London: Faber, 1975).

Speck, W.A., *Reluctant Revolutionaries: Englishmen and the Revolution of 1688* (Oxford: Oxford University Press, 1988).

Spellman, W.M., *The Latitudinarians and the Church of England, 1660-1700* (Athens, GA: University of Georgia Press, 1993).

Spurr, J., '"Latitudinarianism" and the Restoration Church' *HJ*, Vol. 31, 1988, 61-82.

- 'The Church of England, Comprehension and the Toleration Act of 1689', *EHR*, Oct. 1989, 926-946.

- 'Schism and the Restoration Church', *JEH*, Vol. 41, No. 3, July 1990, 408-424.

- '"Virtue, Religion and Government": the Anglican Uses of Providence' in T. Harris, P. Seaward and M. Goldie (eds.), *The Politics of Religion in Restoration England* (Oxford: B. Blackwell, 1990), 29-47.
- *The Restoration Church of England, 1646-1689* (New Haven: Yale University Press, 1991).
- *English Puritanism 1603-1689* (Basingstoke: Macmillan, 1998)

Steneck, N.H., '"The Ballad of Robert Grosse and Joseph Glanvill" and the background to *Plus Ultra*', *The British Journal of the History of Science*, XIV, 1981, 59-74.

Stewart, M.A., 'Rational dissent in early eighteenth-century Ireland' in L. Haakonssen (ed.) *Enlightenment and Religion: Rational dissent in eighteenth-century Britain* (Cambridge: Cambridge University Press, 1996).

Stoughton, J., *History of Religion in England, from the Opening of the Long Parliament to the End of the Eighteenth Century*, (6 vols.) (London: Hodder & Stoughton, 1881).

Sutherland, M.P., 'Protestant Divergence in the Restoration Crisis', *JRH*, 21, No 3, October 1997, 285-301.

Swatos, W.H., Jnr *Into Denominationalism: The Anglican Metamorphosis* (Storrs, Conn: Society for the Scientific Study of Religion, 1979).

Sykes, N., *Old Priest and New Presbyter: The Anglican attitude to episcopacy, presbyterianism and papacy since the Reformation* (Cambridge: Cambridge University Press, 1956).
- *From Sheldon to Secker: Aspects of English Church History 1660-1768* (Cambridge: Cambridge University Press, 1959).

Thomas, K., 'Cases of Conscience in Seventeenth-Century England' in J. Morrill, P. Slack and D. Woolf (eds) *Public Duty and Private Conscience in Seventeenth-Century England* (Oxford: Clarendon, 1993), 29-56.

Thomas, R., 'Philip Doddridge and Liberalism in Religion' in G. Nuttall (ed) *Philip Doddridge 1702-51: His Contribution to English Religion* (London: Independent Press, 1951), 122-153.
- 'The Non-Subscription Controversy amongst Dissenters in 1719: the Salters' Hall Debate', *JEH*, Vol. 4, 1954, 162-186.
- 'The Seven Bishops and Their Petition, 18 May 1688', *JEH*, Vol 12, 1961, 56-70.
- 'Comprehension and Indulgence' in G.F. Nuttall and O. Chadwick (eds), *From Uniformity to Unity 1662-1962* (London: SPCK, 1962), 189-253.
- *Daniel Williams "Presbyterian Bishop"* (London: Dr Williams' Library, 1964).
- 'Presbyterians in Separation: Parties in Nonconformity' and 'Presbyterians in Transition' in Bolam *et al*, *The English Presbyterians: From Elizabethan Puritanism to Modern Unitarianism* (London: Allen & Unwin, 1968), 93-112 & 113-174.

Thomson, A., 'Life of Dr Owen' in W.H. Goold (ed), *The Work of John Owen D.D.*, (16 vols., 1850-53), London: 1965, Vol. 1, XXI-CXXI.

Toon, P., *God's Statesman: The Life and Work of John Owen* (Exeter: Paternoster, 1971).

Trevor-Roper, H., 'Toleration and Religion After 1688' in O.. Grell, J.I. Israel and N. Tyacke (eds), *From Persecution to Toleration: the Glorious Revolution and Religion in England* (Oxford: Clarendon, 1991), 389-408.

Tuck, R., 'The civil religion of Thomas Hobbes' in N. Phillipson and Q. Skinner (eds), *Political Discourse in Early Modern Britain* (Cambridge: Cambridge University Press, 1993), 120-138.

Tulloch, J., *Rational Theology and Christian Philosophy in England in the Seventeenth Century*, (2 vols.) (Edinburgh: Blackwood, 1872).

Turner, G.L. (ed.), *Original Records of Early Nonconformity Under Persecution and Indulgence* (London: Unwin, 1911).

Tyacke, N., 'Puritanism, Arminianism and Counter-Revolution' in C. Russell (ed), *The Origins of the English Civil War* (London: Macmillan, 1973), 119-143.

- *Anti-Calvinists: the Rise of English Arminianism c1590-1640* (Oxford: Clarendon, 1987).

- 'The "Rise of Puritanism" and the Legalizing of Dissent, 1571-1719' in O.. Grell, J.I. Israel and N. Tyacke (eds), *From Persecution to Toleration: the Glorious Revolution and Religion in England* (Oxford: Clarendon, 1991), 17-49.

- 'Archbishop Laud', in K. Fincham (ed), *The Early Stuart Church, 1603-1640* (Basingstoke, Macmillan, 1993), 51-70.

- 'Arminianism and the Theology of the Restoration Church' in *Idem, Aspects of English Protestantism c. 1530-1700* (Manchester: Manchester University Press, 2001), 320-339.

Van Leeuwan, H.G., *The Problem of Certainty in English Thought, 1630-1690* (The Hague: Martinus Nijhoff, 1970).

Venn, J. and J.A. (eds), *Alumni Cantabrigienses* (Cambridge: Cambridge University Press, 1922).

Walker, W., *The Creeds and Platforms of Congregationalism*, (1893)(Boston: Pilgrim Press, 1960).

Wallace D.D., *Puritans and Predestination: Grace in English Protestant Theology 1525-1695* (Chapel Hill, NC: University of North Carolina Press, 1982).

Watts, M.R., *The Dissenters: from the Reformation to the French Revolution* (Oxford: Oxford University Press, 1978).

Webb, R.K., 'From Toleration to Religious Liberty' in J.R. Jones (ed.), *Liberty Secured? Britain Before and After 1688* (Stanford: Stanford University Press, 1992) 158-198.

- 'The emergence of Rational dissent', in K. Haakonssen (ed.) *Enlightenment and Religion: Rational dissent in eighteenth-century Britain* (Cambridge: Cambridge University Press, 1996), 12-41.

White, B.R., 'The Twilight of Puritanism in the Years Before and After 1688' in O.. Grell, J.I. Israel and N. Tyacke (eds.), *From Persecution to Toleration: The Glorious Revolution and Religion in England* (Oxford: Clarendon Press, 1991), 307-330.

White, P., 'The Rise of Arminianism Reconsidered', *P&P*, 101, 1983, 34-54.

- *Predestination, policy and polemic: Conflict and consensus in the English Church from the Reformation to the Civil War* (Cambridge: Cambridge University Press, 1992).

- 'The *via media* in the early Stuart Church', in K. Fincham (ed), *The Early Stuart Church, 1603-1640* (Basingstoke: Macmillan, 1993), 211-230.

Whiteman, A., 'The Re-Establishment of the Church of England, 1660-1663', *TRHS*, Fifth Series, Vol. 5, 1955, 111-131.

- 'The Restoration of the Church of England' in G.F. Nuttall and O. Chadwick (eds), *From Uniformity to Unity 1662-1962* (London: SPCK, 1962), 19-88.

Whiting, C.E., *Studies in English Puritanism From the Restoration to the Revolution, 1660-1688* (London: SPCK, 1931).

Wilkes, J.W., 'The Transformation of Dissent: a Review of the Change from the Seventeenth to the Eighteenth Centuries' in C.R. Cole and M.E. Moody (eds.), *The Dissenting Tradition: Essays for Leland H. Carlson* (Athens, Ohio: Ohio University Press, 1975), 108-122.

Williams, G.H., *The Radical Reformation* (Philadelphia: Westminster Press, 1962).

Wojcik, J.W., *Robert Boyle and the Limits of Reason* (Cambridge: Cambridge University Press, 1997).

Wolterstorff, N., 'Locke's philosophy of religion' in V. Chappell (ed) *The Cambridge Companion to Locke* (Cambridge: Cambridge University Press, 1994), 172-198.

Wood, A.A., *Athenae Oxonienses,* (1813-20) (4 vols.) (New York: Johnson Reprint Corp., 1967).

Wood, A.H., *Church Unity Without Uniformity: A Study of Seventeenth-century English Church Movements and of Richard Baxter's Proposals for a Comprehensive Church* (London: Epworth, 1963).

Woolf, D., 'Conscience, Constancy and Ambition in the Career and Writings of James Howell' in J. Morrill, P. Slack and D. Woolf (eds.), *Public Duty and Private Conscience in Seventeenth-Century England: Essays Presented to G.E. Aylmer* (Oxford: Clarendon Press, 1993), 243-278.

Woolhouse, R., 'Locke's theory of knowledge' in V. Chappell (ed) *The Cambridge Companion to Locke* (Cambridge: Cambridge University Press, 1994), 146-171.

Wootton, D., 'Introduction' in D. Wootton (ed), *John Locke: Political Writings* (Harmondsworth: Penguin, 1993), 7-122.

Worden, B., 'Toleration and the Cromwellian Protectorate' in W.J. Sheils (ed), *Persecution and Toleration,* Studies in Church History 21, (Oxford: B. Blackwell, 1984), 199-233.

Wykes, D.L., '"To let the memory of these men dye is injurious to posterity": Edmund Calamy's *Account* of the Ejected Ministers' in N. Swanson (ed.), *The Church Retrospective, Studies in Church History* 33 (Woodbridge: Ecclesiastical History Society, 1997), 379-392.

- *To Revive the Memory of Some Excellent Men: Edmund Calamy and the Early Historians of Nonconformity* (London: Dr Williams Trust, 1997).

Zakai, A., 'Religious Toleration and its Enemies: The Independent Divines and the Issue of Toleration during the English Civil War', *Albion,* Vol. 21, No. 1 (Spring 1989), 1-33.

- 'Orthodoxy in England and New England: Puritans and the Issue of Religious Toleration, 1640-1650', *Proceedings of the American Philosophical Society,* Vol. 135, No. 3, 1991, 401-441.

- *Exile and Kingdom: History and Apocalypse in the Puritan Migration to America* (Cambridge: Cambridge University Press, 1992).

General Index

Studies in Christian History and Thought

(All titles uniform with this volume)
Dates in bold are of projected publication

David Bebbington
Holiness in Nineteenth-Century England
David Bebbington stresses the relationship of movements of spirituality to changes in their cultural setting, especially the legacies of the Enlightenment and Romanticism. He shows that these broad shifts in ideological mood had a profound effect on the ways in which piety was conceptualized and practised. Holiness was intimately bound up with the spirit of the age.
2000 / 0-85364-981-2 / viii + 98pp

J. William Black
Reformation Pastors
Richard Baxter and the Ideal of the Reformed Pastor
This work examines Richard Baxter's *Gildas Salvianus, The Reformed Pastor* (1656) and explores each aspect of his pastoral strategy in light of his own concern for 'reformation' and in the broader context of Edwardian, Elizabethan and early Stuart pastoral ideals and practice.
2003 / 1-84227-190-3 / xxii + 308pp

James Bruce
Prophecy, Miracles, Angels, *and* Heavenly Light?
The Eschatology, Pneumatology and Missiology of Adomnán's Life of Columba
This book surveys approaches to the marvellous in hagiography, providing the first critique of Plummer's hypothesis of Irish saga origin. It then analyses the uniquely systematized phenomena in the *Life of Columba* from Adomnán's seventh-century theological perspective, identifying the coming of the eschatological Kingdom as the key to understanding.
2004 / 1-84227-227-6 / xviii + 286pp

Colin J. Bulley
The Priesthood of Some Believers
Developments from the General to the Special Priesthood in the Christian Literature of the First Three Centuries
The first in-depth treatment of early Christian texts on the priesthood of all believers shows that the developing priesthood of the ordained related closely to the division between laity and clergy and had deleterious effects on the practice of the general priesthood.
2000 / 1-84227-034-6 / xii + 336pp

July 2005

Anthony R. Cross (ed.)
Ecumenism and History
Studies in Honour of John H.Y. Briggs

This collection of essays examines the inter-relationships between the two fields in which Professor Briggs has contributed so much: history—particularly Baptist and Nonconformist—and the ecumenical movement. With contributions from colleagues and former research students from Britain, Europe and North America, *Ecumenism and History* provides wide-ranging studies in important aspects of Christian history, theology and ecumenical studies.

2002 / 1-84227-135-0 / xx + 362pp

Maggi Dawn
Confessions of an Inquiring Spirit
Form as Constitutive of Meaning in S.T. Coleridge's Theological Writing

This study of Coleridge's *Confessions* focuses on its confessional, epistolary and fragmentary form, suggesting that attention to these features significantly affects its interpretation. Bringing a close study of these three literary forms, the author suggests ways in which they nuance the text with particular understandings of the Trinity, and of a kenotic christology. Some parallels are drawn between Romantic and postmodern dilemmas concerning the authority of the biblical text.

***2006** / 1-84227-255-1 / approx. 224 pp*

Ruth Gouldbourne
The Flesh and the Feminine
Gender and Theology in the Writings of Caspar Schwenckfeld

Caspar Schwenckfeld and his movement exemplify one of the radical communities of the sixteenth century. Challenging theological and liturgical norms, they also found themselves challenging social and particularly gender assumptions. In this book, the issues of the relationship between radical theology and the understanding of gender are considered.

***2005** / 1-84227-048-6 / approx. 304pp*

Crawford Gribben
Puritan Millennialism
Literature and Theology, 1550–1682

Puritan Millennialism surveys the growth, impact and eventual decline of puritan millennialism throughout England, Scotland and Ireland, arguing that it was much more diverse than has frequently been suggested. This Paternoster edition is revised and extended from the original 2000 text.

***2007** / 1-84227-372-8 / approx. 320pp*

July 2005

Galen K. Johnson

Prisoner of Conscience

John Bunyan on Self, Community and Christian Faith

This is an interdisciplinary study of John Bunyan's understanding of conscience across his autobiographical, theological and fictional writings, investigating whether conscience always deserves fidelity, and how Bunyan's view of conscience affects his relationship both to modern Western individualism and historic Christianity.

2003 / 1-84227-223-3 / xvi + 236pp

R.T. Kendall

Calvin and English Calvinism to 1649

The author's thesis is that those who formed the Westminster Confession of Faith, which is regarded as Calvinism, in fact departed from John Calvin on two points: (1) the extent of the atonement and (2) the ground of assurance of salvation.

1997 / 0-85364-827-1 / xii + 264pp

Timothy Larsen

Friends of Religious Equality

Nonconformist Politics in Mid-Victorian England

During the middle decades of the nineteenth century the English Nonconformist community developed a coherent political philosophy of its own, of which a central tenet was the principle of religious equality (in contrast to the stereotype of Evangelical Dissenters). The Dissenting community fought for the civil rights of Roman Catholics, non-Christians and even atheists on an issue of principle which had its flowering in the enthusiastic and undivided support which Nonconformity gave to the campaign for Jewish emancipation. This reissued study examines the political efforts and ideas of English Nonconformists during the period, covering the whole range of national issues raised, from state education to the Crimean War. It offers a case study of a theologically conservative group defending religious pluralism in the civic sphere, showing that the concept of religious equality was a grand vision at the centre of the political philosophy of the Dissenters.

2007 */ 1-84227-402-3 / x + 300pp*

July 2005

Byung-Ho Moon

Christ the Mediator of the Law

Calvin's Christological Understanding of the Law as the Rule of Living and Life-Giving

This book explores the coherence between Christology and soteriology in Calvin's theology of the law, examining its intellectual origins and his position on the concept and extent of Christ's mediation of the law. A comparative study between Calvin and contemporary Reformers—Luther, Bucer, Melancthon and Bullinger—and his opponent Michael Servetus is made for the purpose of pointing out the unique feature of Calvin's Christological understanding of the law.

***2005** / 1-84227-318-3 / approx. 370pp*

John Eifion Morgan-Wynne

Holy Spirit and Religious Experience in Christian Writings, c.AD 90–200

This study examines how far Christians in the third to fifth generations (c.AD 90–200) attributed their sense of encounter with the divine presence, their sense of illumination in the truth or guidance in decision-making, and their sense of ethical empowerment to the activity of the Holy Spirit in their lives.

***2005** / 1-84227-319-1 / approx. 350pp*

James I. Packer

The Redemption and Restoration of Man in the Thought of Richard Baxter

James I. Packer provides a full and sympathetic exposition of Richard Baxter's doctrine of humanity, created and fallen; its redemption by Christ Jesus; and its restoration in the image of God through the obedience of faith by the power of the Holy Spirit.

2002 / 1-84227-147-4 / 432pp

Andrew Partington,

Church and State

The Contribution of the Church of England Bishops to the House of Lords during the Thatcher Years

In *Church and State*, Andrew Partington argues that the contribution of the Church of England bishops to the House of Lords during the Thatcher years was overwhelmingly critical of the government; failed to have a significant influence in the public realm; was inefficient, being undertaken by a minority of those eligible to sit on the Bench of Bishops; and was insufficiently moral and spiritual in its content to be distinctive. On the basis of this, and the likely reduction of the number of places available for Church of England bishops in a fully reformed Second Chamber, the author argues for an evolution in the Church of England's approach to the service of its bishops in the House of Lords. He proposes the Church of England works to overcome the genuine obstacles which hinder busy diocesan bishops from contributing to the debates of the House of Lords and to its life more informally.

***2005** / 1-84227-334-5 / approx. 324pp*

Michael Pasquarello III

God's Ploughman

Hugh Latimer: A 'Preaching Life' (1490–1555)

This construction of a 'preaching life' situates Hugh Latimer within the larger religious, political and intellectual world of late medieval England. Neither biography, intellectual history, nor analysis of discrete sermon texts, this book is a work of homiletic history which draws from the details of Latimer's milieu to construct an interpretive framework for the preaching performances that formed the core of his identity as a religious reformer. Its goal is to illumine the practical wisdom embodied in the content, form and style of Latimer's preaching, and to recapture a sense of its overarching purpose, movement, and transforming force during the reform of sixteenth-century England.

***2006** / 1-84227-336-1 / approx. 250pp*

Alan P.F. Sell

Enlightenment, Ecumenism, Evangel

Theological Themes and Thinkers 1550–2000

This book consists of papers in which such interlocking topics as the Enlightenment, the problem of authority, the development of doctrine, spirituality, ecumenism, theological method and the heart of the gospel are discussed. Issues of significance to the church at large are explored with special reference to writers from the Reformed and Dissenting traditions.

2005 / 1-84227-330-2 / xviii + 422pp

Alan P.F. Sell

Hinterland Theology

Some Reformed and Dissenting Adjustments

Many books have been written on theology's 'giants' and significant trends, but what of those lesser-known writers who adjusted to them? In this book some hinterland theologians of the British Reformed and Dissenting traditions, who followed in the wake of toleration, the Evangelical Revival, the rise of modern biblical criticism and Karl Barth, are allowed to have their say. They include Thomas Ridgley, Ralph Wardlaw, T.V. Tymms and N.H.G. Robinson.

***2006** / 1-84227-331-0 / approx. 350pp*

Alan P.F. Sell and Anthony R. Cross (eds)

Protestant Nonconformity in the Twentieth Century

In this collection of essays scholars representative of a number of Nonconformist traditions reflect thematically on Nonconformists' life and witness during the twentieth century. Among the subjects reviewed are biblical studies, theology, worship, evangelism and spirituality, and ecumenism. Over and above its immediate interest, this collection provides a marker to future scholars and others wishing to know how some of their forebears assessed Nonconformity's contribution to a variety of fields during the century leading up to Christianity's third millennium.

2003 / 1-84227-221-7 / x + 398pp

Mark Smith

Religion in Industrial Society

Oldham and Saddleworth 1740–1865

This book analyses the way British churches sought to meet the challenge of industrialization and urbanization during the period 1740–1865. Working from a case-study of Oldham and Saddleworth, Mark Smith challenges the received view that the Anglican Church in the eighteenth century was characterized by complacency and inertia, and reveals Anglicanism's vigorous and creative response to the new conditions. He reassesses the significance of the centrally directed church reforms of the mid-nineteenth century, and emphasizes the importance of local energy and enthusiasm. Charting the growth of denominational pluralism in Oldham and Saddleworth, Dr Smith compares the strengths and weaknesses of the various Anglican and Nonconformist approaches to promoting church growth. He also demonstrates the extent to which all the churches participated in a common culture shaped by the influence of evangelicalism, and shows that active co-operation between the churches rather than denominational conflict dominated. This revised and updated edition of Dr Smith's challenging and original study makes an important contribution both to the social history of religion and to urban studies.

***2006** / 1-84227-335-3 / approx. 300pp*

Martin Sutherland

Peace, Toleration and Decay

The Ecclesiology of Later Stuart Dissent

This fresh analysis brings to light the complexity and fragility of the later Stuart Nonconformist consensus. Recent findings on wider seventeenth-century thought are incorporated into a new picture of the dynamics of Dissent and the roots of evangelicalism.

2003 / 1-84227-152-0 / xxii + 216pp

G. Michael Thomas

The Extent of the Atonement

A Dilemma for Reformed Theology from Calvin to the Consensus

A study of the way Reformed theology addressed the question, 'Did Christ die for all, or for the elect only?', commencing with John Calvin, and including debates with Lutheranism, the Synod of Dort and the teaching of Moïse Amyraut.

1997 / 0-85364-828-X / x + 278pp

David M. Thompson

Baptism, Church and Society in Britain from the Evangelical Revival to *Baptism, Eucharist and Ministry*

The theology and practice of baptism have not received the attention they deserve. How important is faith? What does baptismal regeneration mean? Is baptism a bond of unity between Christians? This book discusses the theology of baptism and popular belief and practice in England and Wales from the Evangelical Revival to the publication of the World Council of Churches' consensus statement on *Baptism, Eucharist and Ministry* (1982).

***2005** / 1-84227-393-0 / approx. 224pp*

Mark D. Thompson

A Sure Ground on Which to Stand

The Relation of Authority and Interpretive Method of Luther's Approach to Scripture

The best interpreter of Luther is Luther himself. Unfortunately many modern studies have superimposed contemporary agendas upon this sixteenth-century Reformer's writings. This fresh study examines Luther's own words to find an explanation for his robust confidence in the Scriptures, a confidence that generated the famous 'stand' at Worms in 1521.

2004 / 1-84227-145-8 / xvi + 322pp

Carl R. Trueman and R.S. Clark (eds)

Protestant Scholasticism

Essays in Reassessment

Traditionally Protestant theology, between Luther's early reforming career and the dawn of the Enlightenment, has been seen in terms of decline and fall into the wastelands of rationalism and scholastic speculation. In this volume a number of scholars question such an interpretation. The editors argue that the development of post-Reformation Protestantism can only be understood when a proper historical model of doctrinal change is adopted. This historical concern underlies the subsequent studies of theologians such as Calvin, Beza, Olevian, Baxter, and the two Turrentini. The result is a significantly different reading of the development of Protestant Orthodoxy, one which both challenges the older scholarly interpretations and clichés about the relationship of Protestantism to, among other things, scholasticism and rationalism, and which demonstrates the fruitfulness of the new, historical approach.

1999 / 0-85364-853-0 / xx + 344pp

Shawn D. Wright

Our Sovereign Refuge

The Pastoral Theology of Theodore Beza

Our Sovereign Refuge is a study of the pastoral theology of the Protestant reformer who inherited the mantle of leadership in the Reformed church from John Calvin. Countering a common view of Beza as supremely a 'scholastic' theologian who deviated from Calvin's biblical focus, Wright uncovers a new portrait. He was not a cold and rigid academic theologian obsessed with probing the eternal decrees of God. Rather, by placing him in his pastoral context and by noting his concerns in his pastoral and biblical treatises, Wright shows that Beza was fundamentally a committed Christian who was troubled by the vicissitudes of life in the second half of the sixteenth century. He believed that the biblical truth of the supreme sovereignty of God alone could support Christians on their earthly pilgrimage to heaven. This pastoral and personal portrait forms the heart of Wright's argument.

2004 / 1-84227-252-7 / xviii + 308pp

Paternoster
9 Holdom Avenue,
Bletchley,
Milton Keynes MK1 1QR,
United Kingdom
Web: www.authenticmedia.co.uk/paternoster

July 2005

www.ingramcontent.com/pod-product-compliance
Lightning Source LLC
LaVergne TN
LVHW050622100826
845148LV00011B/1690

* 9 7 8 1 5 9 7 5 2 7 9 1 0 *